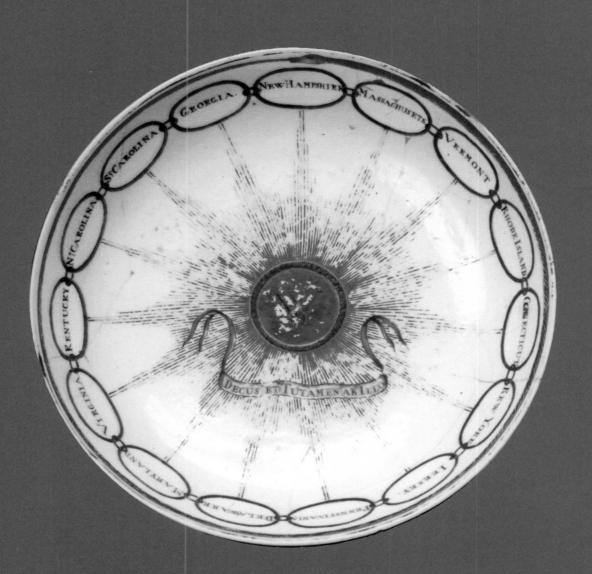

DECUS ET TUTAMEN AB ILLO

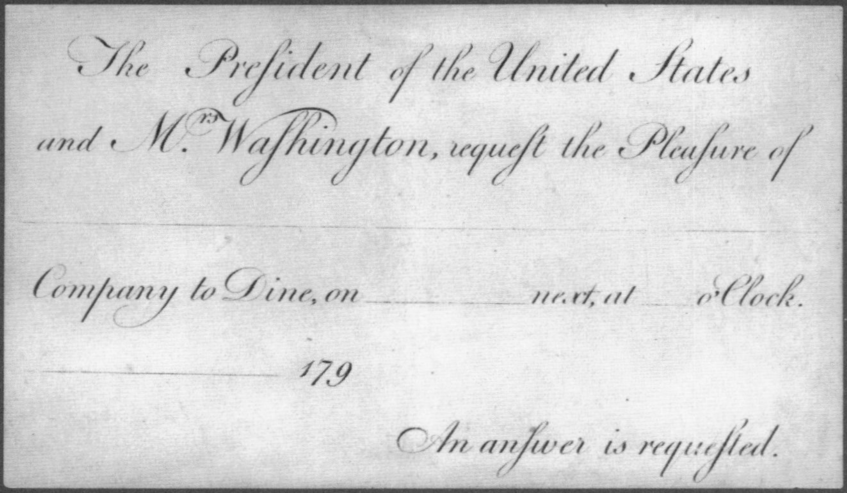

The President of the United States and Mrs Washington, request the Pleasure of

_____

Company to Dine, on _____ next, at ____ o'Clock.

_____ 179

An answer is requested.

Dining with the Washingtons

Dining with the Washingtons

HISTORIC RECIPES, ENTERTAINMENT,
AND HOSPITALITY FROM MOUNT VERNON

———◆———

Essays by MARY V. THOMPSON, DENNIS J. POGUE, CAROL BORCHERT CADOU, *and* J. DEAN NORTON

With contributions by ESTHER C. WHITE *and* STEVEN T. BASHORE

Recipes by NANCY CARTER CRUMP

Foreword by WALTER SCHEIB

———◆———

STEPHEN A. MCLEOD, *Editor*

MOUNT VERNON LADIES' ASSOCIATION

Distributed by the University of North Carolina Press, Chapel Hill

This book is generously supported by

THE FOUNDERS,

Washington Committee for Historic Mount Vernon

Contents

Foreword

—•—

WALTER SCHEIB

****

For years, my view of George Washington was probably similar to that of many Americans. I pictured him as the gracious and influential statesman I had seen in his renowned portraits and learned about in history classes. Beyond that, though, he remained elusive and unreal to me—a mythical figure, a legendary hero.

Strangely enough, it was neither school nor formal study that ultimately led me to understand and appreciate our first president more fully. Of all things, it was cooking—and at the White House, no less. In 2000, during my sixth year as executive chef for the First Family, I was asked to fashion a circa 1800-style menu for a celebration of the two hundredth anniversary of the "people's house." At first, the task seemed overwhelming. I was a chef, after all, not a food historian. And in truth, I had cooked professionally for more than twenty years without having been introduced to significant eighteenth- or early-nineteenth-century cookbooks, such as those by Hannah Glasse and Eliza Leslie.

In preparing for the event, I researched those very cookbooks along with period menus. I also relied on Mount Vernon to educate me about the man and how he dined. As I learned more about Washington the public figure, private citizen, gentleman farmer, and savvy businessman, my image of him as an individual with vivid passions, clear values, and defined tastes began taking shape. I realized, too, that Americans' contemporary enthusiasm for cooking with seasonal local ingredients is nothing new. Indeed, our forefathers had little choice for the most part but to purchase and consume locally sourced foodstuffs in season. I found the self-sufficient realm George Washington created at Mount Vernon to be nothing short of wonderful and inspiring, nonetheless.

My research into early American food practices and rediscovery of Washington and his plantation revealed to me some of the many ways we might gain insight into historical people, events, and culture. This journey not only informed the menu I created for the White House's anniversary, but it also confirmed that food and dining offer singularly colorful windows through which to see into the past.

As we examine George Washington through a culinary lens in this book, an image of him emerges that is both real and approachable. The accounts of those who visited and worked at Mount Vernon reveal much about his personality and character. The president's own words and descriptions further clarify his tastes and values, and invite us to appreciate the many aspects of dining with the Washingtons.

In a 1786 letter to his longtime friend George William Fairfax, George Washington wrote, "My manner of living is plain. . . . A glass of wine and a bit of mutton is [*sic*] always ready—such as will be content to partake of it are welcome—those who look for more will be disappointed."[1] Indeed, much about Washington strikes us as exceedingly modest for a man of his station. His avowedly simple culinary tastes also included the likes of hoecakes and hominy. He chose to wear a Connecticut-made brown broadcloth suit to his first inauguration in April 1789, symbolically rejecting any cor-

OPPOSITE:
George Washington usually donned a black velvet suit for official presidential dinners and receptions, as in this circa 1794–95 portrait by Swedish immigrant painter Adolf Ulrik Wertmüller.

****

relation between the American presidency and the British monarchy. He preferred the company of family and small parties to large formal gatherings. And his happiest days were spent in the country at Mount Vernon, where, dressed in "plain drab clothes, a broad-brimmed white hat . . . and carrying an umbrella with a long staff which is attached to his saddle-bow," he spent much of each day on horseback, surveying his gardens and farms.[2]

Although Washington declared his preference for such living, it would appear to us today, as well as to many people of his time, that his life was hardly simple but rather was characterized by the elegance and finery befitting a man of wealth, a military leader, and a statesman. Indeed, this dichotomy seems to have shaped much of his life. Certainly as a public figure, Washington was not only committed to discipline and hard work but was also renowned for his charm, persuasiveness, and dignity. Indeed, he was much the same in private. It is here, in fact, particularly at Mount Vernon, that we see how his affinity for plainness coexisted with his desires to succeed as an entrepreneurial farmer and to improve the lives of his countrymen.

Although his personal tastes might have been modest, Washington developed Mount Vernon into an elegant and industrious estate of the highest order. Between 1759 and his death in 1799, he expanded upon the original farmhouse his father had built to create a two-and-a-half-story, twenty-room mansion, complete with several kitchens and dining rooms, and he designed and erected the twelve outbuildings that stand today. He also increased the plantation's size from twenty-one hundred to eight thousand acres.

In 1765 Washington abandoned growing tobacco and turned instead primarily to wheat, which he processed at his own gristmill. There were, in fact, five distinct farms at Mount Vernon, each with its own overseer, as well as gardens for vegetables, herbs, and fruit. He also operated a successful fishery, where fish were caught, salted, and sold. Washington explored many avenues of food production not only for his own family's consumption and that of his servants and slaves (at one point numbering as many as three hundred) but also to sell in the colonies and overseas. Particularly in the post–Revolutionary War years, he devoted himself to improving his farms, experimenting with various crops and crop rotation, fertilizers, and the breeding of livestock. He even became president of the Potomac Company and in that role worked to improve navigation on the river so that upstream farmers could take their goods to market more easily.

From his commission to command the Continental Army in Boston in June 1775 until his final retirement from public life in the spring of 1797, Washington spent far less time than he wanted at his beloved estate. His letters reveal that he continued to manage the farms and property improvements during his years away and that he also, while president, had food that was produced there sent to him in New York and Philadelphia. Although he was committed to serving his country, it is clear that he ached to go home to resume the role of gentleman farmer. He returned there to spend time with his family and to host guests as often as possible, and the extant (though limited) menus from Mount Vernon along with the descriptions left by family members and guests reveal that he and Mrs. Washington gave much time and attention to the cultivation of both food and the pleasures of the table.

The food and dining at Mount Vernon reflected the Washingtons' personal tastes as well as the socially accepted styles of the day. Throughout the seasons, its farms yielded a wide selection of vegetables and fruit, including an abundance of root vegetables, beans, lettuces, apples, pears, berries, and figs. Meat, fish, and fowl were also plentiful. Hams cured in the smokehouse under Martha Washington's supervision held particular prominence on the family's tables and were often shipped as gifts domestically and abroad. In addition, George and Martha Washington were especially fond of fish and shellfish, and so oysters, lobsters, shad, and cod were often served.[3]

As noted, Washington preferred a modest style of dining to lavish meals. While supping in Philadelphia one winter, for instance, he was angered when a rare dish of shad his steward had specially ordered was set before him. Discovering the fish had cost three dollars, Washington demanded it be taken away, declaring that he would never set a table with such "luxury and extravagance."[4]

At the same time, however, the Washingtons' high social

status (among the top 3 percent of society at the time) afforded them a wide variety of locally grown and imported foods. The family indeed relied upon Mount Vernon and merchants throughout the colonies for most of their produce, meat, and dairy, but they could also afford to order special or "exotic" foods from abroad. Although after the war Washington decided to forgo purchasing such items as cheese and porter from England and instead buy them at home, he continued to obtain various items from other countries.[5] Indeed, only families of such wealth and prestige as the Washingtons could afford to buy such special edibles as pickled mangoes from India, Lucca olives from Italy, pimentos and sherry from Spain, chocolate from Mexico, and citrus, coconuts, and coffee from the West Indies.

Washington's dining tables, too, present a tension between the simplicity he admired and the elegant array of dishes that a man of his status would have been expected to serve. Whether he was hosting a few close friends or many guests, the style of service and range of offerings would have been much the same. Washington valued punctuality and required those around him—from the kitchen staff to his visitors—to respect it as well. He typically allowed late-arriving guests a grace period of five minutes past the scheduled dining hour to account for any differences in watches, and then would begin the meal whether all were present or not.[6] When the party entered the dining room, slaves dressed in the Washington livery would be standing near the sideboard, ready to serve wine, beer, and porter. The diners would then sit at a table already set with multiple platters of meats and vegetables, which might have included ham, duck or goose, hot roast beef, cold boiled beef, mutton, fish, and of seasonal vegetables such as corn or hominy, cabbage, potatoes, peas, asparagus, salads, and pickles. Typical of the period, a set of cruets or casters filled with salts, dry mustard, vinegar, oil, and nut or mushroom ketchup would also appear on the table. After the platters were removed from the table, the dessert course of pies, tarts, and cheeses would be served, followed by a final course consisting of port, Madeira, nuts, and both fresh and dried fruit.

Such a dinner would have been common at Mount Vernon. To us today it seems quite lavish, but in reality it was typical of those found in affluent homes of that time. In addition, although diners were presented with a spectrum of dishes, they were only expected to choose from among their favorites and refrain from overindulgence. Indeed Washington is said to have often served himself only a bit of meat and cornbread at dinner.[7]

As for the dishes themselves that appeared on the Washingtons' tables, many of us might be surprised to learn how familiar the period recipes seem to our twenty-first-century culinary aesthetic. It is true that they do frequently call for combinations of ingredients that might sound a bit unusual—for instance, seasoning savory foods with sweet spices such as cinnamon and cloves. For the most part, though, the essential components of these dishes and the methods of cooking them seem not so dissimilar from many of our own recipes. They are often so detailed and clearly written, in fact, that most cooking enthusiasts today would be able to follow them successfully. Cookbook authors of the day typically advised, for example, that vegetables should be cooked until just tender to preserve their flavor and texture. We read that meat and fish dishes were often quite delicately seasoned and even brightened with fresh herbs and citrus zest. And not only are many of the confections and sweets just the same as those we enjoy today, but the techniques for preparing them are also virtually unchanged.

Even though culinary memoirs and cookbooks focusing on historical people and places continue to gain in popularity, it might at first seem unusual to examine George and Martha Washington in this manner. Yet as this thorough and appealing book makes clear, such an examination is both appropriate and significant. After all, much of daily life in the eighteenth and early nineteenth centuries was devoted to food preparation and preservation. So when we begin to understand how the president designed his gardens, arranged his dining rooms, and made a business of selling much of what his farm produced—all the while eschewing overindulgence and extravagance at the table—we not only learn more about him, but we also see how he interpreted and even influenced American food and dining. ∗

"That hospitable mansion"

Welcoming Guests at Mount Vernon

Mary V. Thompson

The gracious hospitality extended to guests on plantations in the American South has become legendary over time, but as with many legends, the reality is somewhat complicated. The subject of hospitality at Mount Vernon is especially intriguing because of George Washington's fame and status both in his own country and in Europe.

Various eighteenth-century newcomers to Virginia remarked on the warm welcome they experienced in the homes of prosperous colonists. Philip Vickers Fithian, a Northerner who came to tutor the children of a Virginia planter in 1773, was among those charmed by what he found. "The People are extremely hospitable and very polite," he wrote in his journal, adding that both characteristics "are most certainly universal . . . of the Gentlemen in Virginia." He also noted that "Virginians are so kind one can scarce know how to dispense with, or indeed accept their kindness shown in such a variety of instances."[1]

George and Martha Washington's particular reputation for hospitality is substantiated in diaries and letters written by themselves, by relatives, and by visitors to their home as well as by their descendants. Shortly after the Revolutionary War, an Englishman named Charles Varlo wrote: "The General's house is open to poor travellers as well as rich; he gives diet and lodging to all that come that way."[2] One of Varlo's countrymen, Joseph Hadfield, wrote in 1785 that he was anxious to meet Washington, "this amiable man, who was as much admired and beloved for his domestic virtues, hospitality and agricultural knowledge as for his Fabian prudence and talents when he commanded the American Army." Once at Mount Vernon, Hadfield "experienced . . . the most polite and hospitable reception" and recorded that there "were other strangers besides two of [Washington's] old aides-de-camp."[3] Yet another visitor from England, who spent several days with the Washingtons that same year, noted that people came to see the general "from all parts of the world—hardly a day passes without." He remarked that Washington "always" kept "a genteel table for strangers, that almost daily visit him, as a matter of course."[4]

Washington himself confirmed that many of his guests were virtual strangers to him. In a 1787 letter to his mother, he called Mount Vernon "a well resorted tavern" because "scarcely any strangers who are going from north to south, or from south to north do not spend a day or two at it."[5] The press of visitors continued to such an extent that, in the summer of 1797, Washington commented to a friend, "Unless some one pops in, unexpectedly, Mrs. Washington and myself will do what I believe has not been [done] within the last twenty years by us, that is to set down to dinner by ourselves."[6] Actually, his calculation was slightly off: twelve years earlier, he had confided in his diary that he had just "dined with only Mrs. Washington which I believe is the first instance of it since my retirement from public life."[7]

His diaries vividly convey a sense of the couple's tireless socializing. For example, in 1768, well before the American Revolution made George Washington a household name on two continents, he and his wife had dinner guests on

82 of the 291 days for which there are records. That same year, they had overnight guests on 130 of those 291 days. In 1774, the last full year before he set off for the war, Washington recorded having dinner guests on 136 of the 207 days he was home and overnight guests on 125 of those days. In 1785, two years after the war's official end, the Washingtons welcomed dinner guests 225 times and overnight guests 235 times. Even following Washington's retirement from the presidency, scores of dinner and overnight guests enjoyed the cordial hospitality that the couple provided. Amazingly, in 1798 alone, the Washingtons entertained at least 656 dinner guests and 677 overnight guests at Mount Vernon.[8]

Occasionally, there seem to have been either too many people or too much activity for the Washingtons to keep up with it all. On Christmas Day in 1785, for instance, three men arrived at Mount Vernon: Count Luigi Castiglioni, an Italian scientist who was studying human society, plants,

Colonel Burgess Ball (1749–1800), seen here in a circa 1795 portrait miniature attributed to Raphaelle Peale, undoubtedly received a warm welcome during a Mount Vernon Christmas in 1785. His wife was Frances Washington, George Washington's niece. Ball served as an aide-de-camp to the general during the Revolutionary War.

and animals in the former colonies; Colonel Burgess Ball, the husband of one of Washington's nieces; and William Hunter, a Scottish businessman who lived in Alexandria and belonged to the same Masonic lodge as Washington. Hunter left after dinner that day, but the other two gentlemen stayed. For the next two days, Washington simply jotted notes in his diary about the weather, but on December 28, he made an entry that hinted at the domestic commotion: "Colo. Ball went away yesterday, after breakfast—tho' it was unnoticed in the occurrances of the day."[9]

Contrary to traditional beliefs about unstinting and indiscriminate hospitality in the South, the Washingtons made some distinctions between close friends and associates and those people who arrived on their doorstep simply because they sought a meal, a room for the night, or a chance to see the home of a celebrated figure. An example of this difference is evident in a Washington diary entry from a day in February 1773 when his friend Bryan Fairfax "came here & Stayed all Night—as did three Travellers going to Maryland."[10] Similarly, in the summer of 1785, he noted that "A Mr. Mar[t]el (or some such name) a Frenchman came in and dined, and just before dinner Mr. Arthur Lee, and Mr. P. Fendall got here; all of whom went away after it was over." Lee and Fendall were friends, but Martel, obviously, was something of a mystery.[11] In a letter written shortly after the end of his presidency, he described a typical day, which included the mid-afternoon dinner, "at which I rarely miss seeing strange faces; come, as they say, out of respect to me. Pray, would not the word curiosity answer as well?" He added wistfully, "and how different this, from having a few social friends at a cheerful board?"[12]

Drawing distinctions between the various individuals and groups of people arriving at the Mansion was not always easy. In March 1786, for example, one foreign visitor created something of a conundrum. Here, Washington expresses his confusion: "A Gentleman calling himself the Count de Cheiza D'arteignan Officer of the French Guards came here to dinner; but bringing no letters of introduction, nor any authentic testemonials of his being either; I was at a loss how to receive, or treat him." The count was at Mount Vernon for two days, after which he was "sent, with my horses, to day at his own request, to Alexandri[a]."[13] In a letter written not long afterward, Washington hinted at some of the difficulties inherent in his celebrity. He emphasized that he would always welcome anyone sent to Mount Vernon by some of his friends in England—"no person who shall bear your passport will be an unwelcome guest." But he also noted, "So many come hither without proper introductions that it is a real satisfaction when I am able to discriminate."[14]

Knowing exactly how to rank the many visitors to Mount Vernon was especially difficult when the Washingtons were absent. During the war and the presidency, they had to rely on the judgment of younger relatives or employees, both free and enslaved. In 1794 Washington wrote to his farm manager William Pearce that "persons not always recommended, or introduced in the manner I described [in an earlier letter] may go there, who are entitled to equal civilities; and in such cases you must be governed by your own judgment." Turning to the topic of wine, the president specified that if, in Pearce's judgment, certain guests deserved better treatment, he should "lay in a box of claret, and some Lisbon, or Tenerif wine, that my Madeira may be reserved, as it is old, and not easy to be replaced, for my own use when I get home."[15]

For visitors such as these, Washington had earlier ordered another farm manager to be sure that meals were served with the proper flatware. Instead of the pewter, which was good enough for the majority of strangers passing through, he informed farm manager Anthony Whitting in 1792 that "occasions may occur when Tea or other Spoons (better than Pewter) may be wanted in the absence of my family . . . at Mount Vernon, I do by this conveyance, send half a dozen of each."[16] He also made it clear that visitors unacquainted with the Washingtons should be given accommodations notably different from those provided to guests the hosts either knew personally or through friends. As he wrote to Pearce in 1793, soon after he had joined the estate staff, the "right wing to my dwelling house [the north dependency, opposite the kitchen] as you possibly may have noticed, and heard called the Hall" was "kept altogether for the use of Strangers."[17]

The annual expense of feeding and housing Mount Vernon's visitors was considerable. In June 1798, George Washington expressed to farm manager James Anderson the need

An Englishman hoping to acquire land and settle in America, Nicholas Cresswell (1751–1804), shown here around 1780, traveled widely through various colonies in the years before the American Revolution. He returned home without obtaining any land but carried with him fond memories of the Washingtons' hospitality, as recorded in his journal.

to establish rules for the use of grain and hay for the animals, "without which, wastes, if not embezzlement, is more to be expected than oeconomy." In response, Anderson asserted that "the Maintaining [of] so many Horses of Your own, and those who come to Visit is truly expensive."[18]

Not surprisingly, many who were guests at Mount Vernon had glowing memories of the experience. For example, Englishman Andrew Burnaby stayed there for several days in 1759, a few months after his hosts were wed. He continued to enjoy their hospitality even after leaving the estate—riding to Annapolis in one of Washington's vehicles, driven by a Mount Vernon slave.[19] In 1777 another Englishman, Nicholas Cresswell, who had known George and Martha Washington before the Revolutionary War, wrote:

He keeps an excellent table and a stranger, let him be of what Country or nation, he will always meet with a most hospitable reception at it. His entertainments were

The President exercises it in a superlative degree, from the greatest of its duties to the most trifling minutiae, and Mrs. Washington is the very essence of kindness. Her soul seems to overflow with it like the most abundant fountain, and her happiness is in exact proportion to the number of objects upon which she can dispense her benefits.[21]

At least one visitor in the early 1780s thought the hospitality he encountered there surpassed that of Virginia in general:

The most perfect ease and comfort characterize the mode of receiving strangers in Virginia, but no where are these circumstances more conspicuous than at the house of General Washington. Your apartments are your home, the servants of the house are yours, and whilst every inducement is held out to bring you into the general society in the drawing-room, or at the table, it rests with yourself to be served or not with every thing in your own chamber.[22]

always conducted with the most regularity and in the genteelest manner of any I ever was at on the Continent (and I have been at several of them, that is, before he was made a General). Temperance he always observed, was always cool-headed and exceedingly cautious himself, but took great pleasure in seeing his friends entertained in the way most agreeable to themselves. His lady is of a hospitable disposition, always good-humoured and cheerful, and seems to be actuated by the same motives with himself, but she is rather of a more lively disposition. They are to all appearances a happy pair.[20]

The same spirit of cordiality prevailed after the war. A young Philadelphian wrote his father from Mount Vernon in 1790 to say he had been welcomed "with every most distinguished mark of kindness and attention. Hospitality indeed seems to have spread over the whole place its happiest, kindest influence." He continued:

In a similar vein, Englishman Joseph Hadfield observed in 1785 that the "attentions to [Washington's] guests were extended to your servants and horses. He could entertain and accommodate several families."[23] Thirteen years later, a Polish nobleman named Julian Niemcewicz spent almost two weeks at the plantation. "I was not as a stranger but a member of the family in this estimable house," he wrote. "They took care of me, of my linen, of my clothes, etc."[24] Elkanah Watson, who spent time at Mount Vernon in January 1785, glowingly described the kind of personal attention guests might receive from their host. Watson had arrived bearing letters of introduction from Washington's beloved comrade-in-arms Nathanael Greene and Colonel John Fitzgerald, a former wartime aide, as well as a set of books from British abolitionist Granville Sharp. "Although assured that these credentials would secure me a respectful reception, I trembled with awe as I came into the presence of this great man," he later confessed. Despite his fears, Watson was "soon put . . . at ease" by his host's "free and affable conversation." Watson reveled in being "alone in the enjoyment of the society of Washington, for two of the richest days of my life" and proceeded to relate a telling incident:

The first evening I spent under the wing of his hospitality, we sat a full hour at table by ourselves, without the least interruption, after the family had retired. I was extremely oppressed by a severe cold and excessive coughing, contracted by the exposure of a harsh winter journey. He pressed me to use some remedies, but I declined doing so. As usual after retiring, my coughing increased. When some time had elapsed, the door of my room was gently opened, and on drawing my bed-curtains, to my utter astonishment, I beheld Washington himself, standing at my bed-side, with a bowl of hot tea in his hand. I was mortified and distressed beyond expression. This little incident, occurring in common life with an ordinary man, would not have been noticed; but as a trait of the benevolence and private virtue of Washington, [it] deserves to be recorded.[25]

There is considerable evidence that, as they aged, George and Martha Washington found the entertainment of guests they barely knew to be increasingly burdensome, and so looked to younger family members and to servants for assistance. For example, Washington's nephew George Augustine Washington and his wife, Fanny Bassett, who was Martha Washington's niece, assumed certain domestic responsibilities in the late 1780s and early 1790s. As she prepared for a vacation at home in the summer of 1791, Mrs. Washington alerted Fanny to prepare for an onslaught of guests, adding, "I have been so much indisposed my self that I shall leve the House keeping altogether to you—I shall not conscern in the matter at all,—but leve it to you."[26] The young couple took their duties seriously, and George Augustine proudly assured his uncle in the spring of 1792 that "it affords me pleasure that the Canada Gentlemen left Mount Vernon satisfied with their reception, it being my wish that every person coming here may have their curiocity gratified and be convinced of my disposition towards civility."[27]

Although the Washingtons, like other Virginians, took pleasure in entertaining as lavishly as possible, George

Martha Washington's niece Frances (Fanny) Bassett (1767–1796) assisted her aunt with housekeeping duties at Mount Vernon. English artist Robert Edge Pine painted this delicate portrait of her in 1785, a few months before she married George Washington's favorite nephew, George Augustine Washington (1759–1793).

Washington's status as a world figure attracted a staggering number of guests to their home. The expense of feeding and providing accommodations for these visitors, along with their servants and horses, forced the couple to make some distinctions between people they knew personally, friends or acquaintances of friends, and total strangers. The burden of caring for visitors was not simply financial but also took a toll in terms of time and energy. No wonder, then, that the Washingtons, as they aged, sought the help of younger family members to meet these formidable demands. The journal entries and reminiscences of those fortunate recipients of Mount Vernon hospitality have proved to be a godsend for later generations of historians. Each one illustrates the genial and sociable nature of George and Martha Washington. *

OVERLEAF:
Washington and Lafayette at Mount Vernon, 1784 *(also known as* The Home of Washington after the War*), by Thomas Pritchard Rossiter and Louis Remy Mignot. This 1859 painting offers a romanticized vision of the Washington family enjoying the piazza with one of their favorite guests, the Marquis de Lafayette. Their 1784 visit marked the last time the two men would meet.*

Some Men and Women Who Came to Dinner

Over the course of their forty-year marriage, the famously hospitable George and Martha Washington were dinner hosts not only to family members and close friends but also to numerous strangers and many of the most distinguished figures of their time. Listed here are just some of the notables who graced their table—whether at Mount Vernon, at various headquarters during the Revolutionary War, or at the presidential residences in New York and Philadelphia.

1. ABIGAIL SMITH ADAMS (1744–1818). Wife of John Adams. Among the most intellectually distinguished and influential of American first ladies.

2. JOHN ADAMS (1735–1826). Massachusetts lawyer and signer of the Declaration of Independence. First U.S. vice president (1789–97) and second U.S. president (1797–1801).

3. FRANCIS ASBURY (1745–1816). Methodist missionary, sent to America by John Wesley in 1771. Visited Mount Vernon to ask Washington to sign an antislavery petition that was presented to the Virginia legislature on November 8, 1785, and promptly rejected. Became America's first Methodist bishop that year.

4. FRANÇOIS-RENÉ, VICOMTE DE CHATEAUBRIAND (1768–1848). French writer and statesman. Spent six months touring the United States in 1791. The Chateaubriand steak was named for him.

5. JAMES CRAIK (1730–1814). Scottish physician. Longtime Washington-family friend and doctor. Served with Washington during the French and Indian War. Surgeon-general during the Revolutionary War.

6. ELIZABETH SANDWITH DRINKER (1735–1807). Philadelphia Quaker. Visited Washington's Valley Forge headquarters in 1778 to deliver a petition for the freedom of twenty Quaker men who had been exiled to Virginia after refusing to swear loyalty to the American cause.

7. LORD THOMAS FAIRFAX, SIXTH BARON FAIRFAX OF CAMERON (1693–1781). English nobleman. Proprietor of all land between the Potomac and Rappahannock rivers and an early patron of Washington.

8. HORATIO GATES (1727–1806). English-born major in the British army during the French and Indian War and Continental Army general during the Revolutionary War.

9. CATHERINE SAWBRIDGE MACAULAY GRAHAM (1731–1791). English historian and political activist who was a firm believer in the power of representative institutions to secure freedom and equality. Personally associated with various leaders of the American Revolution, including Washington, whom she visited at Mount Vernon in 1785. The two became frequent correspondents.

10. ELBRIDGE GERRY (1744–1814). Outspoken delegate to the Constitutional Convention (1787) who advocated compromise but refused to sign the final document. Massachusetts U.S. congressman (1789–93), governor (1810–12), and U.S. vice president (1813–14).

11. NATHANAEL GREENE (1742–1786). Rhode Island native. One of Washington's ablest generals in the Continental Army. Named quartermaster general in 1778 and commander of the Southern forces in 1780.

12. ALEXANDER HAMILTON (1757–1804). West Indian-born lawyer and political theorist. Washington's secretary and aide-de-camp during the Revolutionary War. Coauthor (with John Jay and James Madison) of *The Federalist* (1787–88), a series of eighty-five essays urging New York voters to approve the new U.S. Constitution. First U.S. secretary of the treasury (1789–95).

13. PATRICK HENRY (1736–1799). Virginia legislator, orator, and early supporter of American independence. Uttered the famous words, "Give me liberty, or give me death!"

14. JEAN-ANTOINE HOUDON (1741–1828). French neoclassical sculptor. Visited Mount Vernon in 1785 on commission from Benjamin Franklin and Thomas Jefferson to produce a life-size marble statue of Washington for the state of Virginia. A portrait bust modeled during that visit is considered the truest likeness of Washington created during his lifetime.

15. JOHN JAY (1745–1829). Lawyer and jurist. Helped negotiate the 1783 Treaty of Paris that formally ended the Revolutionary War. Coauthor (with Alexander Hamilton and James Madison) of *The Federalist* (1787–88). Negotiated the controversial Jay Treaty with Great Britain (1794). First chief justice of the U.S. Supreme Court (1789–95).

16. THOMAS JEFFERSON (1743–1826). Virginia lawyer and political thinker. Principal author of the Declaration of Independence, American minister to France (1785–89), first U.S. secretary of state (1790–93), U.S. vice president (1797–1801), and third U.S. president (1801–1809).

17. HENRY KNOX (1750–1806). Continental Army chief of artillery and a close adviser to Washington during the Revolutionary War. Commander in chief of the army (1783–84) and first U.S. secretary of war (1789–94).

18. MARIE-JOSEPH-PAUL-YVES-ROCH-GILBERT DU MOTIER, MARQUIS DE LAFAYETTE (1757–1834). French nobleman and close friend of Washington. Volunteered his services to the Continental Army in 1777 and was made a major general by the Continental Congress. Returned to France (1778–80) to win support for the American cause. Served at the Battle of Yorktown (1781).

19. BENJAMIN HENRY LATROBE (1764–1820). English-born civil engineer and architect. Designed parts of the U.S. Capitol and White House as well as the nation's first Roman Catholic cathedral, in Baltimore (1805–18).

20. HENRY (LIGHT-HORSE HARRY) LEE (1756–1818). Virginia soldier and legislator. Served as a cavalry officer in the Continental Army and as governor of Virginia (1791–94). Famously eulogized George Washington as "first in war, first in peace, and first in the hearts of his countrymen."

21. LADY HENRIETTA MARCHANT LISTON (1752–1821). Wife of Sir Robert Liston, British ambassador to the United States. They wed two months before he took up his official duties in the spring of 1796. That December, she saw President Washington deliver his last annual address to Congress. "The Hall was crowded," she wrote, "and a prodigious Mob at the Door, about twelve oClock Washington entered in full dress, as He always is on publick occasion, black velvet, sword, etc." The couple visited Mount Vernon twice, in 1797 and 1799, and Lady Liston called on the widowed Martha Washington in 1800.

22. DOLLEY PAYNE TODD MADISON (1768–1849). Married James Madison in September 1794 at Harewood, home of Washington's nephew George Steptoe Washington and his wife, Lucy Payne, the bride's sister. As President Madison's first lady, rescued a Gilbert Stuart portrait of Washington when British soldiers burned the White House during the War of 1812.

23. JAMES MADISON (1751–1836). Virginia lawyer and statesman. Played a leading role in framing the U.S. Constitution (1787). With Alexander Hamilton and John Jay, wrote *The Federalist* (1787–88), a series of essays promoting ratification of the Constitution. Served as U.S. congressman (1789–97) and fourth U.S. president (1809–17).

24. GEORGE MASON (1725–1792). Virginia legislator and master of Gunston Hall plantation, near Mount Vernon. Author of the Virginia Declaration of Rights (1776) and a delegate to the Constitutional Convention (1787). Long friendship with Washington ended when Mason fought ratification of the Constitution because it lacked a bill of rights guaranteeing individual freedoms.

25. JAMES MONROE (1758–1831). Virginia lawyer and statesman. Served in the Continental Army, Virginia legislature (1782), and Continental Congress (1783–86). Opposed the Constitution for creating an overly centralized government. Helped negotiate the Louisiana Purchase. U.S. secretary of state (1811–17) and fifth U.S. president (1817–25).

26. GOUVERNEUR MORRIS (1752–1816). Lawyer, merchant, and diplomat. Represented New York in the Continental Congress during the Revolutionary War and Pennsylvania at the Constitutional Convention (1787). Major supporter of a strong central government, and of George Washington.

27. ROBERT MORRIS (1734–1806). English-born merchant and signer of the Declaration of Independence. Role in raising money for Washington's army during the Revolutionary War earned him the title "financier of the Revolution." Delegate to the Constitutional Convention (1787) and Pennsylvania U.S. senator (1789–95).

28. CHARLES WILLSON PEALE (1741–1827). Annapolis-born artist. Painted portraits of several members of the Mount Vernon household during his first visit, in 1772, and remained a family friend. Opened a Philadelphia portrait gallery in 1784, celebrating heroes of the Revolutionary War, that later expanded to become a museum of natural history.

29. JEAN-BAPTISTE DONATIEN DE VIMEUR, COMTE DE ROCHAMBEAU (1725–1807). French army general. Came to America to command French troops during the Revolutionary War.

30. JOHN SEVIER (1745–1815). North Carolina-born soldier and politician. During the Revolutionary War, served as a colonel in the North Carolina militia and led troops at the Battle of King's Mountain (1780). As a member of North Carolina's ratifying convention, supported the newly completed U.S. Constitution. Served as North Carolina U.S. congressman (1789–91, 1811–15) and governor of Tennessee (1796–1801, 1803–9).

31. ROGER SHERMAN (1721–1793). Lawyer and politician. Only member of the Continental Congress to sign all four of the nation's generative documents: the Continental Association, Declaration of Independence (which he helped draft), Articles of Confederation, and Constitution. Served as Connecticut U.S. congressman (1789–91) and U.S. senator (1791–93).

32. FRIEDRICH WILHELM VON STEUBEN (a.k.a. Baron von Steuben) (1730–1794). Prussian military officer. Arrived in America in 1777 to help train the Continental Army and mold it into an effective fighting force.

33. THOMAS SUMTER (1734–1832). South Carolina-born soldier and politician. As a leader of guerillas fighting the British in the Carolinas, was dubbed the "Gamecock of the Revolution." As a member of South Carolina's ratifying convention, opposed the newly completed U.S. Constitution. Served as South Carolina U.S. congressman (1789–93, 1797–1801). Fort Sumter in Charleston harbor, where the shots that started the Civil War were fired, is named for him.

34. JOHN TRUMBULL (1756–1843). Connecticut-born artist. Aide-de-camp to Washington during the Revolutionary War. After studying in London under Benjamin West, painted celebrated war-themed canvases and portraits of Washington. In 1817, painted four large scenes for the U.S. Capitol rotunda.

35. ANTHONY WAYNE (1745–1796). Pennsylvania-born Revolutionary War general known as "Mad Anthony." Commanded Fort Ticonderoga, fought at Brandywine, and led American attacks at the battles of Monmouth and Stony Point. In 1793, led an expedition in the Northwest Indian War.

36. NOAH WEBSTER (1758–1843). Connecticut-born lexicographer. Visited Mount Vernon in 1785 while traveling the country to promote enactment of copyright laws. Author of *Grammatical Institute of the English Language* (1783; later known as "Webster's Spelling Book") and *Sketches of American Policy* (1785). Published the landmark two-volume *American Dictionary of the English Language* in 1828. ∗ MVT

****

"THAT HOSPITABLE MANSION" 23

Hercules the Cook

When George Washington made a list of his slaves in February 1786, he noted that there were two male cooks at the "Home House": Hercules and Nathan.[1] Martha Washington's grandson, George Washington Parke Custis, characterized Hercules, a particular favorite of his master, as "a capital cook." He was taken from Mount Vernon to join the presidential household in Philadelphia in the fall of 1790 but often was sent back to the estate for Washington's vacations there.[2] On two occasions in the summer of 1791, for instance, Martha Washington notified her niece that Hercules would precede her and her husband so he could prepare for the couple's arrival.[3]

The family expressed their special feelings for Hercules in various ways. For example, when his wife died in September 1787, Martha Washington directed that three bottles of rum be given to him "to bury his wife."[4] Soon after he began working in the presidential kitchen, Hercules asked to have his son, Richmond, help him as a "scullion" there. George Washington granted him this favor "not from [Richmond's] appearance or merits . . . but because he was the Son of Herculas and [the latter's] desire to have him as an assistant."[5]

George Washington Parke Custis later recalled that Hercules, known in the family as Uncle Harkless, was "as highly accomplished [and] proficient in the culinary art as could be found in the United States." He was of medium height and build, had a dark brown complexion, and was said to be rather "homely" but "possessed of such great muscular power as to entitle him to be compared with his namesake of fabulous history." Described as a "celebrated dandy" during Washington's years as president, Hercules bought clothes with money he earned through the sale of slops from the kitchen.[6] The fact that he could make money this way recalls the English and French tradition of permitting cooks to supplement their income by selling such food-preparation leftovers as animal skins, feathers, tallow, and used tea leaves. At Mount Vernon, these items may well have been put to use as com-post and food for the hogs or in the manufacture of clothing, bedding, candles, and soap. In a city such as New York or Philadelphia, however, where it was possible to buy ready-made products and there was little livestock to feed and few gardens to fertilize, it is understandable why Hercules was permitted this "perquisite."[7]

Everyone in the Washington household treated him with great respect, "as well for his valuable services as for his general good character and pleasing manners." Something of a tyrant in the kitchen, however, Hercules, as Martha Washington's grandson put it, displayed a particular passion for cleanliness:

Under his iron discipline, wo[e] to his underlings if speck or spot could be discovered on the tables or dressers, or if the utensils did not shine like polished silver. With the luckless wights who had offended in these particulars there was no arrest of punishment, for judgment and execution went hand in hand. . . . His underlings flew in all directions to execute his orders, while he, the great master-spirit, seemed to possess the power of ubiquity, and to be everywhere at the same moment.[8]

Hercules was one of several slaves in the president's Philadelphia household considered old enough to qualify under a Pennsylvania law that allowed slaves to claim their freedom after living there for a minimum of six months. When the Washingtons decided to send these people home to Mount Vernon periodically to prevent them from taking advantage of the law, Hercules, having learned about the law and the ramifications of the Washingtons' actions, convinced them of his loyalty.[9] Despite those assurances, Washington wrote to his farm manager William Pearce a few months before the end of his presidency that he suspected the cook was planning to run away.[10] Weekly reports from Mount Vernon from the first two months of 1797 show that Hercules and two other male house servants (Frank Lee, the butler, and Cyrus, a waiter) were working with the bricklayers and gardeners. Probably this was because there wasn't enough work in the Mansion and kitchen to keep them busy while the Washingtons remained for a few final weeks in Philadelphia.

OPPOSITE:
Portrait of George Washington's Cook *(ca. 1795–97), attributed to Gilbert Stuart. This painting of the president's enslaved cook, presumed to be Hercules, underlines his status as perhaps one of America's first celebrity chefs. His reputation as a "celebrated dandy" is borne out by his fine white shirt with high collar and neck ruffle and his elegant white-on-white striped waistcoat. This painting has been in collections in England, France, and Spain since at least the first quarter of the nineteenth century, perhaps suggesting that Hercules made his way to Europe with the help of friends and associates in Philadelphia or New York.*

Perhaps Hercules felt that being asked to dig brick clay and uproot honeysuckle were beneath him and, therefore, demeaning. In the weekly report dated February 25, 1797, the farm manager noted that Hercules had spent two days that week—Monday and Tuesday, February 20 and 21—digging clay and that he had then "absconded."[11] Hercules had left Mount Vernon in the wee hours of February 22, his master's sixty-fifth birthday.

As he traveled back to Mount Vernon after the inauguration of his successor, John Adams, Washington wrote to his trusted friend and secretary, Tobias Lear, asking him to have his Philadelphia steward, Frederick Kitt, "make all the enquiry he can after Hercules, and send him round in the Vessel if he can be discovered & apprehended."[12] A month later, a French visitor to Mount Vernon spoke with the young daughter the cook had left behind. Upon suggesting that she must be very sad at the thought of never seeing her father again, the six-year-old answered that in fact she was "very glad, because he is free now."[13] Hercules was not heard from again. ∗ MVT

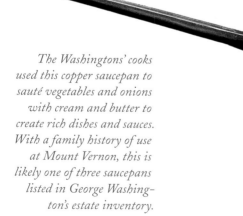

The Washingtons' cooks used this copper saucepan to sauté vegetables and onions with cream and butter to create rich dishes and sauces. With a family history of use at Mount Vernon, this is likely one of three saucepans listed in George Washington's estate inventory.

Serving the Washingtons' Table

Male waiters served meals to George and Martha Washington and their guests. At the presidential residences in New York and Philadelphia, table service was provided by hired white men as well as by enslaved waiters—often of mixed race—who came from Mount Vernon. Louis-Philippe, Duc d'Orleans, visited the estate in the spring of 1797 and noted in his journal:

The general's house servants are mulattoes, some of whom have kinky hair still but skins as light as ours. I noticed one small boy whose hair and skin were so like our own that if I had not been told, I should never have suspected his ancestry. He is nevertheless a slave for the rest of his life.[1]

A prospective waiter's appearance and character were important factors in determining whether or not that individual—be he a free man or a slave—would get the job. In May 1796, when considering the addition of a waiter to the Mount Vernon staff, Washington directed his farm manager William Pearce to have a young slave named Cyrus "taken into the house, and clothes to be made for him. In the meanwhile, get him a strong horn comb and direct him to keep his head well combed, that the hair, or wool may grow long."[2] The black servant depicted in the right-hand corner of the engraving at right, which is based on Edward Savage's 1796 portrait of the Washington family, appears to have long hair tied in a queue, probably the hairstyle Washington wanted Cyrus to wear. Cyrus's job prospects were as dependent on his personal traits as on his appearance:

If Cyrus continues to give evidence of such qualities as would fit him for a waiting man, encourage him to persevere in them; and if they should appear to be sincere and permanent, I will receive him in that character when I retire from public life, if not sooner. To be sober, attentive to his duty, honest, obliging and cleanly, are the qualifications necessary to fit him for my purposes.

This undated hand-colored engraving, after a 1796 portrait of the Washington family by Edward Savage, depicts the president, Mrs. Washington, and her two youngest grandchildren, George Washington (Washy) Parke Custis and Eleanor (Nelly) Parke Custis. One of the family's enslaved black manservants appears in a loose interpretation of the Washington livery.

If he possesses these, or can acquire them, he might become useful to me, at the same time that he would exalt, and benefit himself.[3]

Several months before writing those words, Washington addressed similar points in a letter to his secretary Tobias Lear about the employment of a waiter named William in the presidential residence in Philadelphia. He was willing to pay the young man eight dollars a month, plus other allowances, "being what I am now obliged to give, to the most indifferent set of servants I ever had." The president added that he was not set on hiring William. "Any other genteel looking and well made man (not a giant or dwarf)," he commented, "might answer equally well perhaps, if sober, honest, good tempered, and acquainted with the duties of a house Servant, & footman."[4]

Depending on the formality of the occasion and the number of diners, waiters serving the Washingtons' table might wear the family's red-and-white livery. In his 1786 list of slaves at Mount Vernon, George Washington noted the occupations of two men, Frank Lee and Austin, as "Waiters in the House."[5] Massachusetts representative Theophilus Bradbury, a guest in December 1795 at one of the president's Thursday-afternoon dinners for members of Congress and other public officials, recalled, "We were waited on by four or five men servants dressed in livery."[6] During the same period, another guest noted that breakfast, probably the least formal meal of the day, was attended by "one servant only . . . who had no livery."[7] When Joshua Brookes, a young Englishman in America on business, came to Mount Vernon for dinner in 1799, three servants waited on the table; presumably, they were Frank Lee, Marcus, and Christopher Sheels, each of whom was identified as a house servant on a slave list made four months after Brookes's visit.[8]

Late-eighteenth-century etiquette books spelled out the duties of waiters. According to one such guide, Englishman John Trusler's *The Honours of the Table* (1788), "a good servant will be industrious, and attend to the . . . rules in waiting; but, where he is remiss, it is the duty of the master or mistress to remind him." Among the most crucial of Trusler's numerous rules was the need for waiters to anticipate diners' wishes as well as to "tread lightly across the room, and never to speak, but in reply to a question asked, and then in a modest undervoice."[9]

Although such rules are not known to have been applied per se in the Washington home, waiters at Mount Vernon and in the presidential household no doubt were expected to meet similar high standards. The Reverend Ashbel Green characterized the table servants he observed during George Washington's presidency as being both disciplined and skillful. "Nothing could exceed the order with which [Washington's] table was served," Green recalled many years later. "Every servant knew what he was to do, and did it in the most quiet and yet rapid manner. The dishes and plate were removed and changed, with a silence and speed that seemed like enchantment."[10] ✶ MVT

Martha Washington, Housewife

———◆———

A primary responsibility of the mistresses of upper-class eighteenth-century country houses in both Great Britain and the American South was the orchestration of meals. This task involved determining, among other things, the anticipated number of guests and family members at each meal, what they would be served, and when. At Mount Vernon, this job may have been especially difficult because of the constantly changing number of people in attendance. As the wife of one of the wealthiest and most prominent men in North America, Martha Washington may never have had to cook anything; her many servants, both hired and enslaved, made the meals. Nevertheless, she had to be familiar with all aspects of food preparation and service so that she could supervise activities in her kitchen, larder, dairy, smokehouse, kitchen garden, and dining room.[1]

For a holiday or when hosting important guests, Mrs. Washington may have wanted to prepare something special on her own. According to family lore, a wok-shaped copper vessel, which descended in the family of her second granddaughter, Martha Parke Custis Peter, was a preserving kettle "used by Mrs. Washington herself" and perhaps is physical evidence of her occasional culinary endeavors.[2]

A European guest in 1788 credited Martha Washington with being "an excellent house-wife," whose domain was notable for its "regularity and domestic economy."[3] Her grandson likewise remembered how she excelled in this role: "Mrs. Washington . . . gave her constant attention to all matters of her domestic household, and by her skill and superior management greatly contributed to the comfortable reception and entertainment of the crowds of guests always to be found in the hospitable Mansion of Mount Vernon.[4]

Like her husband, Mrs. Washington was an early riser, up by dawn, and presumably seeing that breakfast was on the table at the family's accustomed hour of 7 a.m.[5] Once that brief meal was over, she "gave orders for dinner, appointing certain provisions, a [pair] of ducks, a goose or a turkey to be laid by, to be put down in case of the arrival of company. . . . A ham was boiled daily."[6] Writing as an elderly man, grandson George Washington Parke Custis tended to idealize the people and events of his childhood at Mount Vernon; his memories of George and Martha Washington were particularly fond—if perhaps unrealistic. His grandmother, he noted, was an extremely neat person, who could "wear a gown for a week, go through her kitchen and laundries, and all the varieties of places in the routine of domestic management, and yet the gown retained its snow-like whiteness, unsullied by even a single speck." She was a firm but fair employer, he added, whose "household was remarkable for the excellence of its domestics."[7]

Mrs. Washington was assisted at various times by a housekeeper, steward, or butler, who performed the more arduous jobs, leaving their mistress free to entertain Mount Vernon's many visitors. The duties and titles of individuals who held these three positions frequently overlapped and often were interchangeable. The first housekeeper for whom records survive was Mary Wilson, who appears to have worked for the family from December 1768 through June the following year and was paid fifteen shillings per month.[8]

In letters written over the years, the Washingtons and, on occasion, their higher-level employees commented on

This pastel portrait of Martha Washington was made around 1862 by French academic painter Charles-François Jalabert, after Gilbert Stuart's unfinished oil portrait of 1796.

the strengths and weaknesses of those who served as housekeeper or steward. For example, in 1783 George Washington's distant cousin and farm manager, Lund Washington, described steward Richard Burnet as

clever in his Way . . . a very good Natured Peacable inoffensive well behaved man, and so far as we have been able to judge will answer the purpose for which he was got, he certainly is a good cook, he appears to be careful active & Industrious, with respect to preservg., Pickling &c.—he is at no loss, but does these things very Ready & Well.[9]

On the other hand, Charles Meunier, who had come to the estate from Philadelphia in 1797, when Washington's presidency ended, quickly proved to be an unsatisfactory steward. As Mrs. Washington complained, the Frenchman was "totally inadequate to the purpose for which he was imployed [*sic*]." She went on to specify that he "knows nothing of cooking—arranging a table—or servants; nor will he assume any authority over them.—Indeed he cannot understand them, nor they him." As a result, she conclud-

*These two pages from the handwritten "Booke of Cookery"
Martha Washington owned include directions for stewing a
neck or loin of lamb and for dressing a dish of "mushrumps"
(mushrooms) in cream. (For a modern adaptation of this
recipe, see page 130.) At least six women of the Culpeper,
Parke, and Custis families recorded favorite recipes in this
cookbook, which apparently dates back to the 1600s.*

ed, "it may readily be conceived then that much confusion ensued."[10]

In October of that year, barely half a year after retiring to Mount Vernon—and despite his step-granddaughter Nelly's earlier proud boast to a friend that she was now "deputy Housekeeper"—the former president wrote to his nephew Bushrod that Mrs. Washington was "exceedingly fatiegued & distressed for want of a good housekeeper." Soon thereafter, the couple found an experienced, competent housekeeper in the person of Mrs. Eleanor Forbes. A childless widow about fifty years old, she had been born in England and previously worked in Richmond for Governor Robert Brooke of Virginia. As the Washingtons' final housekeeper, Mrs. Forbes was altogether satisfactory.[11] * MVT

Martha Washington's Cookbooks

———— ❖ ————

I n carrying out her domestic tasks, Martha Washington had access to at least two cookbooks. The first was a manuscript handed down through several generations of women in the family of her first husband, Daniel Parke Custis, and inherited by Martha when she married him in 1750. The late culinary historian Karen Hess was intrigued to find inside the manuscript eleven pages of recipes, written by six different individuals in seventeenth-century script; their presence convinced her that the cookbook was a copy of an even earlier manuscript and that at least some of its recipes dated to the sixteenth century. This and other bits of evidence suggested to her that the manuscript probably had been in the possession of Daniel's late mother, Frances Parke Custis (1687–1715), who had received it from her own mother, Jane Ludwell Parke. Jane's stepmother, Frances Culpeper, Lady Berkeley, who died around 1691—or perhaps even her mother—had compiled the original text.

Generations later, Martha Washington presented the manuscript cookbook to her youngest granddaughter, Eleanor (Nelly) Parke Custis Lewis, in whose family it remained until 1892, when it was given to the Historical Society of Pennsylvania. Hess believed this heirloom "had not served as a working kitchen manual since the beginning of the [eighteenth] century, perhaps earlier," and that at the time the newly married Martha Dandridge Custis received it, "[m]any of the recipes must have seemed old-fashioned . . . and they became increasingly so as time went on." So although these recipes might not have been followed at Mount Vernon, they do provide valuable insights into the origins of the Virginia cuisine served at the Washingtons' table.[1]

Mrs. Washington's second cookbook was *The Art of Cookery, Made Plain and Easy*, by Hannah Glasse. She probably owned a copy of the sixth edition (1763); seventeen editions were published between 1747 and 1803.[2] Evidence that she used this book—the most popular of its type in both England and the American colonies—is found in a January 1835 letter from Nelly Custis Lewis to her son-in-law Charles M. Conrad. "I am very glad my lip salve pleases you. It was my beloved grandmothers recipe, & she found it I believe in Glass' [*sic*] Cookery." Nelly had sent the same recipe to her longtime friend Elizabeth Bordley Gibson in 1825 and, the year before that, to the Lafayette family in France.[3]

Besides reading these books to understand how certain dishes should be prepared, Mrs. Washington may well have read recipes aloud to the cook, much as Thomas Jefferson's wife, Martha, is said to have done at Monticello.[4] She likely exchanged recipes with friends and neighbors, too. Another manuscript cookbook, said to have descended through a branch of the Jefferson family, contains twenty-five recipes attributed to Mrs. Washington or the kitchen at Mount Vernon.[5] Two similar manuscripts—one compiled by Martha Washington's granddaughter Nelly Custis Lewis in the 1830s (probably for her eldest daughter) and the second by Mrs. Washington's great-granddaughter Mary Randolph Custis Lee (Mrs. Robert E. Lee)—attest to the widespread practice of trading recipes. Recipe number 65 in Nelly's manuscript is an abbreviated version of her grandmother's lip-salve concoction, with a note suggesting the addition of an ingredient to "give the lipsalve a fine odour." Recipe number 145 details the preparation of Martha Washington's remedy for ridding young children of worms.[6] * MVT

Ice Cream

Norborne Berkeley, fourth Baron Botetourt, who was Virginia's colonial governor from 1768 to 1770, may have introduced the Washingtons to ice cream; he served the dish to guests at his residence in Williamsburg.[1] The first known reference to the dessert at Mount Vernon dates to May 1784, when a "Cream Machine for Ice" was acquired for £1.13.3.[2] Subsequently, the Washingtons purchased additional utensils for preparing and serving ice cream; two "dble tin Ice Cream moulds" were acquired for $2.50 in May 1792 and another in June 1795 for $7; the following March, they spent five shillings for an ice cream spoon.[3]

Ice cream was often on the menu at Washington's New York and Philadelphia residences during his presidency. For example, his wife served it at her Friday-night levées (see page 70). Abigail Adams described one such occasion in August 1789, during which guests were "entertained with Ice creems & Lemonade."[4] Pennsylvania Senator William Maclay, who came to dinner later that month, reported, "The dessert was, first Apple pies puddings &ca.; then iced creams Jellies &ca. then Water Melons Musk Melons apples peaches nuts."[5]

The inventory of Washington's estate, completed shortly after his death, lists two pewter ice-cream pots (together valued at $3) and another eight made of tin (together valued at $1) as being stored on the top floor of the kitchen.[6] Today, Mount Vernon's collection contains a late-eighteenth- or early-nineteenth-century tin ice-cream freezer that is not original but probably resembles ice-cream pots the Washingtons owned. To make ices, sherbets, or ice cream, ingredients were put into the pot, or freezer, which was then set into a tub of cracked ice and salt. The pot was turned by means of a loop handle at the top, and its contents were periodically stirred until they achieved the desired consistency.

Martha Washington's copy of the popular English cookbook *The Art of Cookery, Made Plain and Easy* contained the following recipe for ice cream:

Take two pewter basons, one larger than the other; the inward one must have a close cover, into which you are to put your cream, and mix it with raspberries, or whatever you like best, to give it a flavour and a colour. Sweeten it to your palate; then cover it close, and set into the larger bason. Fill it with ice, and a handful of salt: let it stand in this ice three quarters of an hour, then uncover it, and stir the cream well together; cover it close again, and let it stand half an hour longer, after that turn it into your plate. These things are made at the pewterers.[7]

Among the surviving items from the 309-piece white-and-gold French china service George Washington purchased during his presidency are an icery, several serving trays, and small footed cups, known as ice pots. The service originally included "2 Iceries Compleat," twelve "ice plates," and thirty-six "ice pots." The ice plates and pots would have been placed at intervals on the table during dessert and filled from the iceries. Because the eighteenth-century version of ice cream had a relatively liquid consistency, it typically was served in small cups. Two iceries from a blue-and-white china service that the Washingtons gave to their friends Mayor and Mrs. Samuel Powel of Philadelphia also are in the Mount Vernon collection.[8] ✳ MVT

RIGHT:
The Right Honble. Norborne Berkeley, Baron de Bottetourt [*sic*], late Governor of Virginia, *by English engraver Harry Ashby, after a late-eighteenth-century portrait medallion. During his brief term in office (1768–70), Botetourt may have provided the Washingtons and other Virginians who were guests at the Governor's Palace in Williamsburg with their first taste of ice cream.*

In Mount Vernon's spacious kitchen, an early tin ice-cream maker is nestled inside a wooden barrel filled with ice. Ripe berries have been gathered from the kitchen gardens to flavor the cold, sweet confection.

Tea on the Piazza

——— ✦ ———

The two-story piazza (or portico) of George Wash-ington's Mansion offered a commanding view of the Potomac River, a place to catch summer breezes, and a pleasant spot to enjoy refreshments when the weather permitted. As one gentleman recalled: "The situation of Mount Vernon is known to every one to be of surpassing beauty. It stands on the banks of the Potomac, but much elevated above the river, and affords an extensive view of this beautiful piece of water and of the opposite shore. At the back of the house, overlooking the river, is a wide piazza, which was the general resort in the afternoon."[1]

Architect Benjamin Henry Latrobe, who visited Mount Vernon in July 1796, rendered in watercolor a depiction of the Washington family taking tea at the north end of the piazza. Martha Washington is shown seated before a sil-ver hot-water urn and tea ware, placed on one of the card or breakfast tables that could be easily moved outside. Her husband sits in an armchair—possibly one of the thirty Windsor chairs listed after his death as having been "In the Piazza"—his gaze turned toward the horizon and ships in the distance.[2] The children of the household are also in the scene: George Washington (Washy) Parke Custis aims his telescope toward the Potomac; Eleanor (Nelly) Parke Custis leans against a pillar; and young George Washington Motier Lafayette sits on the stone pavers.[3] This charming image suggests not only the portability of Mansion furnishings to accommodate outdoor dining but also the relaxed enjoy-ment of tea on a summer afternoon.

The piazza also was the setting for more elaborate after-noon and evening summertime teas. In June 1796, Philadel-phian Elizabeth Wescott recalled an occasion when "the tea equipage was paraded in order."[4] The formal presentation of tea ware was one means of offering a gracious welcome to distinguished guests. President Washington wrote to his nephew Robert Lewis the same month that he expected his house would "be crowded with company all the while we shall be at it, this Summer, as the Ministers of France, Great Britain and Portugal, in succession, intend to be here. Be-sides other strangers."[5] For entertaining dignitaries as well as "strangers" on warm Virginia days, the piazza must have served as a welcome venue for late afternoon or evening tea. George and Martha Washington could use one or more of their imported porcelain tea services to offer the exotic eighteenth century beverage to guests in an elegant manner befitting their visitors and commensurate with the Wash-ingtons' renowned hospitality. ✦ CBC

OPPOSITE:
A silver urn sits prominently on the tea table in Benjamin Henry Latrobe's 1796 water-color depiction of tea on the Mount Vernon piazza.

RIGHT:
The Washingtons owned a variety of costly and special-ized tea wares, including a silver urn for dispensing hot water into a teapot by means of a spigot. This example, marked by London silver-smith John Carter II and embellished with the Custis coat of arms, was possibly ordered for the 1774 wedding of Martha Washington's son, John (Jacky) Parke Custis.

"Served up in excellent order"

Everyday Dining at Mount Vernon

———•———

Mary V. Thompson

✳✳

The day began early at Mount Vernon, where George Washington expected breakfast to be on the table by 7 a.m.[1] By that time, he had already been up for several hours, gotten dressed, and begun reading or working on his correspondence. Fond of both horses and hounds, he generally made a daily inspection of his stable and kennel around sunrise.[2] Apparently, this routine was altered only on mornings when he went hunting; then, he ate breakfast before dawn, by candlelight.[3]

Others in the household were also up and about before breakfast. One family member recalled that Martha Washington was "an uncommon early riser," who left "her pillow at day-dawn" and immediately set about her "household duties." Occasionally, she indulged in a few minutes of exercise; a female guest in 1801 recalled going for a long walk before breakfast and seeing, in the distance, Martha Washington strolling on the piazza.[4] Nelly Custis, her youngest granddaughter, spent the early morning hours in study and correspondence. As she wrote to a friend in 1794: "I got up this morning at a quarter before five—and sat myself soberly down to get a long Italian lesson—and after that took pen in hand to write to you."[5] Meanwhile, her younger brother, George Washington Parke Custis, was variously involved with both studies and hunting.[6]

With the household engaged in various activities in different locations, a signal was needed to call everyone together. In October 1793, Winthrop Sargent, a government official from the Ohio Territory, was summoned to breakfast at Mount Vernon by "the great Bell," which probably was similar to those at two other sizable Virginia plantations, Monticello and Sabine Hall. One resident at Sabine Hall noted that the bell there, which weighed more than sixty pounds, was "always rung at meal Times."[7]

Architect Benjamin Henry Latrobe wrote in July 1796 that he and other Mount Vernon visitors gathered in "the sitting-room," probably the west parlor, before breakfast, where "all the latest newspapers were laid out." Once in the dining room, he found what he considered a typical Virginia breakfast: tea, coffee, and cold and broiled meats.[8] Early in 1802, Massachusetts Congressman Manasseh Cutler breakfasted on ham, cold corned beef, cold fowl, red herring, and cold mutton, all garnished with parsley and other garden vegetables. At that meal, Martha Washington sat at the head of the table, next to the "tea and coffee equipage," from which she served her guests.[9] Chocolate was another favorite breakfast beverage. Burgess Ball, son-in-law of Washington's brother Charles, asked the president in 1794 to send him two or three bushels of chocolate shells; he had "frequently drank Chocolate . . . at Mt. Vernon, as my Wife thinks it agreed with her better than any other Breakfast."[10] Referring to the fact that no one lingered over this meal, Latrobe commented, "It was very soon over."[11]

Sargent found breakfast with the Washingtons to be a "very substantial Repast," noting that "Indian hoe cake with Butter & Honey seemed the principal Component Parts."[12] Hoecake (also known in the South as Johnnycake), a corn-

✳✳

meal pancake that some historians contend reflects the slave influence on Anglo-American cuisine was mentioned by visitors and by Martha's grandchildren as George Washington's typical breakfast.[13] Julian Niemcewicz, a visitor from Poland, reported that Washington had "tea and caks [sic] made from maize; because of his teeth he makes slices spread with butter and honey."[14] According to Nelly Custis, "he ate three small mush cakes (Indian meal) swimming in butter and honey" and drank three cups of tea without cream." Her younger brother described Washington's Spartan approach: "This meal was with out change to him whose habits were regular, even to matters which others are so apt to indulge themselves in to endless variety. Indian cakes, honey, and tea, formed this temperate repast." On days he went hunting, however, Washington would substitute "a bowl of milk" for the tea.[15]

Breakfast was considered an essential meal, probably because of the eight-hour interval between it and dinner. On the day he left Mount Vernon, Latrobe asked a servant to bring his horses to the door by 10 a.m.; he noted that "as soon as my servant came up [George Washington] went to him and asked him if he had breakfasted."[16] Guests who arrived before eating breakfast were fed, even if the Washingtons had already eaten. In the summer of 1786, a perhaps exasperated George Washington recorded, "Just after we had breakfasted, & my horse was at the door for me to ride, Colonel and Mrs. [Nicholas] Rogers came in. When they sat down to breakfast which was prepared for them, I commenced my ride for Muddy hole, Dogue run & Ferry Plantations [and] to my meadow on Dogue run and the Mill."[17] Twelve years later, Friedrich Wilhelm Hoeninghaus, a young German traveler, reached Mount Vernon one March morning long after breakfast had been served; nevertheless, after George Washington greeted him, he was led into the little parlor and offered breakfast.[18]

After breakfast, while Washington made his habitual eight-to-fourteen-mile ride around the estate, and as visitors rambled about the grounds, preparations began for the family's next—and main—meal, which was dinner.[19] For those who were hungry in the meantime, snacks, both sweet and savory, were available. After visiting with the Washingtons at Tudor Place, the home of Martha's second granddaughter, Martha Parke Custis Peter, Julian Niemcewicz recorded an appealing domestic scene. As the sixteen-month old daughter of Eliza Parke Custis Law (another granddaughter) toddled into the room where the adults were talking, "Gl. Washington called to her; he took from his pocket a roll of peach cheese [a molded paste of fruit and water that is sliced after hardening]; "Here is something for you," he said and gave her a piece and embraced her."[20]

During his rides about the estate, Washington may well have used the "Farmers Luncheon box" that was found in his study after his death.[21] A list of personal belongings sold to his heirs on July 22, 1802, suggests what snack the box might have contained; it records the sale of a "Sandwitch box" to a member of the Washington family.[22]

George Washington generally returned home about half an hour to an hour before dinner.[23] Nelly Custis remembered that the meal usually was served at 3 p.m., which was typical for a Virginia plantation. On Sunday, however, the family ate an hour earlier, in order to "accommodate his servants with a long afternoon."[24] Her recollection of these mealtimes is confirmed in a letter Washington wrote after learning that his nephew Bushrod Washington and his wife were planning to arrive on a Thursday afternoon. After informing the young couple that "my Chariot shall meet you at Colchester at 3 O'clock on that day," he reminded them, "By your Fixing on that hour for its being there, I presume you did not intend to be here at dinner (it being the hour at which we dine) of course shall niether [sic] expect or wait for you [presumably, at the table]."[25]

Changing clothes before dinner seems to have been customary at this level of society. Both step-granddaughter Nelly and Polish visitor Niemcewicz recorded that George Washington dressed for the occasion. And in a letter to Nelly's brother, Washington suggested that the young man, nicknamed Washy, stop what he was doing about an hour before the meal, a time "allowed for dressing, & preparing for [dinner], that you may appear decent."[26] Others followed this practice as well. One of Nelly's friends noted that after breakfast at Mount Vernon, "we either worked, read, or attended to Miss Custis [Nelly,] who plays most charmingly on the piano, until about twelve o'clock, when we dressed for dinner."[27]

As with breakfast, a bell was rung fifteen minutes before dinner was served to call the busy household to the table. Washington wrote a friend in 1763 of his disappointment that an anticipated guest had not arrived at Mount Vernon by dinnertime: "A constant Watch was kept untill the accustomed Bell gave the signal for Dinner, and said it was time to look no more."[28] Martha Washington's grandson remembered that, in his later years, Washington generally rode his horse at a moderate pace, except when running late for dinner. Then, he wrote, this "most punctual of men would display the horsemanship of his better days, and a hard gallop [would] bring him up to time, so that the sound of his horse's hoofs and the first dinner-bell should be heard together at a quarter to three o'clock."[29]

George Washington was as punctilious and precise about mealtimes as he was about other aspects of his life, and he expected the same of others. In September 1797, he closed a quick note to Tobias Lear, his former secretary and longtime friend, with these words: "In much haste dinner waiting."[30] The following year, the former president advised Washy to

make it an invariable rule to be in place . . . at the usual breakfasting, dining, and tea hours. It is not only disagreeable, but it is also very inconvenient, for servants to be running here, and there, and they know not where, to summon you to them, when their duties, and attendance, on the company who are seated, render it improper."[31]

Washington's frequently expressed preference for household design and decor that were straightforward and unpretentious pertained to his food preferences as well. According to Washy, he "ate heartily" at dinner "but was not particular in his diet, with the exception of fish, of which he was excessively fond."[32] Several French officers stopped at Mount

Martha Washington's two youngest grandchildren, George Washington (Washy) Parke Custis and Eleanor (Nelly) Parke Custis, shared fond memories of meals served at Mount Vernon. Around 1796, when they were about fifteen and seventeen, respectively, they posed for these pastel portraits by English artist James Sharples.

Vernon in 1780 to pay their respects to Mrs. Washington, who invited them to dinner. The table was described as "abundantly served, but without profusion," and at least one guest was pleased with his first-ever taste of preserved strawberries.[33] In the spring of 1788, a Mr. Winsor had "an exceeding good dinner" at Mount Vernon that "was served up in excellent order."[34] Scottish artist Archibald Robertson, entertained at a family meal during the presidency, found the dinner "plain, but suitable for a family in genteel and comfortable circumstances."[35] And the Reverend John Latta, who dined at Mount Vernon in July 1799, recorded that the "table is furnished in [a] great, but not luxurious, variety of dishes."[36]

Unfortunately, there are only scant records of significant details about the meals the Washingtons served their guests. Massachusetts jurist Amariah Frost provided a few after enjoying a "very good" dinner in June 1797; it included "a small roasted pigg, boiled leg of lamb, roasted fowles, beef, peas, lettice, cucumbers, artichokes, etc., puddings, tarts, etc., etc." The tablecloth was removed after dinner, as was cus-

A damask napkin bears the Washingtons' laundry mark, carefully embroidered in blue silk on one corner: "1/GW/48." Elegant and expensive table linens were important indicators of genteel manners. Numbering each item avoided wearing out individual napkins by rotating their use.

tomary, and George Washington offered, as a toast, "All our Friends."[37] About a year and a half later, Joshua Brookes described how the food was arranged on the table: a "leg of boiled pork" at the head, a goose at the foot, and, in between, roast beef, a round of cold boiled beef, mutton chops, hominy, cabbage, potatoes, pickles, fried tripe, and onions, among other items. During dinner, wine, porter, and beer were offered. The tablecloth was wiped off before the second course, which included mince pies, tarts, and cheese, was served. After the tablecloth was removed, port, Madeira wine, two kinds of nuts, apples, and raisins were set out. Three servants attended the eight people dining that day.[38]

During the eighteenth century, it was customary in Anglican homes, such as Mount Vernon, for brief prayers to be offered at both the beginning and end of the meal. For instance, while dining at the home of a Virginia minister late in 1773, Philip Vickers Fithian, a Northerner who had come south to work as a tutor, was asked to voice thanks before the meal ("God bless us in what we are to receive") and afterward ("God make us thankful for his mercies").[39] Although Amariah Frost mentioned that no prayers were said before the Mount Vernon dinner he was served in 1797, George Washington, on a later occasion, asked minister John Latta to "officiate in [his] clerical character" at the opening and closing of the meal.[40] According to guests at his table during the Revolutionary War and the presidency, Washington himself generally stood and said grace before headquarters and Congressional dinners, "as fathers of a family do in America"; of course, if a clergyman were present, he might be asked to say the customary prayers instead. One wartime guest supping with Washington for the first time wrote:

> *I did not perceive that he made this prayer; yet I remember that, on taking his place at table, he made a gesture and said a word which I took for a piece of politeness, and which perhaps was a religious action. In this case, his prayer must have been short; the clergyman made use of more forms.*[41]

Dinners with the Washingtons at Mount Vernon ended according to a ritual described in a British etiquette guide of

Blue-and-white Chinese export porcelains fill the butler's pantry, echoing their listing in the inventory of Washington's estate taken soon after he died. Updating his table settings in 1783, at the end of the Revolutionary War, he sent home more than 205 pieces, including tureens, butter boats, salad dishes, and various plates.

the time: "[A]fter the cloth and dessert are removed and two or three glasses of wine are gone round, . . . the ladies . . . retire and leave the men to themselves."[42] Julian Niemcewicz noted that during his 1798 visit, he and Washington talked for hours at a time, both "at the table after the departure of the ladies, or else in the evening seated under the portico [piazza]."[43] One visitor to the presidential household recalled that the gentlemen, not the ladies, withdrew from the dining room after a family dinner he attended. According to artist Archibald Robertson, dinner concluded with a few glasses of champagne, over which people lingered for about forty-five minutes, after which "the General and Colonel [Tobias] Lear retired, leaving the ladies in high glee."[44]

Late in the day, the Washingtons gathered for tea, which actually was a light meal served "at sunset in summer and at candlelight in winter."[45] Accounts left by several visitors enable us to pinpoint the time this meal typically was served. A guest visiting from Philadelphia in June 1796 noted that tea was offered at 7 p.m. and, probably because of the summer heat, was taken on "the large and magnificent Portico at the back of the house where the tea equipage was paraded in order."[46] The following month, Boston merchant Thomas Handasyd Perkins wrote, "[T]he first evening I lodged at Mount Vernon . . . . the day trenched far upon the evening, and at seven or eight o'clock we were taking our tea."[47] In June 1798, Niemcewicz recorded having "Tea at 7 o'clock," after which George Washington "chats until nine, and then he goes to bed."[48] It was customary in the eighteenth century to eat bread, butter, and little "cakes" or cookies at tea; accordingly, George Washington Parke Custis recalled that his step-grandfather "always took a little tea and toast between six and seven in the evening."[49]

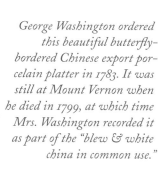

George Washington ordered this beautiful butterfly-bordered Chinese export porcelain platter in 1783. It was still at Mount Vernon when he died in 1799, at which time Mrs. Washington recorded it as part of the "blew & white china in common use."

Occasionally, supper was offered later in the evening, but apparently it was not part of the Washingtons' normal routine; possibly this was because, as a guest in 1793 noted, "Suppers and even a Glass of wine in the Eve[nin]g [afflicted Washington] with the head ache."[50] Martha Washington's grandson recalled that during a typical family evening, George Washington would leaf through newspapers "while taking his single cup of tea (his only supper)," reading aloud "passages of peculiar interest, making remarks upon the same." At nine, he would bid everyone good night and head for his bedroom.[51]

Yet there were notable occasions when the evening did not end so early. When Robert Hunter, Jr., a young British merchant, visited Mount Vernon in the fall of 1785, he noted that Washington retired to his study to write for "two hours, between tea and supper." On that particular day, his host was "anxious to hear the news of Congress" from houseguest Richard Henry Lee; otherwise, he probably "would not have returned to supper, but gone to bed at his usual hour, nine o'clock, for he seldom makes any ceremony." Hunter recalled that everyone in attendance enjoyed "a very elegant supper about that time," at which Washington "with a few glasses of champagne got quite merry, and being with his intimate friends laughed and talked a good deal." Hunter realized his good fortune in observing such exuberance: "Before strangers [Washington] is generally very reserved, and seldom says a word."[52]

Philadelphian Elizabeth Wescott visited Mount Vernon in June 1796. She was close to the young people in the household, who at that time included not only Martha Washington's grandchildren but also the son of the Marquis de Lafayette. An account of her stay includes a description of an early evening concert by Nelly and young Lafayette, followed by supper:

> [W]e again returned to the portico, which commands a most extensive view of the Potomac and the country adjacent. The prospect is most noble indeed, and at the same time beautifully romantic. We sat in this delightful place admiring the scenery around us, rendered more beautiful from the serenity of the evening and the moon

> which played upon the water, together with some beautiful music from Miss Custis and Mr[.] Fayette—indeed it was more like enchantment than anything else. . . . Precisely at nine o'clock my reverie was disturbed by the servant calling us to supper—which consisted of fruits and cream, cakes[,] wine, etc.

She and the Washingtons remained at the table for about an hour before retiring to their respective bedrooms.[53]

Architect Benjamin Henry Latrobe, however, wistfully recorded a different situation about a month later, when "Mrs. Washington and Miss Custis had retired early and the President left the company about 8 o'clock. We soon after retired to bed. There was no hint of Supper."[54] A light meal of bread, butter, cold meats and fruits, supper was typically eaten on other plantations about seven o'clock in the evening, but could be served later, as at Mount Vernon and Sabine Hall, where "We go into Supper commonly about half after eight or at nine."[55]

By the time supper was over and everyone went to their rooms, the kitchen staff had already started making bread for the next day, when the round of meals and arrival of guests (whether expected or unexpected) would begin again. ∗

OVERLEAF:
The piazza, added to the east front of the Mansion in 1777, provided a delightful outdoor living space, sheltered from the Virginia sun and cooled by breezes off the Potomac. During the summer, family and friends would often gather there in the late afternoon for tea.

Dining Rooms at Mount Vernon

———•———

Rooms formally designated to accommodate dining became a common feature in upper-class Virginia homes during the first half of the eighteenth century. Before that, and continuing for many decades in more modest dwellings, people ate in a room called the "hall," which generally served as a multipurpose living space. The popularity of formal dining rooms paralleled the increasing importance of mealtimes as socially significant occasions when hosts could demonstrate their mastery of genteel behavior.[1] The original Mount Vernon house, built in 1735 by George Washington's father, Augustine Washington, included a room designated as the "hall." After George Washington assumed ownership in 1754, the hall was upgraded to become a fashionable dining room. After the Revolutionary War, he added a second dining room as part of an even more ambitious expansion project. What he called the "new room," which dwarfed every other space in the Mansion in size and in grandeur, was a fitting setting in which America's most respected man could entertain friends and other guests.[2]

The house Augustine Washington had built exhibited typical Georgian colonial characteristics, with symmetrical one-and-a-half-story facades and an entry passage flanked by two sets of rooms intended for both public and private use. The hall was one of two larger rooms positioned on the west side—the formal front—of the house.[3] According to an inventory made in 1753 after the death of George Washington's older half-brother, Lawrence, the hall contained, among other objects, a mahogany table, a dozen walnut chairs, two mirrors, a collection of "blew & white china" tableware, silverware, beer and wine glasses, and a punch bowl.[4] The absence of bedding and certain other household items suggests that this space mainly served as a dining room.

When Washington began expanding and redecorating the Mansion in 1775, he was determined to transform the southwest room flanking the passage into an elegantly ornamented dining room. This space may have been the site of the old hall, although it is unclear from documentary evidence which of the two west-front rooms had served that function.[5] Washington spared no expense in redecorating the new dining room. He paid William Sears, a talented craftsman who previously had worked for George Mason at his nearby Gunston Hall estate, to carve a wooden mantelpiece and fireplace surround modeled after a design found in an English "pattern" book, Abraham Swan's *The British Architect* (1745). Washington hired another craftsman, cryptically referred to in records as the "French stucco man," to fabricate an ornate plaster ceiling, also based on an English source—in this case, a plate included in William Pain's *The Practical Builder* (1774).[6] In 1787 the walls were painted in a vibrant verdigris, a shade of green that was then highly fashionable in British America.[7]

In addition to upgrading the existing spaces, Washington planned to add wings to the north and south facades, which effectively doubled the size of the house. The first two floors of the north wing would accommodate a formal dining room. When Washington was called away in May 1775 to command the Continental Army at the outbreak of the Revolutionary War, he appointed his farm manager and distant cousin, Lund Washington, to oversee construction.[8] In a letter to Lund in September 1776, he made clear his high expectations for the "new room," specifying that above all he wanted to "have the whole executed in a masterly manner."[9] But when Washington returned to Mount Vernon in late 1783 and saw that much remained to be done, he himself took charge of some of the work, searching for materials and craftsmen who were sufficiently skilled to carry out his ambitious plans.

Washington wrote to one workman to emphasize that the decoration should be executed "in a plain neat style," and once again he looked to Great Britain for inspiration to guide his design.[10] He selected a plate from Batty Langley's influential *The City and Country Builder's Treasury of Designs* (1756) that served as the model for a three-part Venetian window, the room's dominant architectural feature.[11] Apparently based on an original design by an unknown hand, the plaster ceiling incorporated various agricultural symbols meant to complement those found in the Italian-marble chimneypiece that Samuel Vaughan, an English admirer, had sent to Washington. Applied plaster ornaments in the then-fashionable neoclassical style popularized by English architect Robert Adam adorned the woodwork, the frieze, and the fields on the Venetian window and in the coved portion of the ceiling. As in the smaller dining room, verdigris-green paint on the walls completed the dramatic overall effect.[12]

Besides accommodating large gatherings of friends and family for dining and dancing, the new large dining room was the setting for other, more serious events. In 1781, years before its remodeling was completed, the room may have been the site of a strategy session Washington called in conjunction with the French general Rochambeau and his staff; its purpose was to prepare for the southern campaign that ended with the British surrender at Yorktown. Legend also has it that this was the room where Washington received word in 1789 that he had been unanimously elected president of the United States. Even if that story is apocryphal, it was in this room that George Washington's body lay in state after his death on December 14, 1799, and preceding burial in the family vault four days later.[13] ✳ DJP

This silver-plated candlestick was purchased by President Washington from Philadelphia silversmith Rowland Perry in 1795 for the executive household. After Washington retired from the presidency, the candlestick was used at Mount Vernon.

The Kitchen at Mount Vernon

A standard feature on Virginia plantations from at least the mid-1600s until the mid-nineteenth century was a structure, detached from the main house, where food was prepared. Functional, social, and environmental factors unique to the American South dictated the unusual placement of this architectural feature. These factors included the concern for safety from fire, the desire to escape the heat and "the smell of hot victuals, offensive in hot weather," and the general regional practice of separating domestic functions from the dwelling in order to reinforce the segregation of black servants' activities from those of the planter family.[1] Such a kitchen was built at Mount Vernon before 1753 and was replaced in 1775, the year George Washington undertook a major effort to enlarge the Mansion and alter the layout of various outbuildings as well as of the surrounding gardens and grounds.[2]

The earlier kitchen was one of four outbuildings (along with the dairy, storehouse, and washhouse) that were positioned in two pairs, each of which ran in a line at an angle to a corner of the Mansion's west facade. They formed an open forecourt, framing the house and facing the circle where the formal carriage driveway leading to the Mansion ended. Although these structures no longer stand, archaeological investigations that began in the 1930s unearthed their foundations. Interestingly, the two inner buildings—the dairy and the storehouse—sat on stone foundations, as does the earliest portion of the Mansion, while brick foundations supported the larger kitchen and washhouse. This difference in material suggests that perhaps the dairy and storehouse were built in 1735, the same year the Mansion was constructed, while the other structures were erected somewhat later but before March 1753, when the inventory of the estate of Washington's older half-brother, Lawrence, was compiled.[3]

The expansion-and-redesign project that Washington launched just before leaving Mount Vernon in May 1775 to command American forces outside Boston called for the construction of new outbuildings to match the enlarged Mansion. The outmoded structures were razed, and two buildings—the kitchen and servants' hall—were erected in their stead. They were placed farther back to accommodate the expanded plan and faced each other across the driveway circle. The new buildings were larger and more architecturally significant than the originals, matching the Mansion in many details; most notably, the siding boards on the facade facing the circle were beveled and sanded to resemble stone blocks. Covered walkways, called colonnades, were built to link each of the new structures to the Mansion. Servants carrying food back and forth between the kitchen and the small dining room could now do so along a protected passageway.[4]

The kitchen at Mount Vernon is a substantial structure, with three workrooms on the first floor and a loft above, which variously served as the residence of the cook or the housekeeper. The largest of the three workrooms contains a sizable fireplace and an attached oven; the other two rooms are a scullery, where food was prepared and dishes washed, and a larder (with a subterranean cooling floor) for storage. According to the inventory of the building compiled after George Washington's death, the kitchen boasted an array of cooking equipment that included pots and pans, skillets, a griddle, a toaster, a boiler, spits, chafing dishes, tin and pewter "Ice Cream Pots," coffeepots, strainers, and much more.[5] * DJP

Mount Vernon's kitchen sprang to life about 4:30 each morning, when the cooks would arrive to revive the fire and start preparations for breakfast at 7 a.m.—stirring the batter for hoecakes, grinding beans for coffee, slicing cold meats from the day before, and fetching fresh cream and butter from the dairy.

Martha Washington once remarked that vegetables are "the best part of our living in the country." Shown here in the Mount Vernon kitchen is an array of fresh produce from the garden, including Danver half-long carrots, pattypan squash, savoy cabbage, drum-head cabbage, red potatoes, and Swiss chard.

The Cooks' Day, 1790s

4 A.M. Nathan, one of the Washingtons' two enslaved cooks at the Mansion, wakes up in his bunk in the greenhouse quarters, washes, shaves, and dresses. Around the same time and in a nearby cabin, the other cook, Lucy, and her husband, Frank Lee, the butler, wake up and prepare for work.

4:30 A.M. Lucy and Nathan meet in the kitchen and begin their workday routine by stirring the fire to revive it and drawing and heating water. Throughout the day, their tasks will require at least thirty large pieces of wood and many wooden buckets of water, each weighing about twenty pounds when full.

5 A.M. Mrs. Forbes, the hired housekeeper who lives on the second floor of the kitchen building, awakes to the sounds of breakfast preparations below. She dresses and comes downstairs to supervise Lucy and Nathan, and to check with Frank Lee to ensure that the table is properly set for breakfast in the small dining room.

Lucy stirs the hoecake batter and kneads the bread dough, both of which she started the previous night, while Nathan roasts coffee beans.

6 A.M. Martha Washington goes down to the kitchen to ensure that breakfast is under way, and then walks around the piazza for exercise. Kitty stops by the kitchen, where she delivers fresh cream and butter from the dairy.

6:30 A.M. Lucy and Nathan make hoecakes, coffee, tea, and chocolate for the Washingtons' breakfast. They also slice cold meat left over from the previous day's dinner to supplement the first meal of the day.

6:45 A.M. The plantation bell is rung to announce that breakfast soon will be served. Lucy and Nathan finish their cooking and, with the help of enslaved waiters Frank Lee, Christopher Sheels, and Marcus, send food to the small dining room.

7 A.M. Frank Lee makes sure the breakfast table is properly laid and then leaves Marcus, a young domestic slave, to help serve the meal. Frank goes to the kennel to check on and feed the dogs.

7:30 A.M. The gardener stops by the kitchen with today's basket of ripe fruits and vegetables. Lucy talks to him about getting some mint later in the day, after the dew on the leaves has dried.

8 A.M. Martha Washington returns to the kitchen, where she, Nathan, and Lucy inspect the produce and contents of the larder and discuss the dinner menu; she consults one or more of her cookbooks for guidance in preparing certain dishes. She goes into the scullery to be sure the breakfast dishes are properly washed.

Frank Lee, Christopher Sheels, and Marcus clear the table in the small dining room. Lucy begins cleaning pots and pans, while Nathan and Mrs. Washington go to the poultry yard, where they feed the birds and select the turkey that will soon become one of the dinner entrees.

9 A.M. Lucy and Nathan begin preparing dinner by washing and chopping vegetables. Meanwhile, the turkey is being killed and plucked.

9:45 A.M. Nathan prepares a sandwich for George Washington, who is about to leave on his daily rounds of the plantation.

Danish artist Joachim Ferdinand Richardt depicted the east front of Mount Vernon when he visited in July 1858. This detail highlights a black woman carrying a steaming dish through the south passage, from the kitchen to the Mansion, where the family of John Augustine Washington III, the last Washingtons to own Mount Vernon, presumably waits.

11 A.M. Lucy's mother, Old Doll, is an elderly slave who was the first cook at the Mansion after the Washingtons were wed in 1759. Now she is too old to work on a regular basis, but at the request of Mrs. Washington, she comes to the kitchen to distill some mint water for medicinal purposes.

12 NOON Lucy takes a few minutes to sit down and rest. As per instructions from George Washington, she does not waste this time; picking up her knitting, she resumes working on a pair of stockings.

Father Jack, as the Washingtons call him, is an elderly slave who was born in Africa. Despite his advanced age, he goes down to the Potomac River and fishes from his canoe in order to catch one of George Washington's favorite foods, which will be served at dinner.

2 P.M. Martha Washington stops by the small dining room and the kitchen to oversee dinner preparations. Lucy is responsible for the baking, while Nathan tends the iron and copper pots in the fireplace; temperatures on the hearth can reach 170 degrees Fahrenheit.

Father Jack brings the fish he has caught up to the kitchen and gives them to Nathan.

2:45 P.M. The plantation bell rings to alert everyone that dinner will be served in fifteen minutes. Frank Lee, Christopher Sheels, and Marcus are in the kitchen, helping Lucy and Nathan transfer the foods prepared for dinner into serving dishes and platters. Then the three waiters carry the dishes to the small dining room and finish setting the table.

3 P.M. Lucy and Nathan eat dinner in the kitchen, while the Washingtons and their guests are served in the small dining room.

4:30 P.M. Frank, Christopher, and Marcus clear the table and clean up the dining room after dinner. Then they eat their own meal.

5 P.M. Lucy gives Frank some food scraps that he takes to the dogs, which are down the hill at the kennel. Then she disposes of refuse from the meal by throwing a pail of it into the south grove midden. Nathan chops wood for use in the kitchen the next day.

6 P.M. Assisted by Christopher and Marcus, Lucy and Nathan are in the kitchen, brewing tea and slicing bread and leftover cold meat for the next meal—tea. The Washingtons are expecting to take tea at around 6:30.

7 P.M. Martha Washington goes to the kitchen to oversee Lucy as she mixes bread dough and prepares hoecake batter for the next day.

8 P.M. Lucy and Nathan clean the kitchen one last time and bank the fire for the night, before heading to their respective quarters. Thankfully, the Washingtons have no plans for supper (which would have been served at about 9 p.m. in either of the dining rooms). So the cooks can return to their quarters a bit early.[1] * MVT

Smokehouse

———— ◆ ————

At Mount Vernon as elsewhere during the eighteenth century, salting was the primary means of preserving pork, beef, and mutton. Also, some cuts of pork, such as bacon and ham, were smoked in order to enhance their flavor.[1] During the curing process, the meat was locked in the smokehouse to prevent theft. This precaution was not always successful, however. In May 1795, while President Washington was living in Philadelphia, his farm manager William Pearce wrote to inform him that "some person Riped [*sic*] a plank of the Back part of the smoke House and Took out several pieces of Bacon. . . . I have not been able to find out yet who It is."[2]

When the curing was completed, bacons and hams were stored in barrels filled with ashes or bran. Early in the Revolutionary War, farm manager Lund Washington (a distant cousin of George Washington) wrote his employer that the "Bacon when it is sufficiently smoakd, I think to have put up in Cask with Ashes and if necessary move it, together with some Porck which I have already put up into Barrels."[3] Two years later, Lund sold 1,282 pounds of bacon to one

John Herndon "for the Use of the [Continental Army] and recorded that the buyer also paid for "two cask & 6 Bushels of Bran to pack it in."[4]

According to George Washington, Virginia ladies took particular pride in the quality of the ham and bacon produced on their plantations. He and his wife even sent these meats as gifts to friends in far-off Europe. In 1786 the general wrote the Marquis de Lafayette that Mrs. Washington "had packed & sent . . . a barrel of Virginia Hams. I do not know that they are better, or so good as you make in France but as they are of our own manufacture . . . and we recollect that it is a dish of which you are fond, she prevailed on me to ask your's & Madame de la Fayette's acceptance of them."[5] A dozen years later, as thanks for a gift of cheese from Englishman William Hambly, Washington shipped some pork to him in Falmouth.[6]

The justifiable satisfaction Martha Washington expressed in the quality of meats preserved under her supervision became the stuff of family folklore. Long after her death, her grandson, George Washington Parke Custis, recalled both her pride in her table and her husband's amusement over a lost ham at dinner in an anecdote that no doubt entertained several generations of descendants and their guests.

It happened that upon a large company sitting down to dinner at Mount Vernon one day . . . my grandmother . . . discovered that the ham, the pride of every Virginia housewife's table, was missing from its accustomed post of honor. Upon questioning Frank, the butler, this portly, and at the same time the most polite and accomplished of all butlers, observed that a ham . . . had been prepared, agreeably to the Madam's orders, but lo and behold! who should come into the kitchen, while the savory ham was smoking in its dish, but old Vulcan, the hound [one of several the Marquis de Lafayette had sent to George Washington from France after the Revolutionary War], and without more ado fastened his fangs into it; and although they of the kitchen had stood to such arms as they could get, and had fought the old spoiler desperately, yet Vulcan had finally triumphed, and bore off the prize, ay, "cleanly, under the keeper's nose." The lady by no means

relished the loss of a dish which formed the pride of her table, and uttered some remarks by no means favorable to old Vulcan, or indeed to dogs in general, while the chief, having heard the story, communicated it to his guests, and with them, laughed heartily at the exploit of the stag-hound.[7]

Ham and bacon from Mount Vernon graced the tables of the Washingtons' homes in New York and Philadelphia throughout the presidential years. In July 1794, for example, the president informed his farm manager William Pearce that "Mrs. Washington desires you will send her by the first Vessel to this place one dozn. of the best Hams and half a dozn. Midlings of Bacon."[8] And Mount Vernon was very likely the source of the ham served at a dinner the Washingtons hosted for members of Congress in December of the following year.[9] * MVT

The unprecedented numbers of guests who flocked to meet George Washington, both at Mount Vernon and at the presidential residences, arguably made Martha Washington the premier hostess in late-eighteenth-century America. In 1796, at age sixty-five, she posed for this pastel portrait by James Sharples.

WASHINGTON AND FAIRFAX AT A WAR-DANCE.

NEW YORK. VIRTUE, EMMINS & C.

Entered according to act of Congress, in the year 1857, by Virtue, Emmins & C.º in the clerks office of the district court of the southern district of New York.

Sixteen-year-old George Washington witnessed a Native American war dance while on his first frontier surveying trip in 1748. The description in his diary inspired this 1857 print, Washington and Fairfax at a War-Dance, *engraved by John Rogers after a painting by John McNevin.*

Food on the Frontier

George Washington spent a number of years on the frontier in what is now West Virginia, Ohio, and Pennsylvania, both working as a surveyor and serving as a soldier in the French and Indian War. After the Revolutionary War, he returned to these areas in order to inspect lands he owned and to promote plans for increasing navigation and commerce on the western rivers. Surviving documents indicate that Washington and his companions on these trips hunted for the meat they ate. One record shows that, on his first trip to the frontier as a sixteen-year-old, he cooked food over an open fire, using a forked stick as a spit and "a Large Chip" instead of a plate.[1]

On these expeditions, he spent time in the company of Indians and may well have eaten their traditional foods. For instance, in March 1748, at the home of Colonel Thomas Cresap, a famous frontiersman, Washington encountered a raiding party of about thirty Indians who were heading home after having taken one scalp. Cresap and Washington shared some whiskey with them, and then the Indians began beating a drum—fashioned from a cooking pot and a deerskin—and dancing. Five years later, Washington visited a leader of the Delaware nation known as Queen Aliquippa. When this staunch ally of the British protested that the young Virginian had neglected to visit her on an earlier leg of his trip, he made amends by giving her a matchcoat (a type of woven winter blanket) and a bottle of rum.[2]

Among the foods Washington certainly ate during his frontier travels were buffalo, venison, and wild turkey. He recorded in his diary that during a fall 1770 journey on the Ohio River, near present-day Lee's Creek, West Virginia, he met up with Kiashute, a Seneca Indian who had accompanied him to the Ohio Valley in 1753, when he carried a message from Virginia's governor to the French asking them to leave the valley. The two were pleased to see each other, and Washington's "old acquaintance" gave him "a Quarter of very fine Buffalo." A few days later, his party killed five

buffalo and wounded several more; at the same time, they also killed three deer. "This Country," Washington noted of these western lands, "abounds in Buffalo and Wild game of all kinds as also in all kinds of wild fowl." Among the wild birds he saw at that time were geese, several types of ducks, and turkeys, of which his party killed five in one day.[3]

On his trip to the frontier in the fall of 1784, Washington was well equipped, carrying two tents, bedding (including sheets), and a trunk containing silver camp cups and spoons, canteens, two kegs of "Spirits," and horseshoes. Additionally, there were fishing lines, camp kettles in which to cook stews, two kinds of wine (Madeira and port), another alcoholic drink called cherry bounce (see recipe on page 204), tea, and seven pounds of white sugar. Finally, there were several condiments ("Oyl, Mustard—Vinegar and Spices of all sorts") for seasoning various meats, fish, and fowl.[4] * MVT

Dining under Canvas

Before the Revolutionary War, George and Martha Washington typically dined at home in the company of family members, friends, neighbors, and business acquaintances. But during the war, General Washington (who led a peripatetic life in the field) and his wife (who joined him annually for lengthy visits) played host to military officers, government officials, and prominent citizens from other colonies as well as guests from abroad who came either as military allies to the Americans or as diplomats. As the most prominent American leader of the period, Washington sought to convince these disparate groups that the independence movement was credible and eminently worth supporting.

One way he demonstrated his commitment to the revolution was to equip his headquarters—whether in a private home during the winter or in a tent during a military campaign—in a manner that showed he was a gentleman and a gracious host. To that end, he purchased supplies that reflected the way he provisioned his own home: ivory-handled flatware and mahogany knife boxes for storing them; damask table linens; lacquered serving trays; china and fine-earthenware plates, cups, teapots, sauceboats, and tureens; and cut-glass salt dishes, decanters, and glasses.[1] His purchase in May 1782 of "Scarlet Cloth to face Servants Coats" indicates that men wearing livery served the tables at headquarters, just as they did at Mount Vernon.[2]

When the Continental Army took to the field, Washington used an elaborate mess kit that he had purchased in April 1776 and subsequently added to; it contained, among other items, a set of nested camp kettles, three large canisters, twelve oval tin dishes, and thirty-three tin plates. One of his surviving mess kits, now in the Smithsonian Institution, contains four tin pots with detachable wooden handles, six tin plates, three tin platters, knives and forks with black handles, a gridiron with collapsible legs, two tinder boxes, eight glass bottles with cork stoppers, and two glass bottles for salt and pepper with pewter tops.[3]

In New York in July 1776, Elizabeth Thompson, an elderly Irishwoman, was hired to serve as housekeeper for the general's military household. She remained on his staff until the summer of 1781 and apparently developed a close relationship with both George and Martha Washington during the years they spent under trying conditions.[4]

Washington made an effort to dine regularly with officers other those on his personal staff. As early as 1775, he ordered that "the Field Officer of the day, the Officer of his own guard, and the Adjutant of the day; consider themselves invited to dine at Head Quarters." Three years later, after noticing that the field officers were often too busy to eat with him, he altered the standing invitation somewhat so they would dine at headquarters the day after they were on duty. In September 1782, he asked that the officers of the day, the brigade majors, and quartermaster of the day all come for dinner the day they were relieved of duty.[5]

In July 1779, Washington jokingly cautioned two prominent New York ladies invited to dinner at his field headquarters at West Point that they would be eating on "plates, once tin but now Iron; (not become so by the labor of scowering)," a reference to the dishware in his mess kit. He also alerted

them to the placement of food on the table: "Since our arrival at this happy spot, we have had a Ham (sometimes a shoulder) of Bacon, to grace the head of the table; a piece of roast Beef adorns the foot; and, a small dish of Greens or Beans (almost imperceptable) decorates the center."[6] Because the most important dish was typically placed at the center of the table, Washington was letting the women know that vegetables were a rare treat in camp.

A visiting Frenchman described a West Point dinner the same summer that was served in a tent pitched on the banks of the Hudson River:

> [T]he waves came right up to the tent-pins, where they broke with a solemn roar. A few steps away from us musicians played military and tuneful French airs. The banks and the forests of the mountain answered long to the cannon shots fired to the health of the King and Queen [of France], and the opposite bank shone with the fires which the soldiers had lighted.[7]

According to the recollections of some who dined with both Washingtons during the war, the general thoroughly enjoyed these occasions, which sometimes lasted for hours. George Bennet, an Englishman who visited headquarters in Newburgh, New York, in 1783, noted that he sat to the left of Mrs. Washington, while her husband sat to her right; there were about fifteen officers around the table. Bennet wrote that the "dinner was good . . . we all sat on camp stools . . . Mrs. W. was as plain, easy and affable as [General Washington] was, & one would have thought from the familiarity which prevailed there, that he saw a respectable private gentleman dining at the Head of his own Family."[8] These meals gave Washington an opportunity to learn about the state of his army, about public opinion in the various colonies, and about the wider world beyond the purview of Great Britain. They also helped prepare both George and Martha Washington for the even more nationally significant roles they eventually would assume as the first president and first lady of the new United States. * MVT

"An excellent table"

The Art of Dining at Mount Vernon

Carol Borchert Cadou

For George Washington, who always paid keen attention to his dining spaces and their furnishings, mealtime rituals provided opportunities to present himself as a sophisticated member of the gentry class, an enlightened gentleman, and a gracious host. By the time of his death, in 1799, the former general and president had amassed an impressive array of tableware and household furnishings. During his travels, his service in the Revolutionary War, and his two terms as president, he accumulated the objects that befitted his position. Their purposeful arrangement offered Mount Vernon visitors a window on Washington's interests and accomplishments. Guests were impressed with what they encountered. As one gentleman observed in 1777: "He keeps an excellent table and a stranger, let him be of what Country or nation, he will always meet with a most hospitable reception at it. His entertainments were always conducted with the most regularity and in the genteelest manner of any I ever was at on the Continent."[1]

Two rooms at Mount Vernon (one of modest size, the other quite large) were reserved for formal dining and entertainments. The small dining room, located in the older portion of the house originally constructed by Washington's father, was an elegant and comfortable space suitable for breakfasts as well as for dinners with ten or fewer people. Furniture itemized in Washington's posthumous estate inventory included "2 Dining Tables"—perhaps the "Two neat Mahogany Tables" he had ordered from London in April 1757 with the request that they be "4½ feet square when

spread and to join occasionally," so they were sufficiently flexible to accommodate small or large gatherings. The "10 Mahoganey chairs" that surrounded the table in 1799 could have been from any one of several sets of chairs Washington purchased for his family and guests over the course of forty years. Among those probably intended for dining were the "1 Dozn neat and strong Mahogany chairs" he acquired in 1757, the "12 Chairs covered with Leather and brass naild" he received in 1764, and the "12 Chairs & 2 window curtains for ye dining room" he purchased in 1774, when the Fairfax family vacated nearby Belvoir plantation.[2] In 1783 he asked his nephew Bushrod Washington to seek out "two dozen strong, neat and plain, but fashionable, Table chairs (I mean Chair for a dining room)."[3] Assuming George Washington obtained these, they may well have replaced the outmoded chairs from the prewar years.

Additional furnishings in the so-called family dining room included a "Large Case" valued in 1799 at $40 (perhaps the mahogany spirits case with sixteen gallon-size bottles that Washington had ordered from London in September 1760), a mahogany sideboard on which stood two knife cases, and a tea table.[4] The array of gilt-framed prints lining the bright green painted walls included engraved portraits of Benjamin Franklin, Philadelphia astronomer and mathematician David Rittenhouse, and Revolutionary War generals Nathanael Greene, Anthony Wayne, and the Marquis de Lafayette—all men Washington held in high esteem. In addition to a portrait of Washington himself were engravings

OPPOSITE:
Washington artfully transformed his smaller Mansion dining room into an elegant setting for meals and entertaining. Beneath an ornate plaster ceiling and surrounded by a variety of framed engravings hung on fashionably painted walls, the Washingtons and their guests dined at a table carefully laid out with appropriate ceramics, glass, silver, and linens. Costly mahogany cases, fitted to hold bottles and knives (see pages 98 and 149), neatly stored spirits and cutlery, while expensive silver vessels were used for wine and tea service (see pages 100 and 179).

of historical events, among them *The Death of General Wolfe*, *William Penn's Treaty with the Indians*, and *Alfred the Great Dividing His Loaf with the Pilgrim*.[5]

The Mansion's large dining room provided a fashionable setting for elegant meals and entertainment and could accommodate twice the number of seated guests. With its soaring ceiling (two stories high) and measuring an impressive six hundred square feet, the room reflected the latest in classical design elements inspired by the period excavations at Pompeii and Herculaneum and favored by George Washington and his contemporaries for their references to the republican ideals of ancient Rome. The room's verdigris-based green-painted wallpaper formed an attractive background for a display of artworks that reflected Washington's interests in the land, his military service, and his social and political affiliations. They included American landscape paintings he had purchased as president, scenes of the *Hudson River* (*Morning and Evening*) by William Winstanley, and views

George Washington's presidential purchases included ivory-handled cutlery as well as an assemblage of 309 pieces of white-bodied, gilt-rimmed porcelain from the Sèvres, Angoulême, and Nast factories in France. The Washingtons used these French porcelains in retirement at Mount Vernon, lending their table a simple, elegant neoclassical aesthetic, with subtle echoes of ancient white-marble statuary.

of the Potomac River by George Beck. Perhaps for symmetry, the engravings of military subjects included two sets each of *The Dead Soldier*, *The Death of General Montgomery*, and *The Battle of Bunker's Hill*; Washington bought the latter two sets during the presidency, perhaps as reminders of his war years or of the talents of John Trumbull, whose original canvases the engravings replicated. Trumbull's 1790 portrait *General Washington at Verplanck's Point*, presented by the artist to Martha Washington, also hung in the room. Pastel images of the Virgin Mary and Saint John evidenced the Washingtons' religious beliefs, and an engraved portrait of France's King Louis XVI, who was deposed during President Washington's first term, reflected the American leader's overseas alliances.[6]

Called the "New Room" by Washington, the large dining room contained many of the dwelling's newest furnishings. When he returned to Mount Vernon in 1797 following his presidency, the sloop *Salem* carried to Virginia furniture specifically intended for this room. The ship's cargo included two inlaid-mahogany sideboards and twenty-four carved-mahogany side chairs from Philadelphia cabinetmaker John Aitken—all in the latest neoclassical style. In addition to the landscape paintings that had previously hung on the executive-residence walls, Washington placed in this dining room two large gilt-framed looking glasses (or mirrors) and a pair of sconces purchased in New York and Philadelphia, respectively. Although he installed wall-mounted silver-plated Argand lamps in the room (another presidential purchase), the main source of light during evening meals continued to be from candles placed on the table or on one of the locally crafted candlestands.[7] When Joshua Brookes, a young Englishman, visited Mount Vernon in February 1799, he remarked that the large dining room was "elegantly furnished." He especially noted the mahogany chairs, "white chintz window curtains with deep festoons of green satin, a glass chandelier," and a white-marble mantelpiece displaying "marble jars and blue china ones in which were placed some blue and red bachelor's buttons."[8]

The Washingtons owned an impressive array of ceramics and silver in specialized forms for use in the two dining rooms, including no fewer than six porcelain tea, coffee,

Architectural details of Washington's "New Room" (the large dining room) reflect his interests and alliances. The marble chimneypiece, a gift from English émigré Samuel Vaughan, includes carved plows and agricultural elements appropriate for a Cincinnatus figure. The engraved portrait of France's King Louis XVI, a gift to Washington from the French ambassador, features an elaborate gilded frame with the royal crest and Washington's coat of arms. Several large American landscape paintings, including William Winstanley's views of the Hudson River, hang in this dining room beneath the delicate swags and foliage of neoclassical ornament.

breakfast, and dinner services. Washington's first recorded porcelain purchase was the "Compleat sett Fine Image China" he received from London in 1757. Made in China, the set contained an assortment of elegant tea ware—including a teapot, covered sugar bowl, cream pitcher, and teacups with saucers—all decorated with polychrome vignettes of Chinese women and children. During the eighteenth century, the consumption of imported Chinese tea signified gentility; and these early purchases for Mount Vernon ensured that Washington's guests at his bachelor residence would drink the exotic liquid from highly prized, mysteriously translucent Chinese porcelain. In addition to their porcelain services, the couple had an elegant variety of specialized silver pieces for serving tea, including an urn that dispensed hot water into the teapot through a spigot, glass-lined silver sugar and cream pails, and tongs and ladles for adding sugar and cream to the steaming beverage.[9]

They also owned specially crafted porcelain and silver vessels for coffee. Following the Revolutionary War, Washington purchased a stately silver coffeepot, elaborately engraved with his family's coat of arms, from Philadelphia silversmith Joseph Anthony, Jr.[10] The Comte de Custine-Sarreck, one of several French officers who had served under generals Rochambeau and Washington at Yorktown, presented the Washingtons with an elaborately decorated and monogrammed tea-and-coffee service from his personal factory at Niderviller. During his presidency, Washington added more French porcelains to his growing tableware col-

lection. He purchased from the Comte de Moustier—the outgoing French minister to the United States—a 309-piece assemblage of white-bodied, gilt-rimmed items manufactured at the Nast, Angoulême, and Sèvres factories; these ranged from soup and dinner plates to ice-cream pots, egg dishes, and flowerpots.

Clergyman Manasseh Cutler, a guest at Mount Vernon in 1802, not long before Martha Washington died, recalled that "At the head of the [breakfast] table was the tea and coffee equipage, where [Mrs. Washington] seated herself and sent the tea and coffee to the company."[11] She served breakfast tea and coffee in the presidential years as well, but some of the couple's finer wares, such as the silver coffeepot, may have remained at Mount Vernon during that period. When English traveler Henry Wansey enjoyed breakfast at the executive residence in Philadelphia in 1794, he recalled that "Mrs. Washington herself made tea and coffee for us," but "a silver urn for hot water, was the only article of expense on the table."[12]

Dinner, usually served at 3 p.m., was the most formal meal of the day. Table decorations included such delicate objects as a pyramid of glass salvers crowned with a sweetmeat dish and English porcelain figurines representing the seasons and ancient Greek muses.[13] Perhaps the most impressive table ornaments date from Washington's presidential years, when he sought to establish a style appropriate for the new republic. Aiding him in this endeavor was Philadelphia statesman Gouverneur Morris, who opined in January 1790:

As president, Washington acquired a silver-plated plateau (mirrored set of trays) that served as a frame and reflective backdrop for candelabra, porcelain ornaments (see page 69), and flower vases. This plateau and its ornaments were used at Mount Vernon entertainments after Washington's presidency ended.

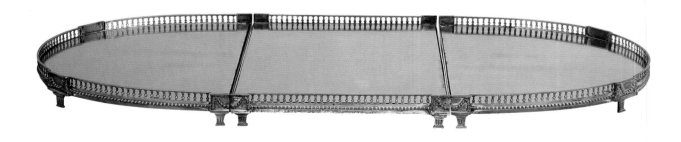

The Washingtons owned a variety of elegant silver and porcelains for serving coffee, a beverage enjoyed regularly at Mount Vernon as early as 1758. In 1782 the couple received the gift of coffee cups and saucers from the Comte de Custine-Sarreck. The following year, they acquired a stately rococo silver coffeepot from Philadelphia—complete with the Washington-family coat of arms.

*The Washingtons' large array of tea wares included
Chinese export porcelains with delicate polychrome scenes,
English silver sugar tongs, and a large silver tea tray
wrought by New York silversmith Ephraim Brasher.*

I think it of very great importance to fix the Taste of our Country properly, and I think your Example will go very far in that Respect. It is therefore my Wish that every Thing about you should be substantially good and majestically plain; made to endure. Nothing is so extravagant in the Event as those buildings and Carriages and Furnitures and Dresses and Ornaments which will want continual Renovation. Where a Taste of this kind prevails, each Generation has to provide for itself whereas in the other there is a vast Accumulation of real Wealth in the space of half a Century."[14]

At his own expense, Washington supplemented the tableware supplied by Congress with items he felt would foster respect for the young nation and establish an appropriate taste. Writing to Morris in the fall of 1789, the president requested a shipment from Paris of "mirrors for a table" as well as "neat and fashionable but not expensive ornaments for them."[15] In selecting the "mirrors for a table" (or plateau) for the president, Morris chose a silver-plated nine-piece set. In addition, he bought an ensemble of classical figures and vases made of unglazed biscuit porcelain. The pure-white-bodied ornaments in classical figures and forms referenced the political ideals and statuary of ancient Greece and Rome, and they also subtly alluded to the founding principles of the new nation. Morris had taken the liberty of buying costly table ornaments, but he felt they would evince "a noble Simplicity" that had been "fashionable above two thousand years" and were, therefore, suitable for the presidential table.[16] Washington's dinner guests evidently appreciated both the appearance and significance of these decorative accessories. Referring to the centerpiece, Massachusetts congressman Theophilus Bradbury noted, "It was very elegant and used for ornament only."[17]

At the conclusion of dinner in both the presidential residences and at Mount Vernon, servants removed the tablecloth and served wine to the gentlemen guests, who lingered over their glasses for further conversation. In November 1785, London merchant Robert Hunter, Jr., reported, "The General sent the bottle about pretty freely after dinner, and gave success to the navigation of the Potomac for his toast."[18] For

wine service during and after dinner, Washington acquired silver salvers, coasters, rollers, and coolers for the easy movement of bottles and decanters around the table and the enjoyment of wine at just the right temperature.[19]

Within the green-painted and -papered walls of Mount Vernon's two dining rooms, and amid an impressive array of artwork and tableware, George and Martha Washington's guests enjoyed meals and conversations nearly every day the couple was in residence. Although they rarely had the opportunity for a private dinner, George Washington was particularly at ease when dining with family or close friends. As Robert Hunter observed one evening in 1785: "The General with a few glasses of champagne got quite merry, and being with his intimate friends laughed and talked a good deal. Before strangers, he is generally very reserved and seldom says a word."[20] On those occasions, Washington's surroundings likely spoke for him, conveying his financial and social position, his military and political accomplishments, his interests and hopes for the new nation—as well as his years of attention to the details of providing gracious hospitality. ✳

In 1759 newlyweds George and Martha Washington received from London "1 pair Seasons" for placement on their table. These two porcelain figurines, likely representing spring and summer, were probably displayed by the couple for most of their forty years together.

OVERLEAF:
The Washingtons' large dining room displayed an array of carefully assembled tableware and dining furniture. Many pieces, including the mahogany sideboards and side chairs, were acquired during the presidential years and returned with the couple to Mount Vernon in 1797.

Presidential Dining

Throughout his presidency, when the seat of national government was in New York and then in Philadelphia, George Washington made a practice of inviting ten to twenty congressmen and other public officials to dine with him on Thursdays at 4 p.m. These meals were more elaborate, both in the number of dishes offered and in the table settings, than family dinners at Mount Vernon. Although the Thursday repasts were mentioned in diaries and letters of individuals who attended, we have only two relatively full descriptions of them, along with a few revealing details from other sources.

In stark contrast to the camaraderie that had characterized meals at Washington's headquarters during the Revolutionary War, these dinners—according to the available evidence—could be tedious for all concerned: conversation was fitful and strained, and one attendee described Washington as bearing "a settled Aspect of Melancholy," drumming on the edge of the table with his silverware. Although the president's increasing deafness no doubt contributed to the tension, the more obvious problem may have been caused by the presence of non-Federalist congressmen, who distrusted and criticized nearly every move Washington made. Of one such occasion, Senator William Maclay of Pennsylvania wrote, "It was a great dinner," but he "considered it part of my duty as a Senator, to submit to it, and am glad it is over." Maclay conceded that his host "treated me with great attention. . . . Yet he knows well how rigid a republican I am. I cannot think that he considers it worth while to soften me. It is not worth his While, I am not an Object if he should gain me, and I trust he cannot do it by any improper means."[1]

At the dinner on August 27, 1789, in New York, George and Martha Washington sat opposite each other at the middle of the table, while the president's two secretaries, Tobias Lear and Robert Lewis, sat at either end. The center of the table was "garnished in the usual tasty way," with small decorative objects, probably made of spun sugar, and artificial flowers. The meal started with some sort of soup, followed by roasted and boiled fish and several types of meat and poultry. The second course included apple pie and puddings. A dessert of "iced creams" and jellies followed, and then fresh fruit—watermelons, muskmelons, apples, and peaches—and nuts were served. Once the dishes had been cleared and the tablecloth removed, the president filled a glass with wine and, Maclay wrote, "with great formality drank to the health of every individual by name round the table. Everybody imitated him, changed glasses, and such a buzz of 'health, sir,' and 'health, madam,' and 'thank you, sir' and 'thank you, madam' never had I heard before."[2]

Six years later, after the government had moved to Philadelphia, the table decorations were made of French bisque porcelain and arranged on a mirrored silver platform known as a plateau. The dishes were arrayed around the plateau

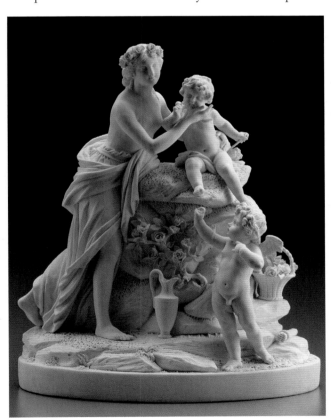

OPPOSITE:
Built in 1785 by Robert Morris, this house was selected by the Philadelphia City Corporation to serve as the executive residence when the seat of government moved from New York. George and Martha Washington lived here from 1790 to 1797.

LEFT:
This biscuit porcelain figural group of Venus and cupids was created at the Angoulême factory in France. It was one of three classically inspired groupings purchased in Paris by Philadelphia statesman Gouverneur Morris in 1789 and sent to America to decorate the first president's dining table.

and included "an elegant variety of roast beef, veal, turkeys, ducks, fowls, hams, puddings, jellies, oranges, apples, nuts, almonds, figs, raisins, and a variety of wines and punch"; probably this abundance constituted three courses. Four or five male servants dressed in livery waited on the table, bringing drinks from the sideboard to the guests and helping pass the plates. Dinner was over by 6 p.m., "more than an hour after the candles were introduced."[3]

Even at the president's table, things didn't always go smoothly. Mary White Morris, wife of businessman and financier Robert Morris, related an unfortunate gaffe that occurred at a dinner party in June 1789, when a "large and fine looking Triffle" [*sic*] was brought to the table, looking "exceeding well indeed." George Washington placed a serving on her plate, but after she had tasted it, Mrs. Morris "had to pass her handkerchief by her mouth, and rid herself of the Morsel." She then whispered to her host that the cream used in the dish had gone off and was "miserable Stale and rancid." Mrs. Morris then noted that Washington "changed his plate immediately," but she giggled when relating that "Mrs. Washington eat [*sic*] a whole heap of it."[4] * MVT

This graceful, serpentine-front sideboard is one of two that George Washington purchased from John Aitken of Philadelphia in February 1797 for his large dining room at Mount Vernon. The versatile case piece held linens and other dining equipage and, when not needed for serving food during meals, provided display space for knife boxes and porcelain figurines.

Levées

During her husband's presidency, Martha Washington hosted a weekly levée, or reception, on Fridays, beginning at 7 p.m. and ending just after 10 p.m. No invitations were issued, it being understood that those residents of the capital city with the proper social credentials were welcome—so long as they were appropriately dressed. Because these occasions were informal, the president wore neither a hat nor a sword. He made a point of talking with women at these events, and women also sought out the president, especially the "young ladies," who "used to throng around him and engage him in conversation. There were some of the well-remembered belles of that day who imagined themselves to be favorites with him. As these were the only opportunities which they had of conversing with him, they were disposed to use them."[1]

Mrs. Washington generally sat with a few of her close friends while receiving the other visiting ladies, who curtsied to her in greeting and then mingled with the other guests, most of whom stood throughout the levée. Refreshments, which were were set out in another room, included tea, coffee, plum and plain cake in winter, and lemonade, orangeade, and ice cream during the summer—all accompanied by candies, fruits, and cheese. At the end of the evening, the ladies would curtsy to Mrs. Washington again as they departed.[2]

Yet despite their informality, the levées were disparaged by the president's political adversaries, who saw in these genteel gatherings hints of an aristocracy and even of a nascent monarchy. After attending one such evening held in New York in 1789, Pennsylvania Senator William Maclay, who was among Washington's opponents, complained in his diary:

Nothing is regarded or valued at such Meetings but the qualifications that flow from the Taylor Barber or dancing Master to be clean shaved Shirted and powdered, to make Your bows with grace and be master of small chat on the Weather play or news paper anecdote of the day, are the highest qualifications necessary—Levees may be extreamely Useful, in old Countries w[h]ere Men of great fortunes are collected. . . . But here I think they are hurtful. . . . Indeed from these small beginnings I fear we shall follow on, nor cease till we have reached the summit of Court Etiquette, and all the frivolities fopperies and Expense practiced in european Governments.[3]

A potentially serious incident occurred at a levée in the summer of that same year, involving a Miss Mary McIvers, who wore a fashionable headdress crowned with tall ostrich feathers. As she walked under one of the chandeliers, which were of course lit with candles, the feathers caught fire, causing "no small alarm" among the guests. An aide to the president, Major William Jackson, "with great presence of mind, and equal gallantry," dashed over to the young lady and, by clapping the burning plumes between his hands, extinguished the flame." Apparently, "the drawing-room went on as usual."[4]

An amusing—and certainly less harrowing—incident occurred at another of the New York levées. The president's twenty-year-old nephew, Robert Lewis, was spending several months with the family while they settled into their new routine. As he came to the door to help several female guests out of their carriage, Lewis heard "the screams and crys [of] a Lady who seemed to be in great distress." The women reported that a member of their party had an insect in her ear. Lewis managed to get all the ladies out of the carriage and into a private room in the president's house, where, after pouring some oil in the sufferer's ear, "the bug instantly run out—which was the cause of much rejoicing."

Later, in his journal account of the evening, honesty compelled Lewis to record "another circumstance which has since caused much laugh[ter], when the bug ran out of . . . [the] . . . ear, it fell in her bosom and I plunged [my] hand into it involuntarily to catch the insect." With all this excitement, one young lady, who had caught Robert Lewis's eye some weeks earlier at church, found herself "near fainting." The young gallant was forced to "support her in my arms and to apply cold water to her face" in order to revive her.

The ladies then rearranged their dresses, "which had been a good deal discomfited," and went in to make their greetings to Mrs. Washington, "who was all this while a stranger to what had happened." The story was told at the party, and Lewis was the hero of the evening. He also noted that "After . . . the company had nearly dispersed," one of the female guests who "had observed my attention to the Lady whilst in distress invited me very politely to come and see her," which Lewis thought he might do "so soon as time and opportunity will admit."[5] ✳ MVT

William Jackson (1759–1828) emigrated from England to Charleston, South Carolina, as a teenager. He served as a staff officer in the Continental Army and as secretary of the Constitutional Convention. Jackson often visited the executive residence while serving as personal secretary to President Washington, from 1789 to 1791.

South Grove Midden

George and Martha Washington presided over a fashionable table laden with an abundance of meats, vegetables, beverages, and sweets. At the end of every meal, the attending household slaves returned the soiled dishes and uneaten food to the kitchen, where the dishes were washed. Following the practice of that time, table scraps and other waste matter were discarded in an outdoor midden, or refuse heap. At Mount Vernon, this was done in the south grove, the lawn between the Mansion and the kitchen. For archaeologists, the discards put there from the 1750s until 1775 have provided clues about daily life on the plantation and in the Mansion.

Mount Vernon's archaeologists discovered the refuse in 1990, during the installation of an irrigation system. Over the next four years, the south grove midden was excavated, yielding some fifty thousand artifacts. This assemblage, which includes more than four hundred fragmentary and intact ceramic and glass vessels and almost twenty-nine thousand bones from sixty animal species, represents the single largest collection of domestic artifacts excavated at the estate to date. As such, the finds from this dig offer singular evidence about the dining habits and dietary preferences of the Washington household in the two decades before the American Revolution.

In 1776 Washington directed his farm manager to plant "groves of Trees at each end of the dwelling House . . . with all the clever kind of Trees (especially flowering ones)" in the south grove.[1] Although this landscaping resulted in less refuse being deposited there, the midden remained a handy receptacle for some kitchen waste for the remainder of Washington's life and well into the nineteenth century.

Many of the remnants found in the south grove midden suggest the variety of beverages that were enjoyed in the Mansion. Clockwise from upper left: a white salt-glaze stoneware slop bowl for tea, an etched glass decanter and wine glass, a Rhenish stoneware jug, a Nottingham stoneware ale mug, and a Chinese export porcelain tea bowl.

Beginning in 1757, when George Washington was settling into his life as a tobacco planter, he placed numerous orders to his English agents for both china (Chinese export porcelain) and "white stone" (English white stoneware) tableware.[2] He received a shipment of a full set of stoneware (plates, tea ware, and serving pieces) in December 1757. In March 1758, a shipment containing various china vessels arrived, followed that summer by a second substantial shipment of white stoneware.[3] Early the next year, the newly wed Martha Washington brought to Mount Vernon her various ceramic, glass, and pewter vessels—all fashionable tableware from the estate of her late first husband, Daniel Parke Custis.

George and Martha Washington used white stoneware for breakfast and dinner, while the more expensive Chinese porcelain typically was reserved for tea and dinner with guests.[4] Fragments of both sets of tableware were unearthed from the south grove midden: the remnants of a small creamer, a porringer with a molded shell motif on its handle, a delicate coffee cup molded with scenes from *Aesop's Fables*, and a large white-stoneware pitcher. Numerous teacups and saucers—one pair elaborately decorated with gilt and overglaze-red and underglaze-blue painting—and two matching sets of plates were part of the Chinese porcelain used for afternoon teas and special dinners during the first years the Washingtons were married.

In addition to the well-documented white stoneware and porcelain that graced the Washingtons' table, there was a tea service of thin brown stoneware, commonly called Nottingham for its place of manufacture in England. Fragments of two teapots from this set were found within the midden as well as several slop bowls—larger containers for discarding cold tea.

The Washingtons served ale and beer in tankards made from Nottingham brown stoneware and a thicker earthenware with a mottled-manganese glaze made in Staffordshire. Fragments from fourteen such tankards were identified; they were of various sizes and decorative styles, perhaps because these beverages were enjoyed during informal occasions. Martha Washington served punch from tin-glazed earthenware bowls shipped from Bristol, while her husband poured

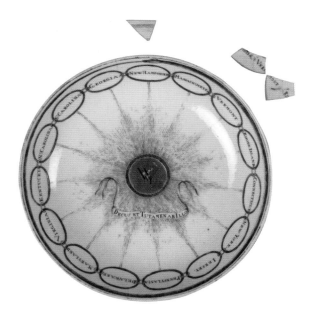

his favorite wine, Madeira, from a delicate decanter etched with flowers into glasses with tulip-shaped bowls. Until archaeologists began excavating the south grove midden, remnants of these vessels had been buried under layers of trash for nearly two centuries.

Besides shedding light on dining practices in the Mansion, the midden finds offer insight into how the enslaved cooks prepared meals and the vessels they used for that purpose. For example, the discovery of earthenware milk pans—wide, shallow bowls for cooling milk—suggest that dairy activities were concentrated near the kitchen during the 1760s and early 1770s. Most of these milk pans came from London, although some were purchased from William Rogers, a potter in Yorktown, Virginia. At least two were fashioned from colonoware, a low-fired, unglazed earthenware made from local clay. Many smaller colonoware bowls were also found. Because there is no evidence that colonoware was manufactured at Mount Vernon, it is assumed that slaves working in the kitchen acquired it from a nearby potter. Perhaps the cooks ate their own meals out of the smaller bowls unearthed in the south grove midden and also used those vessels for food preparation. * ECW

This saucer is from the historic States pattern, a forty-five-piece set of Chinese export porcelain presented to Martha Washington in 1796 by the Dutch East India Company. The pattern features her monogram at the center, encircled by decorative chain-links, each link containing the name of a state. Mount Vernon's archaeologists have excavated three fragments of this historic china pattern, and complete pieces are part of the museum collections.

Setting the Table

When people entered the dining room for afternoon dinner—the main and most formal meal of the day—they found all the food in place, set out in a balanced, symmetrical pattern. For instance, there probably would be a roast of some sort at the center of the table, flanked on either end with fish and soup. These dishes were called "removes" because they were served first and then taken away and replaced by two others, perhaps smaller roasts or fowl. Vegetables, stews, puddings, and "made dishes" (such as veal scallopini, called "Scotch collops" [see recipe on page 144] in the eighteenth century) were arranged on the sides.[1] To make the presentation more dramatic, the large bird or roast at the center might be placed on either a footed tray or an X-shaped piece called a dish cross; at the end of the Revolutionary War, George Washington ordered a "Cross or Stand for the centre of the Dining table" with other silver pieces from France.[2]

Cutlery was set on the table in essentially the same way it is today: fork to the left, knife to the right; the spoon was placed upside down by the knife, to avoid a mishap with dangling lace cuffs. Dessertspoons, knives, and forks were on the sideboard or serving table with the dessert plates. Teaspoons would be on a tray to be used after dinner. Salt and butter dishes and cruets holding condiments were on the table. Serving spoons were either crossed or placed parallel to one another, facing in opposite directions, on the corners of the table.[3]

George Washington bought several types of cutlery for use on his table. His first order, placed in 1757, was for "2 Setts best Silver handle Knives & Forks" with "best London Blades," probably two sizes of pistol-handled cutlery, of which ten pieces survive. Four months after he and Martha were wed, in January 1759, he augmented these with a set of six English carving knives and forks, with handles of stained ivory and silver ferrules. Four years later, he ordered knives and forks with Chinese-porcelain handles, probably in blue and white, from England. Additional silver utensils on the Washingtons' table were dessert, mustard, and salt spoons, teaspoons, and tablespoons.[4]

The man or woman seated closest to each of the large central dishes—be it a roast of meat or fowl—was expected to carve them, from a seated position.[5] Those who wished to learn the fine points of this social skill could consult a book devoted to the subject. *The Honours of the Table* (1788) considered carving to be one of the "accomplishments of a gentleman," and cautioned:

> *We are always in pain for a man, who, instead of cutting up a fowl genteely, is hacking for half an hour across a bone, greasing himself, and bespattering the company with the sauce: but where the master or mistress of a table dissects a bird with ease and grace, or serves her guest with such parts as are best flavoured and most esteemed, they are not only well thought of, but admired.*[6]

This standing tin-plate warmer, with an open back, would have been placed near the fireplace to heat the metal cabinet and warm the Canton plates resting inside.

The carver put slices on a plate held by a servant, who would take it to whichever guest had asked for that particular cut. Side dishes were served by whichever guest sat closest to them; one author characterized the scene at this stage of the meal as "a confusion of passing."[7] Pennsylvania Senator William Maclay described this type of food service in the presidential household; Washington himself, at one of his regular Thursday-afternoon congressional dinners, "offered to help me to . . . part of a Dish which Stood before him" and later was seen "distributing a pudding."[8]

In cold weather, the waiters might keep the dinner plates in a warmer set near the fire until a particular diner had decided which dishes to try. A warmer made of lacquered tin, standing on four legs and fitted with three shelves that were accessed by means of a swinging door on the back, served this purpose at Mount Vernon. Despite all efforts to keep food hot after it left the kitchen, it generally had cooled by the time it was served according to the protocol of the time.

Drinks were kept on the sideboard, or, because eighteenth-century diners preferred their wine as cold as possible, it might be kept in cellarettes or wine coolers; Washington owned lion-headed examples of these, both a wood-and-brass floor model and table models in silver.[9] Glasses were cooled or rinsed in cylindrical glass vessels called wine rinsers; a surviving example from Mount Vernon is made of cobalt-blue glass. Diners indicated their drink preferences to waiters, who would bring them whatever beverage they desired. The practice of placing wine bottles on the table so diners could serve themselves was to emerge early in the nineteenth century.[10]

After the first course, all the dishes and the top tablecloth were removed and the second course served. There would be the same number of dishes as for the previous course, but now the diners were offered a sweet pudding or cream, a tart, or custard. An ordinary dinner ended after dessert was served and eaten.[11] On more formal occasions, the servants left the room after dessert, the diners savored a few glasses of wine together, and the ladies retired to the drawing room for coffee, tea, and conversation. After more drinking and conversation, the gentlemen at the table would join the ladies, perhaps for some card games.[12]

The servants who carried tableware back and forth from the kitchen used glass, plate, and cutlery baskets. Generally, these were made of wood or wicker and might be lined with tin or be lacquered and gilded.[13] Among George Washington's papers are an order and an invoice from the early 1760s for "1 China Plate Basket"; although this might refer to a packing container, the object probably was used for clearing the table.[14] * MVT

Frank Lee the Butler

———————◆———————

Francis (Frank) Lee was a mulatto (mixed-race) slave whom George Washington purchased from Mary Smith Ball Lee, the widow of Colonel John Lee of Westmoreland County, in May 1768 for £50. Frank's brother, William (Billy) Lee, who would become Washington's valet, was acquired at the same time.[1] By the time Washington died, in December 1799, Frank had worked his way up to butler, a position of responsibility that sometimes was held by a hired white man. Washington once described his ideal butler or steward as someone who could "set out a Table, attend at the side board," and act "in the capacity of a head Servant in the family . . . and make all the others do their duty properly."[2] In Frank Lee, he found a man who could do all this as well as graciously greet visitors to the Washingtons' home and make them feel welcome.

One of Frank's responsibilities was seeing that the table was properly set when the Washingtons sat down. Because his master was emphatic about punctuality, insisting that breakfast be on the table at seven every morning, Frank had to rise very early in order to have everything ready by then. He also oversaw the maintenance of the Washingtons' costly linens, china, silver, and glassware. During meals, he was in charge of the waiters who served at the table.[3] Both Frank and the waiters wore uniforms, known as livery, that were variations on the three-piece suits favored by gentlemen of the time. Typically, livery consisted of a coat, a waistcoat or vest, and breeches; these usually were made of fine wool in the colors of the slave owner's coat of arms and edged with woven "livery lace." The livery worn at Mount Vernon featured an off-white suit trimmed with red and a red vest.[4]

Frank Lee had to be sure the house was meticulously cleaned at least once a week, so he also oversaw the work of the maids. During the thorough spring cleaning of the Mansion, he not only directed the maids but also completed some tasks himself. For example, one year Mrs. Washington had him "clanse the House from the garret to the sellers—have all the Beds aird and mended and the Bed cloths of every kind made very clean the Bed steads also well scalded—and the low bed steads put up to be ready to carry out of one room into another as . . . they are often wanted."[5]

When there wasn't enough work in the Mansion to keep Frank busy, he would often be assigned other jobs, such as helping the gardener or painting, both inside and outside the house. Among the seasonal duties he performed in the late fall was putting "long litter," such as straw or cornstalks, against the cellar windows in order to insulate the Mansion in winter. Also during the fall, he gathered black walnuts—one of his master's favorites—for year-round use. Finally, he helped with the care and breeding of George Washington's dogs, particularly the terriers.[6]

Frank was married to Lucy, who worked as a cook and belonged to the estate of Mrs. Washington's first husband, Daniel Parke Custis. The couple lived for some years in two rooms over the kitchen where Lucy worked; there they reared at least three children: Mike, Phil, and Patty.[7] In their family garden, Lucy and Frank raised melons and chickens, some of which they sold to the Washingtons.[8]

George Washington's last will and testament directed that all the slaves at Mount Vernon who belonged to him were to be freed after Mrs. Washington died.[9] Of the 316 slaves named on a list that had been compiled the summer before Washington's death, 40 were rented from a neighbor, 123 belonged to him, and 153 belonged to Mrs. Washington as "dower" property. Her first husband had died in 1757, without leaving a will. According to Virginia law, both under British rule and after the Revolutionary War, in such cases, a man's widow would be able to use one-third of his slaves

for her lifetime. Upon her death, those slaves, including any children born to the women, would become the property of the deceased husband's remaining heirs. Martha Washington could not, therefore, free her slaves.[10] This legal restriction complicated the lives of many enslaved families at Mount Vernon, including that of Frank and Lucy. Frank, who had belonged to George Washington, became free but lived on at the estate until his death, in the summer of 1821. A local newspaper carried this notice: "Died lately at Mount Vernon, at a very advanced age Francis Lee, Butler to that mansion in the days of its ancient master. Francis was the brother of William Lee, body servant to the General in the War of the Revolution, and particularly mentioned in the General's will."[11] Some years after Frank's death, Martha Washington's grandson remembered him as "the most polite and accomplished of all butlers."[12] ∗ MVT

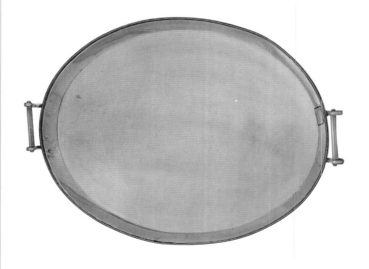

see page 79.

a. Malus oxymela acida, Saurer Hoßhapfel. b. Malus sylvestris fructu rubro minore, Pomme sauvage, Hoßhapfel. c. Malus sylvestris fructu rotundo viridi graue, Hoßhapfel. d. Malus Persica flore pleno. e. Malus Persica Sti Laurentii, dicta. f. Malus Persica minor, Pesche petit, Pfirsig. g. Malus Persica major molle carne, Pfirsigapfel. h. Malus Persica magna, Bohnen Pfirsig.

"An abundance of every thing"

Mount Vernon's Fruit and Vegetable Gardens

J. Dean Norton

During the Washingtons' extended absences from Mount Vernon in the presidential years, George Washington conveyed his wife's wishes regarding the estate's fruit and vegetable gardens in frequent, lengthy letters to his farm managers. For example, a missive to manager Anthony Whitting on February 3, 1793, was accompanied by "some Lima Beans which Mrs. Washington desires may be given to the Gardener."[1] Three months later, he wrote Whitting that "Mrs. Washington desires you will direct old Doll to distill a good deal of Rose and Mint Water, &ca."[2] (Rose and mint water were extensively used to flavor various dishes.) Writing to another farm manager, William Pearce, in September 1794, Washington noted that his wife wanted the gardener to "send her some Artichoke seed of the best kinds he has."[3]

Obviously, the gardens were Martha Washington's domain and were the main source of produce for the family and their many guests. In 1792 she wrote to her niece Fanny Bassett, "I impress it upon the gardener to have everything in his garden that will be necessary in the House keeping way—as vegetable is the best part of our living in the country."[4]

In 1760, a year after marrying Martha Dandridge Custis, George Washington established his first garden plot, subsequently referred to as the lower garden. As might be expected, it existed for the cultivation of vegetables, fruits, and berries. According to a well-respected text of the time, *The Universal Gardener and Botanist*, "The kitchen garden was the most useful and consequential part of gardening." Indeed, it was "a necessary support of life."[5]

Fruit and nut trees grew in a second square garden, which was directly opposite the lower garden to the north. Records kept as this piece of ground was being established indicate Washington's participation in the project. In March 1762, for example, he was "grafting and planting Bullock heart and . . . fine early cherries from Colo. Mason."[6] George Mason, of the Gunston Hall estate, a dozen miles west of Mount Vernon, was, like Washington, an enthusiastic farmer as well as an accomplished grafter and orchardist.

A year later, Washington noted that on four days in late March 1763, nearly two hundred fruit trees were grafted and planted in the new garden. More specifically, the gardener had "grafted 12 Butter pears, 10 black Pear of Worcester, 10 of the Winter Boon Chrns. 8 of the summer Boon Chrns. 10 of the bergamy Pears and 10 New Town Pippin all from Collo. Mason."[7] Records also indicate that he planted many types of apricots, at least two kinds of peaches, three types of plums, seven varieties of apples, eight varieties of cherries, and eighteen types of pears.

Although there is scant information about the gardens at Mount Vernon from the mid-1760s to the mid-1780s, one visitor's account from 1782 suggests that they flourished. "There is an immense, extremely well-cultivated garden behind the right wing [of the house]," Baron Ludwig von Closen, a young aide-de-camp to French general Rochambeau, noted in his journal. "The choicest fruits in the country are to be found there."[8]

In 1785 Washington decided to redesign his estate in a more naturalistic style and change the configuration of his

OPPOSITE:
An illustration of apples from German apothecary and botanist Johann Wilhelm Weimann's Taalryk register *(ca. 1748).*

79

gardens from rectangular to a shape suggestive of a cathedral window. From mid-January 1785 until mid-1786 he wrote extensively in his diary about the progress he was making with his enhanced naturalistic landscape. The lower garden continued yielding a variety of fruits and vegetables, while the upper garden served two purposes. Most of the fruit trees were removed from the upper garden and transplanted to a part of the estate that previously had been a vineyard. Now, roses, other flowers, and shrubs flourished in the upper garden, but space remained there for vegetable cultivation. *The Universal Gardener and Botanist* described the type of garden Washington designed, explaining that such grounds were characterized by having

> *the Kitchen, fruit, and pleasure garden all in one; having*
> *their principal walks spacious, and the borders next them*
> *of considerable breadth; the back part of them planted with*
> *a range of espalier fruit-trees, surrounding the quarters;*
> *the front with flowers and small shrubs; and the inner*
> *quarters for the growth of the kitchen-vegetables, &c.*[9]

George Washington took abiding pride in identifying himself as a farmer, but he relied on a professional gardener to manage and maintain his garden enclosures. As early as

On those occasions "that your Earth grows dry," advised Batty Langley in Washington's copy of New Principles of Gardening (1728), *"'tis requisite to give it a moderate watering […] with a watering Pot and Rose." Accordingly, water was gently spread about from the perforated head, or "rose" of watering cans, such as this one used at Mount Vernon.*

1771, he wrote to his local friend Robert Adam: "In short a good Kitchen Gardener is what I want—If he undersd something of fruit Trees & could graft and Innoculate so much the better."[10] In 1788, a year after the greenhouse was completed and the upper garden transformed into a blooming pleasure garden, he sought "a complete Kitchen Gardener with a competent knowledge of Flowers and a Green House."[11] In late March 1790, his nephew George A. Washington, then serving as farm manager, wrote reassuringly to the president that "the gardener . . . seems fond of flours but says he will pay strick attention to more necessary parts of Gardening by furnishing a good supply to the kitchen."[12]

Washington was adamant about including vegetables in every proper dinner. In the spring of 1796, anticipating the end of his presidency and retirement to Mount Vernon, he wrote to William Pearce, "I shall expect an abundance of every thing in the gardens."[13] Past experience, he noted in a letter to his nephew Robert Lewis the following month, had showed that the Mansion would be "crowded with company . . . as the Ministers of France, Great Britain and Portugal, in succession, intend to be here. Besides other strangers."[14] And he insisted that his head gardener submit weekly reports documenting the types of vegetables, fruits, and berries that were being cultivated. These reports indicate that the garden workers spent most of their time growing vegetables in all the main garden enclosures.

Sometimes, the reports would detail the activities in the individual gardens. For example, on March 17, 1798, the head gardener, William Spence, wrote that his workers were "planting Kidney Beans, pease Onions, Carrots &c in the lower Garden"; on April 21, they were "Digging, Transplanting horse radish, planting Beans, peas, & Simlens, in Vineyard"; and on June 2, he and his laborers were "Dressing the flower plants, plantg beans. & Celery weeding onions in the high garden."[15]

Although the reports contain no specific information about the types of beans, cabbage, and so on in the gardens, a few references to specific vegetables can be found in the product orders Washington sent to London. In 1766, for instance, he sent off for "Garden peas, dwarf Martow peas, white non parl peas, green peas, early Sugr loaf cabbage, late

The lower terrace of the kitchen garden features a cistern or aboveground dipping well, which allows water to be softened and warmed before being applied to plants, a treatment that is conducive to good growth. This area of the garden also includes pole teepees for growing pole beans, trellises for grapes, and beds for herbs.

LEFT: *Mount Vernon strawberries and raspberries.*
RIGHT: *An illustration of grapes from German apothecary and botanist Johann Wilhelm Weimann's* Taalryk register *(ca. 1748).*

Sug loaf cabbage, scarlet raddish, short raddish, best Savoy, lattice and scarlet onion."[16]

Three vegetables in particular—artichokes, asparagus, and celery—required the skills of a professional gardener and his workers. Their tasks included trenching, covering, and ridging the plants. The vegetables were then served as part of an elegant meal, evidence of the premium the Washingtons placed on offering choice delicacies to their guests. Other delectable treats were berries of all types, which were planted in the lower garden and in a section of the fruit-garden enclosure devoted to their cultivation. Reports from the gardener indicate that during the week of January 13, 1798, gooseberry and currant bushes were pruned and that strawberries were gathered during the week of May 26.[17] Visitors to Mount Vernon extolled the quality of the berries they enjoyed there. For example, in 1790, French jurist and linguist Peter Stephen Duponceau wrote that he was delighted to see "for the first time preserved strawberries. . . . Those were large and beautiful, and I indulged in eating a few of them. I have been fond of them ever since."[18]

The gardeners' reports give us further information about the plants and trees that were tended within the garden walls at Mount Vernon during the Washingtons' years there. For instance, one notes that during the week of February 18, 1798, the gardeners are "Digging and pruning Fig trees in the under garden," probably referring to the lower garden, where they still grow today. During the week of December 30, 1797, the peach trees were being pruned, and gardeners were "nailing them to the walls." A week later, cherry trees are being "pruned and fastened to the wall."[19] These reports confirm that the gardener was directing his workers to espalier the fruit trees—that is, to train them to grow flat against a wall or support. This practice was common in the eighteenth century because it allowed several trees to grow in a limited space, and so leave more room for the production of vegetables.

George Washington's service to his country and dedication to farming left him little time to oversee the cultivation and harvesting of fruits and vegetables in person. So it was essential that he employ professional gardeners in order to assure the provision of ample quantities for the cooks in the

Globe artichokes were a favorite of Mrs. Washington and a garden vegetable often grown in the Mansion's "upper bordr."

family kitchen. It was up to Martha Washington to supervise the preparation and presentation of meals that capitalized on the bounty of Mount Vernon's gardens. After Amariah Frost, a Massachusetts clergyman, visited the estate in June 1797, he recorded in his diary that he had "viewed the garden and walks, which are very elegant, abounding with many curiosities, Fig trees, raisins, limes, oranges, etc., large English mulberries, artichokes, etc."[20] He and countless other guests were impressed by the abundance of fresh, wholesome food served at Mount Vernon and perhaps concurred with Mrs. Washington's opinion that vegetables were "the best part of our living in the country." *

OVERLEAF:
A Virginia summertime breakfast of ham, hoecakes, toast, tea, fresh peaches, and berries, served in Mount Vernon's lower garden.

The Upper Garden

———◆———

Mount Vernon's upper garden boasted a profusion of vegetables and flowers. As visitors strolled its wide paths, they marveled at the greenhouse and the "great variety of tree, flowers and plants of foreign growth collected from almost every part of the world . . . wonderful in their appearance, exquisite in their perfume and delightful to the eye."[1] For George Washington, however, the area was not so much a verdant retreat as it was a one-acre space that provided vegetables and fruits for his family and guests.

Archaeologists investigating the upper garden from 2005 to 2010 discovered how the area was laid out during the last years of Washington's life, and how various gardening approaches changed the space over time. For example, variations in soil color and texture offered valuable clues to early botanical practices, and they indicated how the garden evolved from Washington's era through the twentieth century.

Entries in Washington's diary suggest that the upper garden (also called the "new garden" and the "high garden" during his time) began to be cultivated by 1762, primarily as a nursery for grafts of fruit and nut trees.[2] His diary also documents the variety and scale of such work. For example, between February 1785 and February 1786, trees were planted there to produce English walnuts, apricots, peaches, pears, plums, and cherries.[3] Archaeological evidence for this activity exists more than two feet below the present grade, where the bottoms of some two hundred small rectangular holes, arranged in ordered rows, still survive. These depressions are filled with dark, rich soil, and their smooth bottoms suggest that the trees planted there did not remain in the ground long enough to reach maturity.

Archaeologists also discovered the long, linear beds spaced throughout the garden that they think are the remains of vegetable or flower beds; these are approximately three feet wide and filled with loamy soil. When amateur landscape architect Samuel Vaughan drew up his plan of Mount Vernon in 1787, he labeled both the upper and lower gardens as kitchen gardens, suggesting their function as spaces reserved for vegetable cultivation. Possibly, these linear beds once contained the vegetables that Vaughan suggested should be grown in a proper kitchen garden.

It is also clear from the archaeological record that major changes were made in the garden during the mid-1780s, when Washington transformed the landscape design of his estate—from a formal geometric layout to one that emphasizes curvilinear lines and naturalistic plantings. This project included altering the spatial orientation of the gardens and changing their boundaries from rectangles to the shieldlike shapes seen today. Buried soils still bear evidence of these changes; silty loams and narrow linear trenches appear to confirm that the ground originally was prepared for cultivation by means of a technique called double digging.

The layout of the upper garden featured four wide paths that provided the primary access around three large geometric planting beds, an area of fruit and nut trees to the northwest, and two boxwood parterres. The central path allowed visitors to enter from the north serpentine and immediately view the brick greenhouse—the garden's focal point. Trimmed boxwoods lined these ten-foot-wide graveled paths and also edged the rectangular garden beds. A ten-foot-wide border of flowers interspersed with fruit trees surrounded these large beds and the vegetables that were grown in the center. During the last decade of Washington's life, visitors characterized the upper garden as both a utilitarian kitchen garden and a flower garden, undoubtedly because vegetables and flowers were integrated within its large beds. There is scant archaeological evidence indicating the specific plants grown there, but visitor accounts and gardeners' reports list various vegetables (artichokes, peas, onions, celery, broccoli, beets), fruits (raspberries, strawberries, gooseberries, peaches, cherries), and flowers (poppies, lilies, roses, pinks).[4]

Archaeological evidence indicates that Washington's garden configuration survived until the 1870s, when the Mount Vernon Ladies' Association undertook an extensive renovation. At that time, the creation of an elaborate rose garden and a series of crescent-shaped beds and paths following the curve of the garden walls transformed Washington's mixed-use garden into one mainly devoted to flowers. ✳ ECW

OPPOSITE:
Mount Vernon's upper-garden beds provided a bountiful array for the Washingtons' table, including nasturtiums, savoy cabbage, red cabbage, beets, and leeks.

Batty Langley was an eccentric English garden designer and a prolific writer. George Washington owned a copy of Langley's New Principles of Gardening *(1728), a volume of enormous influence in Britain's American colonies. This portrait is a mezzotint engraving by J. Carwitham, published in 1741.*

M.ͬ *Batty Langley Architect.*

I. Carwitham fecit 1741.

Melior eſt conſulta Tarditas, quam temeraria Celeritas.

George Washington's Books on Gardening

———•———

Among the approximately one thousand books in George Washington's personal library, seven focused on the subject of gardening. These volumes offer practical advice, ranging from how to prepare flower and vegetable beds and apply fertilizers to instructions on pruning and grafting fruit trees and concocting the proper mixture of gravels for garden paths. One of the books, Philip Miller's *The Abridgment of the Gardeners Dictionary*, was particularly popular in both Britain and America, and Washington probably consulted it frequently. He noted in a 1785 letter to New York Governor George Clinton that Miller "seems to understand the culture of Trees equal to any other writer I have met with."[1]

Although most of the books deal with the actual practice of gardening rather than the design of garden spaces, Batty Langley's *New Principles of Gardening*, published in London in 1728, definitely influenced Washington's overall layout of the Mount Vernon landscape. The son of a Middlesex gardener, Langley was a prolific author of several architectural "pattern" books intended as guides for builders and craftsmen. His garden books are credited with helping to popularize the "picturesque," or "natural," garden style, which became the most fashionable design approach in Britain and among elite American gardeners in the second half of the eighteenth century. Langley argued against the elaborate, geometric layouts that had dominated European landscape designs, favoring instead a style that emphasized curving pathways, seemingly randomly placed groves and "wildernesses" of trees and shrubs, and above all, pleasing vistas of natural beauty.[2]

At Mount Vernon, Washington followed Langley's directions for landscaping in a "more grand and rural manner" as he planned and planted his parterres, groves, wildernesses, and labyrinths. He completed the redesign in 1786, after an eight-year hiatus, when he was away from home during the Revolutionary War. Among the many visitors impressed with the beauty of the new layout was a Polish nobleman, Julian Niemcewicz, who wrote in 1798: "The G[enera]l has never left America. After seeing his house and his gardens one would say that he had seen the most beautiful examples in England of this style."[3] ✳ DJP *and* JDN

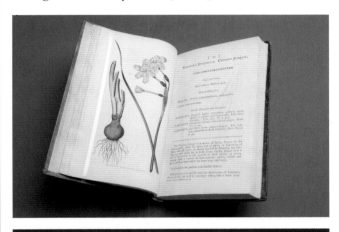

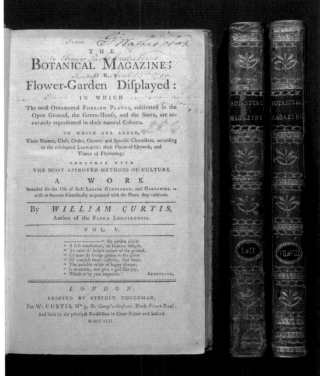

Shown here are George Washington's personal copies of several volumes of the Botanical Magazine, *part of a series of fourteen published by William Curtis from 1787 to 1800. For each plant, this series includes a few pages describing its characteristics, history, and common names as well as a hand-colored copperplate engraved illustration. As a gesture of their shared passion for horticulture, Washington presented these and other volumes from the series to his step-granddaughter Nelly Custis Lewis in 1799.*

Food Preservation

Maintaining an adequate supply of food year-round was a vital task for the Washingtons and other Southern plantation owners in the late eighteenth century. Although both husband and wife were involved in the production of provisions at Mount Vernon, Mrs. Washington was in charge of domestic operations. She—and the housekeepers, stewards, cooks, and scullions she supervised—were responsible for preserving and properly storing enough food for consumption during the winter and early spring. Unless these essential chores were correctly performed, members of the household would face hunger.

Root vegetables such as turnips, radishes, potatoes, and carrots, all staples of the winter diet, generally were stored in layers of dry sand in a cellar.[1] Even buried in sand, this produce could still be damaged by freezing temperatures, damp conditions, and contamination by rats and mice. In their efforts to mitigate these threats, the Washingtons used methods that were familiar to other Americans of the time.[2] Keeping the storage space sanitary was crucial, so Martha Washington regularly ordered that Frank Lee, the enslaved

On April 25, 1788, George Washington recorded in his diary that "4 rows of potatoes the red kind were planted."

butler, clean and whitewash in the cellar.[3] In the fall of 1792, for example, two days were spent "Cleaning the Cellar to Stow potatoes."[4] An extensive drainage system was constructed around the Mansion, including at least one drain that ran through the basement, to reduce dampness. To prevent freezing of the stored produce, late in the year Lee put "long litter"—presumably straw or cornstalks—"against the Cellar Windows."[5] Between five and seven hundred bushels of potatoes and one hundred bushels of turnips, the principal root crops at Mount Vernon, were stored in at least one of the vaulted stone sections of the Mansion cellar at the beginning of winter.[6]

Corn and peas were commonly dried, put in containers, and then placed in a clean, dry, and airy place.[7] Mrs. Washington owned a popular eighteenth-century cookbook that suggested two methods for preserving peas. In the first, young peas were shelled, boiled, and dried, after which they were put into bottles and covered with mutton fat before the bottles were corked. The second involved gathering peas on a very dry day, then shelling them and putting them directly into quart bottles, which were corked and sealed with rosin.[8] Corn, either "in ears" or "shel'ed," was stored in barrels and/or bushels.[9] As with other foodstuffs, the crop had to be monitored even after it was harvested and stored. In March 1786, George Washington bought a thousand bushels of corn after his previous year's crop provided only a fraction of what was needed to get through the year. About two weeks later, someone noticed that the corn was so hot it might spontaneously combust. Washington "was obliged to send part of it to be spread in my Mill loft—part . . . on the Barn floor at Muddy hole—part . . . above stairs in the servants Hall and part . . . on Carpets in the yard." Fortunately for Martha Washington's rugs, her husband noted that rain was threatening and soon had the corn in the yard "taken in again."[10]

More delicate vegetables, preserved by pickling, were integral to the winter diet in Virginia.[11] The many pickle recipes in Martha Washington's cookbooks and the presence of twenty-seven "Pickle Pots" found in the Mansion cellar shortly after her husband's death indicate the popularity of this technique for preserving homegrown vegetables, which

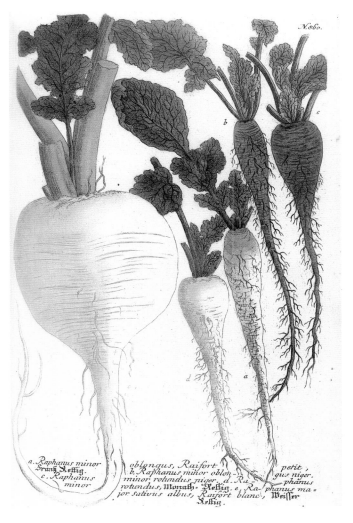

Mrs. Washington asserted were "the best part of our living in the country."[12]

Methods used to preserve fruits included candying, drying, pickling, and preserving with sugar to form "conserves" (jams or jellies) or "preserves" (whole canned fruit). Martha Washington, like many of her contemporaries, would have taken great pride in the quality of fruit confections prepared in her kitchen.[13] One Frenchman who visited Mount Vernon in 1780 fondly recalled a novelty he was served at dinner: "I can only say that I saw there for the first time preserved strawberries. . . . Those were large and beautiful, and I indulged in eating a few of them."[14] Preserved apricots, bottled gooseberries, and dried cherries also appeared on the Washingtons' table.[15] Many of these treasured items were stored in pottery jars covered with coarse white paper and tied with string.[16]

Obviously, it was necessary to eat meat soon after an animal was killed in order to prevent spoilage. Chickens and other fowls, fish, and rabbits could be consumed in one or two meals, but the meat of large animals, such as cattle and pigs, was placed on ice, which was taken from the river during the winter and stored in the hope that it would remain frozen. As George Washington wrote to his farm manager William Pearce in 1794: "I was in hopes the last spell of freezing weather wd. have enabled you to fill the Ice house. It is very desirable it should be so, as the convenience on acct. of fresh meat &ca. in the Summer is inconceivably great in the Country."[17] Only the most prosperous landowners of the day could afford ice houses, which involved considerable labor to fill, and, if the results at Mount Vernon were typical, rarely kept ice from melting by summer's end. * MVT

Milling Flour at Mount Vernon

When George Washington inherited Mount Vernon following the death of his older half-brother, Lawrence, in 1752, the property included a small water-powered gristmill located on Dogue Run Creek in an area Washington initially referred to as Mill Plantation. Slaves ran this mill, which ground mainly corn and wheat for daily sustenance. As Washington increased the size of the property and developed his tobacco business during the 1750s and early 1760s, he also studied the latest methods of farming, known then as the "new husbandry." Based on this research and on his close monitoring of fluctuations in the tobacco market, he decided, in 1766, to introduce a new agricultural and business model for his estate.

Years of tobacco cultivation had exhausted the soils at Mount Vernon. The lower quality of the leaf Washington grew could not compete with that produced by other growers in Tidewater Virginia. This fact, along with the rising volatility of tobacco markets and the fees charged by British business agents, made profits in the trade increasingly weak. Fearing debt, Washington abandoned the production of tobacco in favor of wheat. The change would not be easily implemented. Conversion from tobacco to wheat required new work methods, new farm machinery and tools, and new barns. Most significantly, the plan also involved a major building project: construction of a new, larger water-powered gristmill capable of producing the superfine flour desired in overseas markets. The development of foreign markets for flour began in the seventeenth century, long before Washington was born; they would prove profitable and a much more reliable resource for him for the rest of his life.

The first market for Colonial America's surplus flour and cornmeal was the West Indies, where the sugar trade flourished. With large slave populations engaged in sugar production, outside sources were needed to supply rations. Caribbean merchants and traders also needed these grain products. The mills and millers of English North America—

chiefly in New York, New Jersey, Pennsylvania, Delaware, Maryland, and Virginia—met the demand for flour, cornmeal, and even bread.

According to Charles Kuhlmann, in his 1929 history of flour milling in America: "By 1723 flour and other provisions were being shipped to Barbados, Montserrat, St. Christopher's, Nevis, Antigua, and Jamaica in the British West Indies, to Surinam and Curacao in the Dutch possessions, and the Danish island of St. Thomas. Curacao and Jamaica took large supplies not only for their own needs but for reshipment to the Spanish possessions." At the same time, European markets were opening up as well. Kuhlmann noted that "wheat and flour were being carried to the countries of southern Europe, Portugal especially, and from thence to France. Gradually there was built up a considerable trade with the Madeira Islands, Tenerife, and the Spanish ports of the Bay of Biscay."[1]

Four years after deciding to abandon tobacco cultivation for wheat, Washington hired millwright Jonathan Ball to build the new gristmill (also known as a merchant mill). Work began in February 1770. One of the most difficult aspects of the project involved the digging of a new millrace and a new dam to supply water to the mill. The race was about two miles long, starting at the millpond at the upper end of Dogue Run Farm; from there, water flowed gradually downhill to the waterwheel. Washington's diaries indicate that he closely monitored construction of the mill, visiting the site often. The structure was completed in March 1771, and by June 128,000 pounds of flour had been produced there and shipped to market.[2]

Washington made sure his millwright outfitted the mill with all the proper components. The sixteen-foot-diameter waterwheel was powerful enough to run two sets of millstones, one for grinding corn and the other for grinding wheat. Corn was a dietary staple on the plantation for the Washingtons and their free and enslaved workers. Washington himself was especially partial to corn-based hoecakes, which he enjoyed "swimming in honey and butter."[3] A portion of the cornmeal at Mount Vernon was fed to livestock. The set of millstones for grinding wheat, known as French burrstones, were imported from quarries along the Marne

The reconstruction of George Washington's gristmill has an interior waterwheel, protected from the elements. The mill grinds corn and wheat and is the only one in the United States with an operating Oliver Evans automated-milling system.

River. Made of so-called freshwater quartz, these extremely hard stones were ideal for grinding wheat into superfine flour. European millers had been using them since the fourteenth century, and by the seventeenth century, so were millers in Colonial America. Washington noted that the millstones were "an Article of more consequence than all the rest to me."[4]

The grain was ground between two large millstones, which sometimes measured four to five feet in diameter and weighed a ton apiece. The lower stone, known as the bed stone, remained stationary, while the upper, or runner stone rotated upon an iron spindle driven by the waterwheel and gearing, both of which were made of wood. As the runner stone turned over the bed stone, wheat was ground into wheat meal. The furrows and lands on the grinding face of each stone worked together like scissors, cutting and slicing the grain. The miller used a long compound lever, called a lighter staff, to adjust the height of the runner stone. This lever allowed him to set the gap between the two stones and thus control how coarse or fine the flour would be: the closer the stones were set to each other, the finer the flour. Once ground, the wheat meal was hoisted to the upper floor of the mill for sifting.

Washington's millwright had two large rectangular bolting chests installed for sifting flour into various grades. Located on the upper floor of the mill and powered by the

Correctly cutting the dressing pattern into the grinding face of each millstone was especially critical. The dressing consisted of two parts: the furrows, or grooves, and the flat, higher surfaces between the furrows, called lands.

During that time, several men operated and maintained the facility. Washington's first miller was William Roberts, a Pennsylvanian who possessed the rare skills of both a miller and a millwright. As a millwright—that is, a builder of mills—he could construct waterwheels, gears, and shafts and care for all other components, ensuring the machinery was in good working order. In a 1785 letter to his business associates Robert Lewis and Sons, Washington declared that "for skill in grinding, and keeping a Mill in order, [Roberts is] inferior to No Man. . . . He is an excellent Cooper & Millwright, he has lived with me near fifteen years, during which period I have not paid a shilling for repairs."[6] Unfortunately, Roberts had such a serious drinking problem that Washington had to fire him, that same year. Replacing him was Joseph Davenport, who died suddenly in 1796. Patrick Callahan handled the mill until late summer 1799. That June, Washington contacted Roberts to say he was willing to hire him again, providing he would "refrain from drink, & the evils which it has produced," and to indicate that neither Callahan nor Davenport had been as skilled as Roberts.[7]

In 1791 Washington became one of the first in the country to install the latest in milling technology, the recently patented automated-milling system invented by Oliver Evans. With this system, bucket elevators transported wheat and flour throughout the mill; an automatic flour cooler, called the "hopper boy," prepared the flour for sifting. Cooling was essential because wheat meal became quite warm during the grinding process. Before the advent of Evans's invention, young men known as hopper boys had used rakes to cool the meal—hence the name of the new device. These innovations greatly increased the efficiency of the operation while reducing the number of laborers needed.

waterwheel, the bolters contained hexagonal wood-frame reels fitted with silk bolting cloth. As wheat meal was fed into the bolting chests, the reels rotated, sifting the meal through the extremely fine cloth to yield superfine white flour. "At present my Mill has the reputation of turning out superfine flour of the first quality," Washington proudly wrote in April 1785. It "commands a higher price in this Country & the West Indies than any other."[5] A section of each reel was fitted with a coarser bolting cloth that produced somewhat less refined flour. Known at the time as fine flour, it contained some bran; today, it would be called whole wheat flour. Fine flour was also shipped to overseas markets, bringing in a decent profit. The final product separated by the bolting chests was the remaining bran, called ships stuff; Washington sold this in nearby Alexandria for ship's biscuit, also known as hardtack.

George Washington's wheat crops and the mill that processed them yielded solid profits for nearly thirty years.

OPPOSITE:

The lower floor of the gristmill contains large wooden gears made of white oak and maple. These massive gears, powered by a sixteen-foot waterwheel, drive two sets of millstones for grinding corn and wheat.

Milling at Mount Vernon provided both profit and sustenance. Farm reports for the estate indicate that tremendous numbers of barrels were sold and shipped to domestic and overseas markets. In addition, George Washington's paid staff received barrels of flour, and his family, friends, and many guests also benefited from the successful milling operation. Early in 1799, Washington wrote, "As a Farmer, Wheat and Flour constitute my principal concerns, it behoves me therefore to dispose of them upon the best terms."[8] * STB

Drink and Be Merry

Liquor and Wine at Mount Vernon

DENNIS J. POGUE

From the perspective provided by the passage of more than two hundred years, George Washington might be described as having a "modern" attitude toward alcohol. He drank a range of "spirituous liquors" (as they were then typically called), both in private and in public, and he conscientiously supplied his family and guests, the soldiers he commanded during two wars, and even his hired and enslaved workers with appropriate beverages. Yet he also was fully aware of the dangers of drinking to excess, and on two occasions was forced to discharge highly valued employees because they were unable to control their thirst for strong drink. It was the continued inability of one of these men to curb his drinking that led Washington sadly to observe, "An aching head and trimbling limbs are the inevitable effects of drinking [and] disincline the hands from work; hence begins sloth and that Lestlessness which end in idleness."[1] Nevertheless, he remained convinced of the benefits of moderate alcohol consumption, and late in his life he had no qualms about operating one of the country's largest and most profitable whiskey distilleries.

Beverage alcohol served a range of purposes in American society during George Washington's day. In an era when the practice of medicine was still rudimentary, drinking alcohol was considered a healthful practice, and doctors routinely prescribed spirits to ward off, or even cure, a host of ailments. Securing dependable sources of potable water had been a challenge in much of Western Europe for centuries, and it persisted in America as well. Ale, beer, hard cider, wine, and distilled spirits were all deemed healthier alternatives to water. As in almost every Western nation, alcohol consumption was an intrinsic feature of social gatherings within all classes of American society. Mount Vernon account books and correspondence contain many references to Washington's purchasing and imbibing a variety of alcohols, with Madeira—a fortified wine from Portugal—ale, and beer qualifying as his favorites.[2]

"Hard," or fermented cider was popular in Britain's American colonies during the eighteenth century, with most farmers cultivating their own orchards in order to have enough apples to make the drink themselves. Cider was made at Mount Vernon during all the years Washington owned the estate, with various entries in the plantation records testifying to its production as well as to its consumption by the Washingtons and their employees and slaves. Washington obtained cider from England early on, buying, for example, "12 dozn. Best Herfordshire Cyder in best Mould Bottles, wyred Corks" in 1757 and 128 bottles of the same a year later. Apparently, however, enough cider was routinely produced at Mount Vernon to meet most of the needs of the plantation community.[3]

Washington purchased substantial quantities of beer, ale, and porter (a darker variety of the brew) throughout his adult life, using American and English suppliers at different times. Initially, he ordered these drinks from England: in 1757 he imported twelve dozen bottles of "fine Porter," then 139 bottles of beer in 1758, a hogshead (typically 63 gallons)

97

of "best Porter" in 1760, one hogshead of "fine old Porter" in 1761, and so on, up until the Revolutionary War. He frequently specified that the bottles should be packed in wood shavings to guard against breakage, a precaution resulting from unfortunate past experiences. In 1762, he recalled that the bottles had not been packed that way the previous year and, as a consequence, had been "lost."[4]

After the war, Washington decided to replace imported English ale and beer with American brews. Nationalist sentiment may partially have prompted the change. "We have already been too long subject to British prejudices," he wrote the Marquis de Lafayette in January 1789. "I use no porter or cheese in my family, but such as is made in America; both these articles may now be purchased of an excellent quality." A particular favorite was the porter Robert Hare brewed in

In 1761 George Washington admonished his London agent about the high price he was charged for this sixteen-bottle liquor chest, complaining he could have had it made locally at a much lower cost.

Philadelphia. The previous July, Washington had asked his purchasing agent Clement Biddle to secure him "a gross of Mr. [Hare's] best bottled Porter." Unfortunately, the brewery burned down two years later; the president wrote that he was sorry "on public as well as private accts. to hear of Mr. Hares loss."[5]

The Washingtons favored several types of brandy, both imported and local. In 1774 George Washington bought two kegs of French brandy from a friend. In 1786 he wrote to Lafayette in France, complaining that he had been unable to acquire "an anchor of old Peach Brandy" to accompany the barrel of Mrs. Washington's "Virginia Hams" he was shipping as a gift to his old comrade. Interestingly, in 1788 he claimed brandy was a healthier drink than rum, adding that wine and brandy from France were not as dangerous to the well-being of the people as the "thousands of Hogsheads of poisonous Rum which are annually consumed in the United States." Possibly, his praise here of brandy over rum had a political dimension, as his correspondent was the Comte de Moustier, who was then France's ambassador to the United States. Brandy made from peaches and from apples was produced by Washington's distillery when it was established in 1797; records show that sixty-seven gallons of apple and sixty gallons of peach brandy were sent to the Mansion House Farm in October 1799.[6]

Of the various alcoholic beverages George Washington consumed, Madeira was clearly his favorite. Many visitors noted his fondness for the drink and how he "loved to chat after dinner with a glass of Madeira in his hand." As early as 1759, he ordered a pipe (a cask normally containing 126 gallons) of the "best Old Wine" from "the best House in Madeira." Subsequent orders generally called for substantial quantities of the drink, ranging up to several hundred gallons at a time, and they usually included the request that the wine be of the highest quality. After Martha Washington's death in 1802, one of the men sent to inventory the contents and assess the value of the estate found eight pipes of "old Wine"—probably Madeira—believed to be "about to 25 to 30 years old," in the Mansion cellar.[7]

Wines from Portugal were by far the most popular in America during much of the eighteenth century, while those produced in France and other European countries commanded only a negligible share of the market. One reason for this marked preference was that Madeira, the most sought after of the Portuguese wines, improved in quality under the rigors of a transatlantic crossing, unlike others that were adversely affected. The highly charged political climate of the time also influenced the initial popularity of such wines. Portugal was a longtime ally of Great Britain, while warfare with France from 1754 to 1763 made trade between the American colonies and France illegal. Eventually, Franco-American relations warmed considerably when the two nations formed an alliance during the Revolutionary War, and trade opportunities between them naturally increased. Washington ordered 312 bottles each of French Champagne and claret in 1789; four years later, he bought 485 bottles, combined, of Champagne and burgundy. Guests' accounts include several mentions of Champagne being served during dinner at Mount Vernon and at the president's residence in Philadelphia.[8]

Because wine was among Washington's favorite alcoholic beverages, it is not surprising that he attempted to cultivate wine grapes on his estate. Like many of his fellow Virginians, he was convinced that the profusion of grapes indigenous to the region practically guaranteed successful wine-making. "I have long been of opinion, from the spontaneous growth of the vine," he wrote to his Italian physician friend Philip Mazzei in 1779, "that the climate and soil in many parts of Virginia were well fitted for Vineyards and that Wine, sooner or later would become a valuable article of produce." As early as 1763, Washington acquired and planted fifty-five cuttings of the Madeira grape, and more than twenty years later he received several barrels containing cuttings of the stock. He also experimented with native varieties, as well as with grapes imported from Spain. All his attempts at establishing a vineyard failed, however, and it would be almost two centuries before Virginia's wine industry approached the level of success he had envisioned.[9]

Rum was the most popular distilled spirit in America before the Revolutionary War. George Washington is known to have enjoyed it most often in a punch made of rum, sugar, spices, water, and fruit juices that normally was mixed

Glass stemware from the Mount Vernon collection. At the end of his presidency, Washington noted that he had replaced broken glassware "over and over again" at his own expense.

and served in a large bowl. According to visitors' accounts, punch was offered regularly at Mount Vernon. In June 1798 a visitor from Poland related that when he arrived unexpectedly at the plantation, Martha Washington "appeared after a few minutes, welcomed us most graciously and had punch served."[10]

The record of the Rum Account entered in the Mount Vernon plantation records for 1787 provides insight into the ways alcohol was used to encourage and reward the desired behavior of both free and enslaved workers on the plantation. Washington acquired 491 gallons of rum that year, purchased in eight shipments from five merchants; these ranged in volume from a single barrel (thirty-one gallons) to a hogshead containing 125 gallons. Various hired skilled workers were allotted a daily ration of between two and three pints of rum, for a weekly total of three and five-eighths gallons. Rum also was distributed almost daily to workers, in amounts above the basic ration, for various specific reasons—for example, as a reward to Sam "for burn[in]g the brick kiln," to "the Carpenters [for] raising the [roof of the] Green Ho[use]," and to "the people who assisted in getting the cow out of the mire." After setting up his own distillery in 1797, Washington substituted whiskey for the rum he previously had given to his slaves and employees. In March 1798, forty-five gallons of whiskey were distributed to the fishery workers. And in July of the following year, each group of "cradlers" (workers who cut and gathered grain at the four outlying farms that were part of the estate) received between seventeen and a half and twenty-two and a half gallons of whiskey, presumably both as an incentive and as a reward for a job well done.[11]

Given the many positive references to "old" spirits and wine found in Washington's papers, he no doubt understood that aging in barrels generally improved the taste of such drinks. In October 1797, he received a gift of "a Dozen Bot-tles" of aged rum from architect William Thornton, whose friendship with Washington began when they worked together on the design of the U.S. Capitol in 1793. A native of the Virgin Islands, Thornton described the rum he sent to his friend as "the heart of Oak. It is old Spirit that was distill'd upon my own Estate in the Island of Tortola, 28 years ago, and has obtained the deep colour by standing in Oak Casks ever since." Thornton continued, "It is as good as a Tincture of Bark, and would be of no disservice to a Virginia Planter in a Dram Fog." In a letter written a few days later, Washington expressed his thanks "for the rare & valuable present you have made me. Being the produce of your own Estate renders it more acceptable, and nothing will add more to the go'vt of it, than your coming sometimes to participate in the taste—fog or no fog."[12]

During the Christmas season, it was customary for family and friends to spend the holiday at Mount Vernon, where the consumption of alcohol doubtless contributed to the festive atmosphere. The slaves apparently benefited as well from the celebratory mood, as they usually were given sev-

One of George Washington's silver-plated four-bottle wine coolers, designed to serve wine from glass decanters during the dessert course. This cooler was made in England around 1789.

eral days off work and, at least occasionally, received an allotment of drink. When Philip Bater was hired as a gardener in 1787, his contract included the stipulation that "George Washington doth agree to allow him . . . four Dollars at Christmas, with which he may be drunk 4 days and 4 nights." Additionally, Bater was to receive "two Dollars at Easter to effect the same purpose; two Dollars also at Whitsontide, to be drunk in two days." On December 24, 1799—incidentally, the week after Washington's funeral—the Mansion House Farm slaves were given thirty gallons of whiskey, valued at $17.50, for "a Christmas Dram."[13]

William Roberts came to Mount Vernon in 1770 to operate Mount Vernon's gristmill, a vital component of the overall plantation enterprise. Washington had high regard for Roberts, who operated the mill as a profitable venture for most of the fifteen years he worked at the estate. But he also described Roberts as a "madman" when under the influence of alcohol, and unfortunately the miller's addiction worsened over time. In 1785 Washington was forced to fire him. In a letter to a business contact in which he expressed his need for a new miller, Washington lamented: "My Miller is now become such an intolerable sot . . . that however unwilling I am to part with an old Servant . . . I cannot with propriety or common justice to myself bear with him any longer."[14]

The international fame Washington enjoyed following the stunning victory of American forces in the Revolutionary War spurred many admirers from Europe to make a pilgrimage to Mount Vernon to meet him. Several of those visitors provided written accounts of the hospitality they received upon reaching the plantation; these indicate that alcohol played an important role in the gatherings. According to the reports of his dinner companions, he habitually "had a silver pint cup or mug of beer, placed by his plate, which he drank while dining." Along with the beer, he usually consumed two or more glasses of wine. According to the diary of Robert Hunter, Jr., a Scotsman who visited in November 1785, "The General sent the bottle about pretty freely after dinner, and gave success to the navigation of the Potomac for his toast." Washington often was described as somewhat reserved on these occasions, especially when he

did not know the guests well. But in this instance, Hunter commented, "The General with a few glasses of champagne got quite merry, and being with his intimate friends laughed and talked a good deal."[15]

Washington ordered that even when he was absent from the plantation, visitors should continue to be entertained in a manner befitting their station. It was understood that wine would be served on these occasions, but after learning that guests had drunk more than fifty bottles during a brief span while he was in Philadelphia during the presidency, Washington clarified his desires: "It is not my intention that [wine] should be given to every one who may incline to make a convenience of the house in traveling or who may be induced to visit it from motives of curiosity." He did, however, authorize providing alcohol to his "particular and intimate acquaintances" who might happen to arrive in his absence, or to "the most respectable foreigners" and "persons of distinction (such as members of Congress)." Even so, there was a limit to Washington's largesse, as he made it clear that he preferred that claret be served instead of his much-loved and more costly Madeira.[16]

In January 1797, as he planned his forthcoming return to Mount Vernon upon the end of his presidency, Washington decided—though hesitantly—to heed the advice of his farm manager James Anderson and enter the liquor business by building a whiskey distillery. Although the president freely admitted that he lacked firsthand knowledge of alcohol production, he was persuaded by Anderson's argument that the distillery would be a profitable enterprise. The manager proved to be right: the operation produced almost ten thousand five hundred gallons of spirits in 1799, primarily rye whiskey and small quantities of brandy valued at more than $7,500, making it one of the most successful such distilleries in the land. Thus, along with the distinctions of being "First in war, first in peace, and first in the hearts of his countrymen," it seems fitting to add another, rather surprising item to George Washington's long list of accomplishments—(almost) first in whiskey distilling.[17] *

OVERLEAF:
Washington Taking Leave of the Officers of His Army, at Fraunces Tavern, Broad Street, New York, Decr. 4th. 1783, *engraved by Nathaniel Currier in 1847.*

Barbecues

———— ❖ ————

Barbecues featuring roasted pig were popular summer entertainments in Virginia around the time of the Revolutionary War. Guests would arrive, by carriage or boat, at a prearranged gathering place, where they would dance to fiddle and banjo music while the food was prepared.[1] Here's how one guest at a late-eighteenth- or early-nineteenth-century Virginia barbecue near Richmond recalled the event:

> On the day I was present, dinner was ready at half past three o'clock, and consisted of excellent meats and fish, well prepared and well served, with the vegetables of the season. Your veritable gourmand never fails to regale himself on his favorite barbecue, which is a fine fat pig called a shoat, cooked on or over the coals and highly seasoned with cayenne. A dessert of melons and fruits follows, and punch, porter, and toddy are the table liquors; but with the fruits comes on the favorite beverage of the Virginians—mint-julep, in place of wine. I never witnessed more festivity and good humor than prevailed at this club.[2]

A cookbook by a prominent Virginia hostess of the day included a recipe titled "To Barbecue Shote," which specified that the head and feet should be removed and the carcass divided into four quarters, each weighing about six pounds. While cooking, the meat was to be basted with a sauce consisting of water, garlic, pepper, salt, red wine, and mushroom catsup and thickened with butter and flour.[3] The pepper used in this recipe may well have been cayenne (also known as long pepper), which George Washington ordered in large quantities in 1760 and 1772 (four pounds and one pound, respectively). Thomas Jefferson was growing cayenne by 1767, as was George Washington in the 1780s.[4]

Before the Revolutionary War, Washington attended a number of barbecues, generally on Saturdays, in Alexandria, as well as at the home of his brother-in-law Colonel Fielding Lewis in Fredericksburg, and, closer to Mount Vernon, at Accotink and Johnson's Ferry. Washington himself apparently hosted one or two in September 1773, noting in his diary that he went "to a Barbicue of my own giving at Accatinck."[5]

One of the most significant barbecues Washington attended occurred during his presidency, when he participated in the Masonic ceremony in September 1793 that was part of the cornerstone laying for the U.S. Capitol. Martha Washington's granddaughter Martha Parke Custis (later Mrs. Thomas Peter) was there that day. As her daughter Britannia reminisced many years later:

> She was a girl at the time and drove up from "Hope Park," where she lived, with other members of the family. There was an ox killed and barbecued on the occasion, and, after the corner-stone was put in place by General Washington, and the speaches made, every one went and partook of the repast. Of course, they did not go, being but girls; but the general came to them, mother said, and told them they must have something before they left and escorted them to the table. I have often heard her tell of it![6]

Barbecues were lively social events. At one that Washington attended in August 1770, there was "a great deal of other Company" present and he "stayd there till Sunset."[7] It was not unusual for him to bring overnight guests home afterward, or to spend the night at others' homes as a post–barbecue guest.[8]

Along with dancing, socializing, and of course, feasting, some barbecues featured boat races and games of chance and skill. Washington referred in his diary to a boat race at a barbecue at Johnson's Ferry in May 1774. No doubt the competition prompted a lively round of betting, possibly helped along by the forty-eight bottles of claret he supplied for the occasion.[9] He also enjoyed various outdoor games, any one of which he and his friends may have played while the pig was roasting. During the Christmas season of 1773, he came outside to find his stepson and some visiting friends

OPPOSITE:
Cayenne peppers, gathered from the Mount Vernon garden, are the key ingredient in barbeque sauce.

"pitching the bar," which was probably similar to horseshoes. Painter Charles Willson Peale later recorded that

[Washington] requested to be shown the pegs that marked the bounds of our efforts; then, smiling, and without putting off his coat, held out his hand for the missile. No sooner . . . did the heavy iron bar feel the grasp of his mighty hand than it lost the power of gravitation, and whizzed through the air, striking the ground far, very far, beyond our utmost limits. We were indeed amazed, as we stood around, all stripped to the buff, with shirt sleeves rolled up, and having thought ourselves very clever fellows, while the colonel, on retiring, pleasantly observed, "When you beat my pitch, young gentlemen, I'll try again."[10] * MVT

Fisheries

❖

The Potomac River shoreline that stretched along almost ten miles of Mount Vernon's eastern boundary provided George Washington with a highly profitable commercial opportunity. By catching some of the millions of herring and thousands of shad that passed the plantation during their spring migration to spawn, he not only supplied his own table and secured a major food supply for his slaves but also increased his personal income. In some years, his workers caught more than one million fish, and the revenue from selling the excess usually netted more than £100.[1]

During the approximately six-week period in April and May when the fish were running, slaves from all the Mount Vernon farms were pressed into service, sometimes working day and night. Two men rowed a small boat into the stream following a semicircular path, paying out a seine net over the vessel's stern as they went. The seine was up to four hundred fifty feet long, with lead weights attached to one edge and corks tied to the opposite side; attached to either end were

hauling lines—ropes up to fifteen hundred feet long. After the boats returned to shore, gangs of workers hauled in the lines, causing the net to close and trap the fish. Once the net reached the shallows, the fishermen waded into the water to retrieve the catch in bushel baskets. The fish were beheaded, gutted, and salted, and then packed about eight hundred to the barrel to be preserved. If this procedure was carefully followed, the fish could remain edible for more than a year.[2]

In the spring of 1772—to offer one season as an example—Washington's slaves caught about 1.3 million herring and more than eleven thousand shad. A portion of the catch was distributed to the slaves as rations, and the bulk was sold to local merchants. That year, Washington sold 929,700 herring and 10,894 shad to the Alexandria merchant firm Robert Adam and Company for £184. The sale of fish continued to be an important source of ready money for Washington until the end of his life; for example, in 1797 fishery profits were listed as just over £165. Occasionally, he marketed fish in places as far away as the West Indies. In 1774 one Caribbean commodity he acquired in exchange for fish and flour was several hundred gallons of "Jamaica Rum," which he then sold at a profit to several of his Virginia neighbors.[3] * DJP

This page from one of Washington's ledger books provides a detailed accounting of his fishing enterprises at Mount Vernon. The record for April–May 1799 includes purchases of salt and barrels, expenditures for fishing boat repairs, and a list of workers.

Exotic Foods and Beverages

———— ◆ ————

For a family like the Washingtons, with considerable financial means and a prominent position in society, it was possible to acquire exotic foods and beverages from around the world. When George Washington desired, say, Cheshire cheese, he would place an order that seems quite large by today's standards, because the amount purchased was expected to last for about a year. Regardless of where most such foodstuffs originated—whether in Europe, the Middle East, or Asia—they first went through merchants in England before being shipped to America, a process that could take months.

In the years just prior to the Revolutionary War, as well as during the conflict itself, imported and exotic foods were often unavailable—so Americans were either resigned to doing without, or they sought substitutes for what they couldn't obtain. In March 1778, George Washington learned that his farm manager Lund Washington was going to "attempt to make molasses, sugar, rum and etc. from corn next Fall"; by summer, Lund had a mill ready for pressing corn stalks to make molasses.[1] Faced with a shortage of salt for preserving fish, Lund planned that same year to dip the fish in brine "for but a short time" and then to "hang them up and cure them by smoke, or dry them in the Sun."[2]

After the war, it could still take weeks or months for imported foods sent from a major hub, such as New York or Philadelphia, to reach Mount Vernon. Not surprisingly, the war prompted many to change their purchasing habits, with Washington himself making an effort to "buy American" once peace had been restored. For example, he noted in a 1789 letter to the Marquis de Lafayette that he no longer used either cheese or porter from England but chose instead "such as is made in America," for "both those articles may now be purchased of an excellent quality."[3]

The following selected list of food and drink that George Washington ordered from distant places is derived from his financial papers over a period of about forty years, roughly from the time of his marriage to Martha Dandridge Custis in January 1759 until his death in December 1799. ✳ MVT

CANARY ISLANDS: Canary wine
ENGLAND: Cheese (cheddar, Cheshire, double Gloucester), beer (from Dorset), mustard (from Durham), porter, salt (from Bristol), walnuts
FRANCE: Brandy, olives, wine (burgundy, Champagne, claret)
GERMANY: Rhenish wine
INDIA: Pickled mangoes
ITALY: Lucca olives
MADEIRA ISLANDS: Citron, lemons, Madeira wine
MEDITERRANEAN: Anchovies, capers, citron, currants, olive oil, raisins
MEXICO AND CENTRAL AMERICA: Chocolate
PORTUGAL: Lisbon wine, port wine, salt, sugar
SOUTHERN AND SOUTHEAST ASIA: Cinnamon, cloves (Moluccas, a.k.a. Spice Islands), long peppers, mace, nutmeg (Moluccas)
SPAIN: Pimentos (cherry peppers), sherry
SURINAM: Coffee
WEST INDIES: Coconuts, coffee, lemons, limes, molasses, oranges, pineapples, rum, sugar, turtles
YEMEN: Coffee

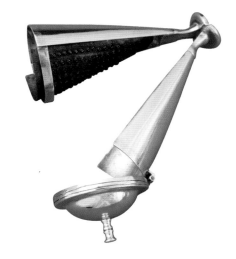

This sleek, silver urn-shaped object opens to reveal a compartment and grater for storing, grinding, and serving nutmeg, a spice used in a variety of eighteenth-century recipes. Portable and convenient devices such as this were occasionally given as gifts or tokens of affection.

Dairying

One of George Washington's fondest wishes during his later years was that his cattle would provide income from the sale of their dairy products in nearby Alexandria, Georgetown, and the District of Columbia. He dreamed of building "large dayries" on his farms and considered his goal of furthering that business as "much more desirable . . . than to push the best of my fields, out of their regular course, with a view to encrease [*sic*] the next, or any other year's crops of grain."[1] For most of his life at Mount Vernon, however, dairying—even for home use—had been a disappointment, an experience he apparently shared with other Virginians of the period. According to Audrey Nöel Hume, an archaeologist at Colonial Williamsburg, most sizable houses in that town, for example, had a dairy or milk house near the kitchen. But contemporary accounts record that of "milk, cream, butter and cheese . . . [the Virginia colonists] made very little—indeed so to speak almost none."[2]

Problems with dairy production in Virginia and elsewhere in the South—mainly due to the poor quality of the cattle—would continue well into the nineteenth century. According to historians Kenneth Kiple and Virginia Himmelsteib King, only progressive farming operations (such as at Mount Vernon) were able to produce significant quantities of milk, and even then the quality was poor.[3]

Dairying at Mount Vernon began in earnest shortly after George Washington married Martha Dandridge Custis, a young widow, in 1759. Before then, his financial records show purchases of milk; after that, he seems to have bought milk only when traveling or living away from Mount Vernon.[4] In September 1760, he ordered six dozen earthenware milk pans, used for setting milk so the cream would rise to the top, from England. Over the next five years, he purchased many more such items in a variety of sizes and materials and bought still more milk pans in the 1790s.[5] Nearly two hundred years later, fragments of some of these utensils were

excavated at the former site of a slave quarter near the Mansion known as the House for Families.[6]

Washington had dairy operations on at least three of the five farms of his estate. At the Mansion House Farm, slaves milked cows and churned butter—among other chores—between two and six days a week.[7] In a February 1794 letter to his farm manager William Pearce, Washington discussed the possibility of constructing a dairy at Union Farm (which was built) and another at Dogue Run (which apparently wasn't), "to see if the Milk at each could not be turned to some account." He wanted these new dairies to be built like the one at River Farm, with a lower section of brick.[8] Financial records from four years later note the purchase of milk pans specifically for the dairies at Union and River farms.[9]

Traditionally, dairying was considered "women's work," at least before mechanized milking machines were introduced in the late nineteenth century. No doubt this explains the absence of such activity at Mount Vernon before the arrival of Martha Washington, who ultimately oversaw the plantation's dairy functions.[10] Working under her supervision were female slaves—including Kitty, Sinah, Anna, and Grace—from the dairy at the Mansion House Farm.[11] Washington also expected the wives of some of his hired white workers to supervise the slave women in the dairy. For instance, in 1797, when he was considering hiring a new gardener, Washington mused that he would prefer a man who was single but wouldn't object to a married man with no more than two children if the employee's wife "would undertake to superintend my Spinners, & if required a small dairy at the Mansion house (where the Gardens are)."[12] Thirty-five years earlier, the employment contract between Washington and a man named Edward Violet spelled out the role of Violet's wife:

> "[George Washington] doth also agree to allow the said Edd Voilett [sic] to employ one of the Negroe women upon the said Plantation to assist at proper times his the said Edwards Wife to Milk[,] Churn and do the necessary Services of the Dairy and for his Wife's trouble and management of the same to allow her one-fourth part of what Butter she can make. [T]he said Geo: being at the expence of Building a good Dairy and furnishing it with Milk Pans[,] Pails, &ca."[13]

Dairying at Mount Vernon was only intermittently profitable. Occasionally, there was enough surplus butter for the estate to sell it to people in the neighborhood, including one baker.[14] In 1793, for instance, Martha Washington wrote to her niece Fanny Bassett Washington, who was managing domestic affairs at Mount Vernon in the owners' absence, about the disposition of surplus butter: "[T]his fine wet summer I should think there must be a great quantity of Butter made—which might be sold to bye such necessaries as one wanted about the House—as it will be needless to put up a large quantity for winter."[15] (The president's immediate family would be staying in Philadelphia.) In 1797 the dairy supervised by farm manager James Anderson made a profit of £30.12.3 through the sale of related products.[16] Yet despite these sporadic successes, butter sometimes had to be purchased for the plantation. As Washington complained just a few days before his death, "It is hoped, and will be expected, that more effectual measures will be pursued to make butter another year; for it is almost beyond belief, that from 101 Cows actually reported on a late enumeration of the Cattle, that I am obliged to buy butter for the use of my family."[17] ✱ MVT

The Slave Diet

———◆———

Julian Niemcewicz, a Polish guest at Mount Vernon in 1798, left an invaluable description of the people and animals he encountered on the estate. Particularly significant is his recollection of a brief visit to a slave cabin on one of the outlying farms. Upon entering the cabin, shared by a woman named Delia and her children, Niemcewicz saw a dwelling that was "more miserable than the most miserable of the cottages of our peasants [in Poland]." He was surprised to find "in the middle of this poverty some cups and a teapot." Near the cabin was a "very small garden planted with vegetables" and "5 or 6 hens, each one leading ten to fifteen chickens." He noted that the slaves "sell the poultry in Alexandria and procure for themselves a few amenities." Niemcewicz learned that each slave was given one peck, plus one gallon, of corn and five herrings per week, with children getting half the amount of the adults.[1]

Washington's writings confirm Niemcewicz's observation that this standard diet consisted of rations supplied by George Washington and foods the slaves could provide for themselves. Typically, a working slave at Mount Vernon daily received slightly more than one quart of cornmeal and between five and eight ounces of salted fish; those who were too young or too old to work received half these amounts. Supplementing this allotment were occasional distributions of fresh meat, fat, offal, and, perhaps for the children, buttermilk.[2] These rations would have provided each adult slave with almost four thousand calories per day, which was comparable to the daily intake of soldiers in the Continental Army during the Revolutionary War as well as of Tory prisoners confined in Maryland during the conflict.[3] Although sufficient calorically, the slaves' rations were deficient in terms of vitamins, a factor that may have predisposed them to disease.[4]

Some slaves added both variety and nutrients to their basic diet with the vegetables, fruit, eggs, domestic fowl, and honey they cultivated on the small plots surrounding their cabins. Still others sold these products in order to buy luxuries such as tea and sugar, ceramics and other household furnishings, or articles of clothing.[5] Archaeologists, who found the remains of at least sixteen types of fish in the cellar of a slave dwelling known as the House for Families, at Mount Vernon's Mansion House Farm, confirm the speculation that some slaves fished for food.[6] Gunflints and lead shot excavated in the cellar, as well as the physical remains of their prey, demonstrate that they also hunted various fowl—wild ducks, grouse, pheasant, quail, and pigeons—in addition to small mammals, such as squirrels, rabbits, opossums, and raccoons.[7]

Numerous artifacts found in the House for Families cellar reveal how these enslaved people prepared and ate their meals. For example, those living near the Mansion used a wider variety of ceramics for food service—and possibly for storage—than did Delia's family on the outlying farm. Among the vessel types excavated from the cellar were fragments of mugs and cups, teapots, bowls, plates and saucers, jugs, and jars. These pieces were variously made of colonoware, a type of pottery crafted either by local Indians or by the slaves themselves; European ceramics such as slipware, tin-glazed earthenware, refined earthenware, creamware, pearlware, Rhenish stoneware, and brown stoneware; and even Chinese porcelain. Slightly more than a quarter of all the ceramics found at the site were made of white salt-glazed stoneware from Britain, which the Washingtons used for about a decade beginning around the time they were wed, in 1759; possibly, they passed these objects along to the slaves when that type of ware went out of fashion.[8]

Other objects related to food preparation and service found in the House for Families cellar included glassware

Slaves might use their cornmeal rations to cook hoecakes, pancakelike batter breads made of cornmeal and fried on a griddle (originally a hoe). Sweet potatoes roasted in the ashes contributed valuable nutrients. Some of the sweet potatoes and other produce from the slaves' gardens may also have been sold at market in Alexandria.

(both wine bottles and stemware), bone-handled table knives and pewter spoons, and cooking implements such as an iron pothook and fragments of an iron pot that may have been used for making soups or stews. Although the slaves may have received some of these objects as hand-me-downs from the Mansion, they perhaps bought others with money earned by selling produce or small, homemade items such as brooms. In some cases, slaves may have resorted to stealing certain implements needed for making and serving their basic meals.[9]

Comparing the humble diet consumed in the slave quarters with the lavish meals served in the Mansion suggests how it felt to be Hercules or Lucy, preparing a sumptuous feast for the Washingtons, or to be a hungry slave child, watching a parent at work in the Mansion kitchen but forbidden to have even a bite of the aromatic dishes destined for the dining room. ✳ MVT

Favorite Foods

Everyone has favorite foods, and the Washingtons were no exception. Martha Washington's grandson recalled that his step-grandfather was particularly fond of fish, a preference that was known even beyond the family circle. According to Washy (as George Washington Parke Custis was familiarly known), "It was the habit for New England ladies frequently to prepare the codfish in a very nice manner, and send it enveloped in cloths, so as to arrive quite warm for the president's Saturday dinner. [He always ate] codfish on that day in compliment to his New England recollections."[1] It is unclear whether George Washington received these gifts in New England during the Revolutionary War, or if "the New England ladies" were the wives of government officials living in Philadelphia.

Custis also remembered when Samuel Fraunces, the household steward in the executive residence, was excited to find "a single shad" for sale in the Philadelphia market one February, the first to be caught that season and, therefore, expensive. Nevertheless, Fraunces purchased the delicacy, anticipating the pleasure it would give the president. But when the fish was prepared and brought to the table, Washington realized it was early in the year for shad and grilled his steward about how much he had paid for it. When Fraunces quoted the outrageous sum of three dollars, Washington roared, "Take it away, sir; it shall never be said that my table sets such an example of luxury and extravagance." As Custis noted, "[P]oor Fraunces tremblingly obeyed, and the first shad of the season was removed untouched."[2]

Martha Washington also was partial to seafood, with a special liking for shellfish. She did not accompany her husband to New York in April 1789 for his inauguration but instead spent about six weeks preparing herself, the two grandchildren they were raising (Nelly and Washy), and the household slaves for the move to the new capital city. Tobias Lear, the president's secretary, wrote back to Mount Vernon to tell of the house awaiting her there. He noted that Fraunces, who had been hired as "Steward & superintendent of the Kitchen," was proving to be "a very excellent fellow . . . in the latter department," because "he tosses up such a number of fine dishes that we are distracted in our choice when we set down to table, and obliged to hold a long consultation upon the subject before we can determine what to attack." Lear then pointedly mentioned that "Oysters & Lobsters make a very conspicuous figure upon the ta[ble] and never go off untouched." He asked his correspondent—the president's nephew, George Augustine Washington—to "tell Madam Washington this," in the hope that such tidings would "hasten her advancing towards New York . . . as she is remarkably fond of these fish."[3] ✳ MVT

The RECIPES

Nancy Carter Crump

THE
ART of COOKERY,
MADE
PLAIN and EASY.

CHAP. I.

Of ROASTING, BOILING, &c.

THAT profeſſed cooks will find fault with touching upon a branch of cookery which they never thought worth their notice, is what I expect: however, this I know, it is the moſt neceſſary part of it; and few ſervants there are, that know how to roaſt and boil to perfection.

I don't pretend to teach profeſſed cooks, but my deſign is to inſtruct the ignorant and unlearned (which will likewiſe be of great uſe in all private families) and in ſo plain and full a manner, that the moſt illiterate and ignorant perſon, who can but read, will know how to do every thing in cookery well.

I ſhall firſt begin with roaſt and boil'd of all ſorts, and muſt deſire the cook to order her fire according to what ſhe is to dreſs; if any thing very little or thin, then a pretty little briſk fire, that it may be done quick and nice; if a very large joint, then be ſure a good fire be laid to cake. Let it be clear at the bottom; and when your meat is half done, move the dripping-pan and ſpit a little from the fire, and ſtir up a good briſk fire;

B   for

Introduction

Although there are numerous contemporary descriptions of meals at the Washingtons' table, Martha Washington herself is known to have followed only a few of the recipes served at those meals. Certainly, she was familiar with Hannah Glasse's *The Art of Cookery, Made Plain and Easy*, first published in 1747; her personal copy is today in Mount Vernon's library. Her younger sister Anna Maria (Nancy) Dandridge Bassett, who lived with the Washingtons, owned and used *The Lady's Companion*. And Mrs. Washington's sister-in-law, Betty Washington Lewis, who lived in nearby Fredericksburg, had a copy of E. Smith's *The Compleat Housewife*, another well-known cookbook of the period; Mrs. Washington might have had access to these as well. During her first marriage, to Daniel Parke Custis, Martha acquired a seventeenth-century manuscript cookbook. She passed this heirloom on to granddaughter Nelly Custis when the young woman was wed in 1799.

In developing the recipes included in *Dining with the Washingtons*, the author consulted these and other cookbooks, including works by Martha Bradley, Mary Kettilby, Eliza Leslie, Elizabeth Raffald, Mary Randolph, and Maria Rundell, as well as several manuscript collections. For reference details, see the chapter notes beginning on page 214.

Keep in mind that the recipes presented here reflect the Washingtons' tastes and times. Some ingredients used then are less familiar to today's cooks—rose water and orange-flower water, for example—as are some cooking methods, including thickening sweet and savory sauces with various combinations of eggs, cream, butter, and flour. Indeed, butter and cream as well as lard and sugar were used in abundance, ingredients that twenty-first-century readers with concerns about calories and cholesterol will especially notice.

Please note that each recipe has been tested to assure that the final results will provide a flavor of the past—foods and beverages that the Washington family and their many guests would have enjoyed.

SOUPS

Soup was an important dish served at the beginning of the midday meal by the mistress of the house. According to British food historian C. Anne Wilson, early-eighteenth-century "menus and table plans . . . show that soup . . . was always set at the top of the table" as part of the first course at dinner and was followed by fish. "Thus the way was paved," Wilson continued, "for the division of the meal into four separate courses of soup, fish, entrée, and sweets together with savouries." It took another century for this arrangement to become an established pattern.[1]

In August 1789, Pennsylvania Senator William Maclay listed in his diary the foods the Washingtons served at a "great dinner" in New York at which he was a guest. Maclay wrote, "[F]irst was soup [followed by] Fish, roasted & boiled meats Gammon Fowls &ca."[2]

Although there are no known soup recipes directly associated with the Washingtons, the ones that follow are representative of the soups that might have appeared on their table.

A Chinese porcelain soup plate (1784-85) from a 302-piece service of "Cincinnati China" sent to George Washington in 1786 by his friend and fellow Revolutionary War veteran Henry (Light-Horse Harry) Lee. The plate shows the winged figure of Fame carrying the insignia of the Society of the Cincinnati, the nation's first veterans' organization. Washington served as the society's first president general from 1783 until his death in 1799.

Basic Beef Stock

This hearty stock, based on Hannah Glasse's Strong Broth for Soup or Gravy recipe, combines beef and beef bones with root vegetables, herbs, and spices to produce a broth or stock that is the foundation for a number of sauces and gravies.[3] Recipes for broths, often referred to as gravies, are found in virtually all the old cookbooks, as broth was used to soften tough cuts of meat or root vegetables and was kept on hand as a base for ragouts and stews.

Makes about 2 quarts

2 tablespoons olive oil
1 pound beef stew meat, cut into chunks
5 to 6 pounds beef bones
1 turnip, peeled and sliced
3 large onions, peeled and quartered
4 large carrots, trimmed and chopped
4 ribs celery, trimmed and chopped
2 leeks, white parts only, trimmed, rinsed thoroughly, and chopped
1 bunch parsley
1 heaping tablespoon dried marjoram
1 tablespoon dried thyme
2 teaspoons dried chervil
6 cloves
7 allspice berries
8 black peppercorns
1 tablespoon salt
3½ quarts water

1. In a large Dutch oven or saucepan, heat the olive oil over medium-high heat. Add the beef and bones, and brown thoroughly, stirring occasionally to brown on all sides.

2. Add the vegetables along with all the remaining ingredients, cover, and bring to a boil. Reduce the heat and simmer gently for 5 to 6 hours, stirring occasionally.

3. Remove the Dutch oven from the heat, let the stock cool to room temperature, and refrigerate in the pan for at least 8 hours, or overnight. Remove the grease and any scum that has risen to the top. Strain the stock thoroughly through a colander into a large saucepan, discarding the solids.

4. Heat the stock over low heat, bring to a low simmer, and simmer for about 1 hour, stirring occasionally and skimming as needed to remove any more scum that rises to the surface.

5. Strain the stock thoroughly through a fine-mesh strainer as many times as necessary until it is clear. Pour it into a large bowl, and set aside to cool completely. Refrigerate in airtight containers for up to 3 days, or in the freezer for up to 6 months.

Asparagus Soup

———————

In January 1791, James McHenry, a Maryland physician who had served under George Washington during the Revolutionary War, sent "a small parcel of asparagus . . . carefully packed up in dry earth" to the president, who assured McHenry that the vegetable had arrived "in very good condition."[4] Because asparagus is an early-spring vegetable, the Washingtons would have been pleased to receive this edible wintertime gift. More than likely, it had been grown in a greenhouse or an orangerie, where vegetables and fruits were often cultivated during the cold months.

This asparagus soup, adapted from Mary Randolph's version in *The Virginia House-Wife*, can be served either hot or chilled.[5]

Makes 2½ to 3 quarts

2 pounds asparagus, tips trimmed and reserved, and stalks cut into 3 to 4 pieces
8 cups chicken broth (preferably homemade)
½ cup diced salt pork
1 medium onion, peeled and finely chopped (about 1 cup)
¼ teaspoon ground white pepper
4 tablespoons unsalted butter, softened
5 tablespoons all-purpose flour
¾ cup heavy cream
Salt

1. In a large saucepan, combine the asparagus stalks with the broth, salt pork, onion, and white pepper. Cover and bring to a boil. Reduce the heat and simmer for about 1 hour, until the asparagus is very soft.

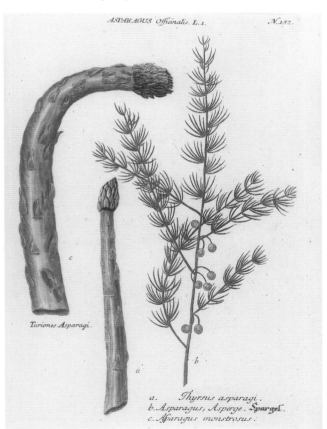

A botanical illustration of asparagus from the Taalryk *register (ca. 1748), published by German apothecary and botanist Johann Wilhelm Weimann.*

2. Remove from the heat, strain the broth into a large bowl, and set aside to cool. Discard the salt pork. Using a potato masher or large metal spoon, crush the asparagus, and then press it through a sieve into the strained broth, mashing to extract as much pulp as possible.

3. Return the broth and asparagus to the saucepan. Set over medium-low heat, cover, and bring to a simmer. Stir the asparagus tips into the soup, and simmer gently for 3 to 5 minutes, until just tender.

4. Combine the butter and flour to form a paste. Add to the soup, stirring until well combined. Stir in the cream, and season with salt and additional pepper, if necessary. Simmer, stirring frequently, for about 3 minutes until the soup thickens.

5. Serve the soup in a tureen.

Chicken Soup

A combination of several eighteenth-century recipes, this flavorful chicken soup can be served as is. Or it can be strained, and the broth topped with stewed celery and toasted bread, to begin the first course—as Hannah Glasse suggested.[6]

Makes about 3 quarts

5 tablespoons unsalted butter, softened and divided
1 cup slivered country ham
¾ cup diced celery
2 large onions, peeled, halved, and thinly sliced crosswise
5½ to 6 cups shredded cooked chicken
5 cups chicken broth (preferably homemade)
1¼ teaspoons salt
½ teaspoon ground black pepper
3 teaspoons dried thyme
1 teaspoon dried chervil
2 tablespoons chopped fresh parsley, plus more for garnish
3 tablespoons all-purpose flour

3 large egg yolks
¾ cup heavy cream

Stewed celery for garnish (optional)
Croutons for garnish (optional)

1. In a large saucepan, melt 2 tablespoons of the butter over medium-low heat. Add the ham, celery, and onions, increase the heat to medium, and cook, stirring occasionally, until the vegetables have softened and onions are slightly browned.

2. Stir in the shredded chicken and heat through, stirring often to prevent it from sticking to the pan.

3. Add the broth, salt, pepper, thyme, chervil, and parsley, cover, and bring to a boil. Reduce the heat and simmer gently for about 2 hours, stirring occasionally.

4. In a small bowl, combine the remaining 3 tablespoons of butter with the flour to form a paste. Add to the soup, stirring until it dissolves and the soup is slightly thickened.

5. Beat the egg yolks with the cream in a separate bowl. Gradually blend about 1 cup of the hot soup into the egg mixture, stirring constantly to prevent the eggs from curdling. Pour the mixture back into the soup. Continue stirring just until the soup has thickened further and is steaming hot. Again, do not allow the soup to boil, or the egg yolks will curdle. Season with additional salt and pepper, if necessary.

6. Serve the soup garnished with chopped parsley and with stewed celery and croutons, if desired.

Oyster Soup

———— ◆ ————

Typically, oyster soup would have been served at Mount Vernon during the winter, when the oysters were not only firm and especially flavorful but also when they could easily be kept fresh and cold. Oysters were abundant in the Potomac River; they could also be purchased in quantity from nearby markets.

Delicately flavored with herbs, this creamy soup recipe is adapted from one in Eliza Leslie's *Seventy-five Receipts*.[7]

Makes 1½ to 2 quarts

1 pint oysters in their liquor
3 slices bacon
1 small onion, peeled and chopped
2 tablespoons all-purpose flour
2 tablespoons unsalted butter, softened
½ teaspoon dried marjoram
½ teaspoon dried thyme
¼ teaspoon dried chervil
¾ teaspoon salt
¼ teaspoon ground black pepper
1½ cups whole milk
1 cup heavy cream
2 large egg yolks, lightly beaten

Minced fresh parsley for garnish

1. Place the oysters in a strainer set over a large bowl and drain thoroughly, reserving the liquor.
2. In a large saucepan, fry the bacon until crisp. Drain on paper towels, crumble into pieces, and set aside. Discard all but 1 tablespoon of the rendered bacon fat. Add the onion, and sauté until softened and just beginning to brown.
3. Blend the flour and butter together to form a paste. Stir into the sautéed onion and cook, stirring frequently, until the butter is melted and the onion is well coated.
4. Measure the oyster liquor, and, if necessary, add enough water to make ½ cup. Stir into the sautéed onion along with the marjoram, thyme, chervil, salt, and pepper and cook, stirring constantly, until the mixture is slightly thickened.
5. Gradually blend in the milk and cream, stirring continuously until the mixture is steaming and comes just below a boil.
6. Remove the saucepan from the heat. Stir together the egg yolks and about 1 cup of the hot liquid, stirring constantly to prevent the yolks from curdling. Gradually blend the egg yolks into the onion mixture and cook, stirring constantly until the soup barely begins to simmer. Again, do not allow the soup to boil, or the egg yolks will curdle.
7. Add the oysters to the soup and cook for 3 to 5 minutes, just until they are nicely plumped and heated through. Season with additional salt and pepper, if necessary.
8. To serve, pour the soup into a tureen, sprinkle with the reserved bacon, and garnish with minced parsley.

This Philadelphia-made side chair was one of sixty-eight purchased by Congress from New York cabinetmaker and retailer Thomas Burling for America's first executive residence.

A Green Peas Soup, without Meat

This Mary Kettilby recipe produces a classic Potage St. Germain. The name comes from the Paris suburb of St.-Germain-en-Laye, where young peas, a rarity in the early eighteenth century, were sown in boxes for early-spring cultivation. The addition of onions and spinach provide a traditional French touch, making this soup a flavorsome beginning for a spring menu.

Calendulas, also known as pot marigolds, make a lovely garnish for this soup. They were used as both a flavoring and a medicinal herb. According to one source, calendulas could be added to dishes in place of saffron, an affordable alternative in the days before saffron was grown in England. Sprinkle the shredded blossoms over the soup just before serving it. Please note that the calendula/pot marigold should not be confused with the African marigold, which is used as an insect repellent in vegetable gardens.[8]

Makes 2 quarts

10 cups fresh or frozen peas or *petits pois* (small, young
    green peas), divided
6 cups water, divided
1½ teaspoons salt
¼ teaspoon ground black pepper
½ teaspoon ground mace
2 cloves
2 teaspoons dried thyme
1 teaspoon dried marjoram
4 tablespoons unsalted butter
3 to 4 green onions, trimmed and sliced crosswise into
    ½-inch pieces
¼ pound fresh baby spinach, coarsely chopped
2 teaspoons minced fresh mint
3 tablespoons all-purpose flour

Diced toast for garnish (optional)
Shredded fresh calendula blossoms for garnish (optional)

1. Put 8 cups of the peas and 4 cups of the water in a large saucepan or Dutch oven. Add the salt, pepper, mace, cloves, thyme, and marjoram, cover, and bring to a boil. Reduce the heat, and simmer for about 45 minutes, until the peas are very tender.

2. Drain the peas, reserving the cooking liquid in the saucepan. Puree the peas in a food processor or with a food mill. If using a food mill, discard the skins. Press the puree through a sieve into the reserved liquid, stirring to combine thoroughly. Cover and set aside to keep warm.

3. Combine the remaining 2 cups of peas with the remaining 2 cups of water in a medium saucepan. Cover and bring to a boil. Reduce the heat and simmer for 20 to 25 minutes, until the peas are just tender.

4. While the second batch of peas is cooking, melt the butter in a sauté pan. Add the green onions, and sauté for about 2 minutes. Add the spinach and mint and stir together, cooking until the spinach has just wilted. Blend in the flour, and cook for about 1 minute.

5. Drain the peas, reserving the cooking liquid, and stir the peas into the warm soup along with the spinach mixture. Heat until it begins to simmer, adding the reserved pea-cooking liquid—a little at a time—if the soup is too thick. Season with additional salt and pepper, if necessary.

6. Pour the soup into a tureen, and garnish with diced toast and shredded calendula blossoms, if desired.

RIGHT:
George Washington's handwriting is evident on this small printed invitation form, which was sent to friends Thomas and Sarah Ramsay Porter of Alexandria. Washington made sure the invitation to dine on "Monday, 19 May 1788," came also from his wife and that "an answer is requested."

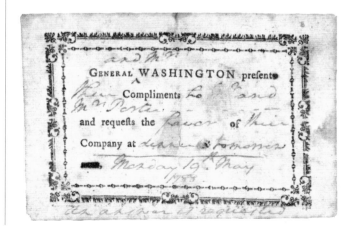

Green pea soup garnished with fresh calendula petals and dry toast. The recipe is served in a Prosperity soup bowl, a historic pattern re-created by Mottahedeh especially for Mount Vernon. It is based on eighteenth-century Stafford-shire creamware shards found in the south grove midden (see pages 72 and 73).

Hannah Glasse's classic eighteenth-century recipe for onion soup is revived in this hearty modern adaptation.

To Make an Onion Soup

Hannah Glasse's classic recipe for onion soup makes, as she asserted, "a delicious dish."[9]

Makes about 2½ quarts

½ cup (1 stick) unsalted butter
2½ pounds onions, peeled and coarsely chopped (7 to 8 cups)
⅓ cup all-purpose flour
4 cups water
2 cups Basic Beef Stock (page 116)
1 teaspoon salt
1 slice bread, toasted and diced
2 large egg yolks, lightly beaten
1 tablespoon balsamic vinegar
Ground black pepper

1. Melt the butter in a heavy skillet over medium heat. When the butter is sizzling, add the onions, cover, and cook for about 15 minutes, stirring often to prevent them from sticking to the pan, until they are very soft and caramelized. Add the flour, stirring to coat the onions, and cook for about 1 minute.

2. While the onions are cooking, combine the water and stock, and bring to a boil over medium-high heat. When the onions are ready, mix them into the hot stock, stirring until well combined.

3. Pour a little of the hot stock into the skillet and stir, scraping up any onion particles that remain. Pour the stock into the stock and onions, and add the salt.

4. Stir in the diced toast, cover, and simmer for about 10 minutes.

5. Combine the egg yolks and vinegar. Gradually blend ½ to 1 cup of the hot soup into the egg yolk-and-vinegar mixture, stirring constantly to prevent the yolks from curdling. Stir the mixture into the soup, and simmer, stirring constantly for several minutes until the soup thickens just slightly. Again, do not let the soup boil, or the egg yolks will curdle.

6. Season with pepper and additional salt, if necessary, and serve hot.

Philadelphia silversmith Richard Humphreys created this silver tablespoon, engraved with the Washington family crest (a winged griffin), in 1780. Such a spoon would likely have been used when soup was being served.

VEGETABLES

A variety of vegetables could be found on colonial tables, prepared with an eye toward presentation as well as taste. Instructions given by early cookbook writers demonstrate a careful attention to vegetables. Hannah Glasse's *The Art of Cookery* alone contains some seventy such recipes, from the simplest preparations to extravagant ragouts and side dishes in which vegetables played a prominent part.

Glasse, whose cookbook was used at Mount Vernon, is one of many writers of the period who stressed the importance of proper cooking techniques. "Most People spoil Garden things by over boiling them," she wrote. "All things that are Green should have a little Crispness, for if they are over boil'd, they neither have any Sweetness or Beauty."[1] The writers likewise emphasized flavor and appearance. E. Smith, for example, singled out asparagus, warning her readers that "if they boil too long, they will lose both their colour and taste."[2] Elizabeth Raffald and Maria Rundell were among those who provided similar instructions for asparagus as well as other vegetables.[3]

Early cookbooks placed a clear emphasis on seasoning, too. Many of their vegetable recipes call for straightforward treatment, with the use of butter and cream being most prevalent. One can also find such dishes as cauliflower simmered in broth and seasoned with "a bit of mace . . . and a dust of white pepper or peas flavored with mint."[4] Other recipes indicate the use of various fresh herbs.

"Every sort of culinary vegetable is infinitely best when fresh from the garden," Eliza Leslie wrote in *Directions for Cookery in Its Various Branches*, "and gathered a short a time as possible before it is cooked."[5] At Mount Vernon, Martha Washington oversaw an extensive vegetable garden; the produce grown there furnished the family's table with abundant foodstuffs. George Washington himself constantly experimented with the cultivation of various plants, trees, and field crops as he focused on improving and adding to the varieties available on his estate.

Although she lacked the kinds of conveniences available today for storing food, Mrs. Washington was diligent in her efforts to provide a year-round supply of vegetables and fruits for her family and their many guests. The recipe books of the day provided her and other gentlewomen with ample instructions to aid in those efforts. Preserving, drying, salting, pickling, and sugaring went on from the beginning of the growing season up through the first frost.

The following recipes reflect the array of vegetables that were available to the Washingtons, whether from their gardens at Mount Vernon or from markets in nearby Alexandria as well as in New York and Philadelphia during the presidential years.

LEFT:
An eighteenth-century Chinese export porcelain dish in the colorful Tobacco Leaf pattern.

OPPOSITE:
Mount Vernon's kitchen garden, dappled with summer-morning sun, includes beds of Swiss chard (front), with plantings of green and red cabbages encircling the artichokes. The red-brick building beyond the wall is George Washington's stable.

A Ragoo of Asparagus

Adapted from Hannah Glasse's *The Art of Cookery*, the recipe for this tasty, easy-to-prepare ragout combines asparagus with several other vegetables that were grown at Mount Vernon.[6]

Serves 6 to 8

3 pounds asparagus, trimmed and cut into thirds
5 tablespoons unsalted butter
1 medium onion, peeled and chopped
2 Belgian endives, trimmed and thinly sliced lengthwise
1 small head soft-leaf lettuce, such as Bibb or Boston, cored and shredded
1½ teaspoons salt
½ teaspoon ground black pepper
4 tablespoons all-purpose flour
2 cups chicken stock (preferably homemade)

1. Bring about 2 cups water to boil over medium heat. Add the asparagus, reduce the heat, and simmer until the asparagus is barely tender. Drain thoroughly, cover, and set aside to keep warm.
2. In a saucepan, melt the butter over medium heat. Add the onion and endives, cooking for 5 to 7 minutes until they begin to soften. Stir in the lettuce, salt, and pepper, and continue cooking until the vegetables are just tender.
3. Sprinkle the flour over the vegetables, and stir to blend well. Gradually add the stock, stirring until it begins to simmer and thickens slightly.
4. Add the asparagus, reserving a few of the tips for garnish, and heat until warmed.
5. Pour the ragout into a serving dish, and garnish with the reserved asparagus tips.

Asparagus and Eggs

Hannah Glasse recommended this simple recipe as a "pretty Side-dish for a second Course, or a Corner-plate."[7] Each course included an equal number of serving dishes, set on the table at the same time. As food historian Jane Carson wrote: "A balanced arrangement of dishes was of first importance. Featured dishes [such as a ham, roast beef, or turkey] occupied the top, bottom, and central positions on the table."[8] Side dishes were also equal in number, lining the table on either side. "Corner-plate[s]" would have been placed exactly where Glasse implied, at the corners of the table.

Glasse recommended serving the dish with toast points. "Toast a Toast as big as you have Occasion for," she instructed, meaning enough for each person. Then "butter it and lay it in your Dish."[9] Follow her directions to complete the recipe, appropriate today for a brunch or Sunday supper.

Serves 6 to 8

2½ pounds asparagus, trimmed and cut into 3 or 4 pieces
Salt
6 large eggs
3 tablespoons heavy cream
Ground black pepper
2 tablespoons unsalted butter

6 to 8 buttered toast points for serving

1. Steam or simmer the asparagus until just tender. Drain well, and season lightly with salt. Cover and set aside to keep warm.
2. Whisk the eggs until foamy. Add the cream, and blend well. Season with salt and pepper. Melt the butter in a large sauté pan over medium-low heat. Add the eggs and cook, stirring often, until just set.
3. To serve, place the toast points on a large platter with the points extending from the sides of the platter. Spoon the eggs over the toast, and arrange the asparagus in the middle of the eggs.

The flavors of endive, onion, lettuce, and chicken stock combine in this adaptation of Hannah Glasse's Ragoo of Asparagus.

French Beans (or Carrots) Dressed the Dutch Way

——— • ———

In *The Art of Cookery*, Hannah Glasse wrote: "Where there is a great Variety of Dishes and a large Table to cover, so there must be a Variety of Names for them; and it matters not whether they be call'd by a French, Dutch or English Name, for they are good, and done with as little Expence as the Dish will allow of."[10] Like many of her contemporaries, Glasse added the names of European countries to certain dishes, perhaps intending to lend them a note of sophistication.[11]

George Washington ordered vegetable seeds of varying kinds from his agents in London, bean seeds among them. He noted in his diary on March 31, 1787, that he was planting twenty acres in carrots and other vegetables, "if Carrot Seed can be obtained."[12]

The recipe below is for green beans, but you can prepare carrots in the same manner. Simply substitute the same weight of carrots for the beans. Peel the carrots, slice them thinly, and boil for about 15 minutes, or until they are just tender.

Serves 6 to 8

1 pound young green beans or haricots verts, trimmed
¾ teaspoon salt
¼ teaspoon ground black pepper
3 medium shallots, peeled and finely chopped
    (about ½ cup)
¼ cup plus 1 tablespoon minced fresh parsley, divided
2 tablespoons unsalted butter

1. Put the beans in a saucepan. Add 2 cups of water, and bring to a boil over medium-high heat.
2. Add the salt, pepper, shallots, and 3 to 4 tablespoons of the parsley. Cover, reduce the heat to low, and simmer for about 5 minutes, until the beans are crisp-tender. Immediately remove from the heat, and drain thoroughly. Return the beans to the pan, and add the butter.

3. Arrange the beans in a serving dish, and garnish with the remaining minced parsley.

Corn Fritters

——— • ———

George Washington's papers contain many references to corn, a popular vegetable that was enjoyed fresh during the summer, or dried for winter use, ground into meal for breads, or made into mush.

This recipe, virtually identical to most modern versions, is adapted from one in the Mary Custis Lee Papers at the Virginia Historical Society in Richmond.[13]

Serves 6 to 8

3 large eggs, separated
½ cup half-and-half
1 cup sifted all-purpose flour
½ teaspoon salt
4 cups fresh corn kernels (about 12 ears corn)
About 1 cup lard or vegetable oil

1. In a large bowl, beat the egg yolks until foamy. Add the half-and-half, flour, and salt, combining well. Stir in the corn.
2. Beat the egg whites to stiff peaks. Gently fold into the corn mixture until well combined.
3. Melt the lard in a frying pan over medium-high heat. (Once melted, it should be about 2 inches deep.) Heat until the oil sizzles when a small amount of batter is dropped into it.
4. Reduce the heat to medium, and drop in tablespoonfuls of the batter, frying the fritters on both sides until golden brown. (To prevent the fritters from touching and maintain the oil's temperature, do not crowd the pan.) Set the fritters on paper towels to remove the excess oil, and set each batch aside to keep warm while frying the remaining batter.
5. Pile the fritters into a serving bowl, and serve hot.

Cauliflower in White Sauce

A favorite vegetable during the colonial period, cauliflower was grown in the gardens of many gentlemen, including those of George Washington.

This recipe for a creamed cauliflower, adapted from Maria Rundell's *A New System of Domestic Cookery*, includes mace—adding a pleasant grace note to an otherwise standard dish.[14] Rundell also suggested adding grated Parmesan cheese to vary the basic recipe.

Serves 6 to 8

1½ cups whole milk

1 cup water

2 large heads cauliflower, cored, outer leaves discarded, and quartered

1½ cups chicken broth (preferably homemade)

¾ teaspoon ground mace

¼ teaspoon ground white pepper

1½ teaspoons salt

3 tablespoons unsalted butter, softened

1½ tablespoons all-purpose flour

⅓ cup heavy cream

1. In a large saucepan, bring the milk and water to a boil over medium heat. Reduce the heat, and add the cauliflower. Cover and simmer for 5 to 10 minutes, until the cauliflower is just tender. Drain the cauliflower thoroughly, discarding the cooking liquid.

2. Return the cauliflower to the saucepan, and add the broth, mace, white pepper, and salt. Cover and bring to a boil. Immediately reduce the heat, and simmer for about 10 minutes, occasionally turning the cauliflower in the broth, until it is nearly tender but still firm.

3. Add the butter, stirring until it melts and is combined with the broth.

4. Sprinkle in the flour, and continue to stir until it is well combined with the broth.

5. Stir in the cream until well blended, and then simmer for about 3 minutes, until the cauliflower is fork-tender and heated through.

6. Season with additional salt and pepper, if necessary, and serve warm.

Washington acquired silver flatware, including salt spoons, in the 1780s. These diminitive spoons were paired with small glass or silver salt cellars and placed around the table, within easy reach of diners. This spoon, fashioned by Philadelphia silversmith Richard Humphreys, features a feather-edged border and Washington's engraved crest.

To Stew Parsnips

———◆———

In June 1787, while presiding at the Constitutional Convention in Philadelphia, Washington wrote to his nephew and farm manager, George Augustine Washington, about the parsnip and carrot plants recently sown at his Dogue Run Farm. "I am really sorry to hear that [they] are so thinly come up," he fretted on June 3. "Does this appear to be the effect of bad Seed, unfavourable Seasons, improper ground, or want of proper Culture?" And a week later, he wrote, "It gives me concern to hear that the prospect of obtaining a Crop of Carrots & parsnips is so unpromising—To ascertain the value of these articles, & their product, was my grand object; in which I must be disappointed if they do not come up."[17]

In this simple recipe, Hannah Glasse noted that readers should pour the parsnips "into a plate for a corner-dish, or a side-dish at supper."[18]

Serves 6 to 8

**2 pounds parsnips, trimmed, peeled, cut crosswise into
   1-inch pieces, and set in cold water**
4 tablespoons unsalted butter, softened
3 tablespoons all-purpose flour
1 cup half-and-half
1 teaspoon salt

1. Drain the parsnips thoroughly, and put them in a large saucepan or Dutch oven. Add just enough water to cover. Cover the pan, and bring to a boil over medium-high heat. Reduce the heat, and simmer for 25 to 30 minutes, until tender. Remove from the heat, and drain thoroughly. Cover and set aside to keep warm.
2. Combine the butter and flour, and cook over low heat until the butter has melted and begins simmering. Gradually add the half-and-half, stirring constantly until well blended and slightly thickened. Add the salt.
3. Add the parsnips to the sauce, and heat through for about 5 minutes, stirring often.

4. Season the parsnips with additional salt and pepper, if necessary, and transfer to a serving bowl.

To Dress Turnips

———◆———

On May 2, 1787, George Washington noted in his diary that the turnip patch had been sown "in front of the Mansion house."[19] That summer, which he spent presiding at the Constitutional Convention in Philadelphia, he stayed in touch with his farm manager, sending questions about the turnips' welfare as well as that of other vegetables planted at his various farms.

Harvested for winter use, turnips prepared with this straightforward Hannah Glasse recipe provide a tasty, easy-to-prepare cold-weather dish.[20] Serve the diced turnips in pieces tossed with butter and cream, as suggested below, or mash them roughly or until creamy, if preferred.

Serves 6 to 8

2½ pounds turnips, peeled and diced (about 4 cups)
4 tablespoons unsalted butter, softened
⅓ cup heavy cream
Salt
Ground black pepper

1. Put the turnips in a large saucepan, barely cover with water, and bring to a boil. Reduce the heat, cover, and simmer for 10 to 12 minutes, until the turnips are fork-tender. Remove from the heat, and drain thoroughly.
2. Return the turnips to the saucepan, and set over low heat. Add the butter and stir until melted. Stir in the cream, and season with salt and pepper. Stir until well blended and heated through.
3. Pour the turnips into a serving dish, and send to the table.

Green Peas with Cream

Delicate green peas were a favored spring vegetable, eagerly anticipated by Virginians after long winters during which fresh vegetables were at a premium. Washington noted in his diary on May 25, 1785, that the family "Had Peas for the [first] time in the season at Dinner."[21] Writing three years later, Virginia planter Robert Carter III of Nomini Hall likewise heralded their arrival, asserting that "Pease ought to be preferred, they being a more succulent Vegetable."[22]

Hannah Glasse's delectable recipe makes a welcome addition to a spring menu.[23]

Serves 6 to 8

6 cups small fresh or frozen green peas
4 tablespoons unsalted butter, softened
1½ teaspoons salt
¼ teaspoon ground nutmeg
1 tablespoon sugar
1½ teaspoons dried thyme
1½ teaspoons dried marjoram
½ teaspoon dried savory
4 sprigs fresh parsley, stemmed and chopped
½ cup boiling water
1 cup heavy cream

1. Combine the peas, butter, salt, nutmeg, sugar, thyme, marjoram, savory, and parsley in a saucepan over medium heat.
2. Pour in the boiling water, cover, and bring to a simmer. Reduce the heat, and cook at a slow simmer for 20 to 30 minutes, stirring occasionally, until tender.
3. Add the cream and heat through.
4. Pour into a serving dish, and serve immediately.

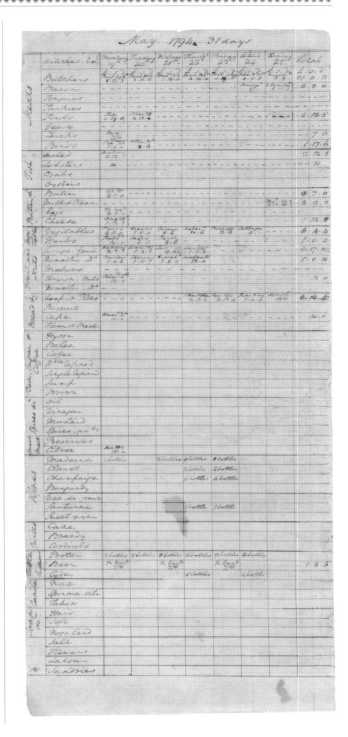

George Washington was a meticulous record-keeper who often kept day-by-day accounts of the amounts and prices of foodstuffs purchased for his Mount Vernon estate. His list from "May 1794 31 days" illustrates the variety of foods served at the Washingtons' table.

LEFT: *An early English garden pea from the Mount Vernon garden, similar to those ordered by George Washington from Robert Cary and Company, London, on June 20, 1768: one peck of "earliest garden peas."*
RIGHT: *Botanical illustration of two varieties of peas from the Taalryk register (ca. 1748), published by German apothecary and botanist Johann Wilhelm Weimann.*

Stewed Peas and Lettuce

———•———

After her husband's death in December 1799, Martha Washington supervised some of the planting at Mount Vernon. On February 11, 1802, she noted in her almanac that she had "sewed peases . . . under the wall in the lower garden."[24]

Hannah Glasse's combination of vegetables and herbs makes another appetizing addition to a spring menu. "If you find the Sauce not thick enough," Glasse suggested, "shake in a little more Flour, and let it simmer, then take it up."[25]

Serves 6 to 8

4 cups fresh or frozen green peas
About 1 head soft-leaf lettuce, such as Bibb or Boston, cored and thinly sliced (about 4 cups loosely packed)
4 tablespoons unsalted butter, softened
¾ teaspoon salt
¼ teaspoon ground black pepper
⅛ teaspoon ground mace
2 to 4 tablespoons all-purpose flour
1 cup chicken broth (preferably homemade)
¼ teaspoon dried chervil
¼ teaspoon dried marjoram
¼ teaspoon dried thyme
¼ teaspoon dried winter savory
2 cloves
1 medium onion, peeled

1. Combine the peas and lettuce in a saucepan over medium-low heat. Add the butter, salt, pepper, and mace, and stir to combine. Cover, bring to a boil, and then reduce the heat and simmer for about 10 minutes.
2. Combine 2 tablespoons of the flour with the broth. Stir into the peas, along with the chervil, marjoram, thyme, and winter savory. Bring back to a simmer.
3. Stick the cloves in the onion, and add to the simmering peas. Cover and continue simmering for about 15 minutes, until the peas are tender. If you find the broth needs to be thicker, spoon about 3 tablespoons of the hot broth into a small bowl, and stir in the remaining 2 tablespoons of flour. Stir the flour and broth back into the stewed peas, and simmer for about 3 more minutes, until thickened. Remove and discard the onion.
4. Season the peas with additional salt and pepper, if necessary, and pour into a serving dish.

Sallad

———•———

In the Washingtons' day, as in ours, salads were a welcome presence on the table, valued for their healthful qualities. Assorted greens were used, including watercress, parsley, sorrel, and different leaf lettuces, often topped with colorful and edible flowers, such as nasturtiums or calendula. Endive and spinach were planted for winter use, as Colonial-era housewives sought to bring variety to the table during the cold months.

Greens of various kinds were grown at Mount Vernon, both in the gardens and the greenhouse. George Washington imported his salad oil from London.

E. Taylor, whose 1769 recipe is adapted here, recommended serving the salad in a china or earthen bowl.[26]

Serves 6 to 8

2 to 3 pounds assorted lettuces—such as romaine, mache, or soft-leaf lettuces such as Bibb or Boston—trimmed and leaves separated
Assorted fresh herbs, such as basil, lemon thyme, and salad burnet
1 bunch watercress, trimmed and stems separated
About 3 ribs celery, diced (about 1 cup)
3 to 4 green onions, trimmed and cut into ½-inch pieces

Mrs. Taylor's Sallad Dressing (page 166)

1. Toss together the lettuces, herbs, watercress, celery, green onions, and dressing in a large serving bowl and serve immediately.

To Make Salamongundy

Salamongundy is a late-seventeenth-century term for what we might call a main-dish salad. According to British food historian C. Anne Wilson, it was composed of ingredients that ranged from greens, herbs, cucumbers, edible flowers, and lemons to roast chicken, anchovies, and other meat or fish "suitable for the table of a great house or to be offered to special guests."[26]

Hannah Glasse recommended this grand composed salad as part of a first course. She advised the reader to wash the lettuce leaves clean and then "swing them pretty dry in a cloth" before cutting them "cross-ways, as fine as a good big Thread."[27]

Some diners at Mount Vernon needed a boost to reach the table. This Windsor-style child's high chair has a family history of use at Mount Vernon. Probably made in Philadelphia in the 1780s, it was later given by Martha Washington to her granddaughter Nelly.

Serves 10 to 12

2 heads romaine lettuce, cored and thinly sliced crosswise
1 roasted chicken (about 3 pounds), carved into breasts, wings, and legs
10 to 12 anchovies
1 lemon, diced
4 yolks of hardboiled large eggs, minced
1 bunch fresh parsley, stemmed and chopped
½ pound small white onions (can use pearl onions), cooked and peeled
Salt
Ground black pepper

Mrs. Taylor's Sallad Dressing (page 136)
Blanched red grapes for garnish
Blanched young green beans or haricots verts for garnish
Nasturtium blossoms for garnish

1. Arrange the lettuce in a serving dish.
2. Remove the skin and meat from the chicken wings and breasts, and cut the meat into thin slices. Alternate the slices with about 10 of the anchovies, sliced if desired, on top of the lettuce and around the dish.
3. Remove the skin and meat from the chicken legs, and cut the meat into small dice. Combine with the lemon, egg yolks, parsley, and any remaining anchovies, if desired. Heap the mixture in the middle of the dish, piling it up as high as possible.
4. Place the largest onions on top of the salamongundy. Arrange the rest of the onions around the edges of the dish. If you are holding the salad to serve later, cover with plastic wrap and refrigerate for up to 2 hours.
5. To serve, pour Mrs. Taylor's Sallad Dressing over the salad, season with salt and pepper, and garnish with grapes, green beans, and nasturtium flowers.

Salamongundy makes a hearty and healthy main dish.

MEAT, POULTRY & FISH

The quantities of meat that were always part of the Washingtons' dinners dominated many descriptions left by guests, Massachusetts Congressman Theophilus Bradbury among them. In a December 1795 letter to his daughter recounting a meal taken with President Washington and others, he wrote, "The dishes were placed all around, and there was an elegant variety of roast beef, veal, turkeys, ducks, fowls, hams &c."[1]

Washington himself commented on the importance of serving fine meat at his table. In an August 1791 letter from Philadelphia to his farm manager, he wrote that he and Mrs. Washington expected to be at Mount Vernon the following month. "I request that you would pay particular attention to the Meats," he advised, "that I may have such as are fat, and Proper for the Table while I am at home. . . . By fat meats— I mean Mutton, Lamb, Veal (if there are any calves young enough)—perhaps a small Beef also."[2]

Chickens were also raised on his farms, and fish were readily available from the Potomac River. Slaves were assigned the task of catching fish in large numbers for meals at the Mansion table.

Forced Beef Tenderloin

Recipes from *The Lady's Companion* and Hannah Glasse's *The Art of Cookery* are combined in this recipe for beef tenderloin stuffed with forcemeat. Forcemeat can be made up of a variety of ingredients, including ground raw or cooked meat, poultry, fish and/or vegetables. Traditionally, ingredients such as fresh or dried fruit, breadcrumbs, herbs, and spices are also added to bind and flavor the mixture.[3]

Serves 6 to 8

1 beef tenderloin (4½ to 5 pounds)
Salt
Ground black pepper
4 shallots, peeled and divided
3 cups fresh breadcrumbs
4 teaspoons freshly grated lemon zest
½ teaspoon ground nutmeg
1½ teaspoons dried thyme
1 teaspoon dried rosemary, divided
1½ cups dry red wine, divided
About ¼ cup melted lard or olive oil
5 tablespoons unsalted butter
1 cup Basic Beef Stock (page 116)

Fresh rosemary and thyme sprigs for garnish

1. Preheat the oven to 425°F. Set a rack in a roasting pan.
2. Season the tenderloin all over with salt and pepper, rubbing into the surface. With a sharp fillet knife (or other thin-blade, medium-size knife), cut a pocket in the side of the tenderloin, being careful not to cut all the way through

to the other side. Reserve any meat removed from the pocket during this process.

3. Finely chop or grind the reserved meat. Finely chop 2 of the shallots, and mix with the chopped meat, bread-crumbs, lemon zest, nutmeg, thyme, and ½ teaspoon of the rosemary. Combine this forcemeat with about ¼ cup of the red wine, just enough to bind the mixture. Stuff it into the tenderloin pocket, packing tightly. Close the pocket with skewers or by tying the loin with kitchen twine at 6- to 8-inch intervals along the length of the roast. Brush the surface with melted lard.

4. Set the tenderloin in the prepared roasting pan, and roast for 15 minutes. Reduce the heat to 400°F, and roast for about 20 minutes, until an instant-read thermometer inserted into the center of the meat registers 130°F to 135°F for medium-rare, or to desired doneness.

5. While the beef is roasting, begin making the sauce. Thinly slice the remaining 2 shallots. In a skillet set over medium heat, melt 3 tablespoons of the butter. Add the shallots, and cook for about 5 minutes, until softened. Raise the heat to medium high, and stir in the remain-ing 1¼ cups of red wine. Bring to a boil, reduce the heat to medium, and cook at a rapid simmer until the sauce is reduced to about 1 cup. Stir in the remaining ½ teaspoon of rosemary and the stock. Bring the sauce back to a boil. Then reduce the heat, and simmer uncovered for 5 to 8 minutes, until reduced by half. Remove the sauce from the heat, cover, and set aside.

6. Remove the tenderloin from the oven, and let rest for about 15 minutes before slicing.

7. To finish the sauce while the tenderloin rests, set it over low heat. Cut the remaining 2 tablespoons of butter into small pieces and whisk into the sauce, a few pieces at a time, until it is incorporated and the sauce is smooth. Pour any juices that have accumulated from the rested tender-loin into the sauce, and stir well to combine. Season with salt and pepper, if necessary.

8. To serve, cut the tenderloin into ¼-inch-thick slices, or as desired, and arrange on a platter. Spoon sauce over the top, and garnish with sprigs of rosemary and thyme. Pour the remaining sauce into a sauceboat, and serve on the side.

Rump of Beef to Stew

———— •◆• ————

This recipe is adapted from one in *The Lady's Companion* (1753), a popular cookbook of the time.[4] Mrs. Washington's sister Anna Maria (Nancy) Dandridge Bassett owned a copy that is now in the Mount Vernon library. This is an example of one of many "made dishes," including fricassees, hashes, and ragouts, enjoyed by the gentry from the Elizabethan period onward; these comprised "meat cooked and served in a flavoured sauce." Sauce was considered "an important part of all such dishes."[5]

This stew is best when made a day or so before it is served, giving the flavors time to blend.

Serves 6 to 8

1 boneless rump roast (3½ to 4 pounds)
Water as needed
2 teaspoons salt
1 teaspoon ground black pepper
¼ teaspoon ground cloves
½ teaspoon ground nutmeg
½ teaspoon ground mace
1 teaspoon dried marjoram
¾ teaspoon dried savory
2 teaspoons dried thyme
2 tablespoons chopped fresh parsley
1 large egg yolk, lightly beaten
2 cups dry red wine, such as claret or merlot
½ cup balsamic vinegar
1 medium onion, peeled, halved lengthwise,
    and thinly sliced
2 tablespoons unsalted butter

Peeled boiled new potatoes for serving
Orange slices for garnish

1. Rinse the roast, and pat it dry. Place in a Dutch oven, and pour in enough water to come halfway up the sides of the roast. Cover and bring to a boil. Reduce the heat and simmer for about 1 hour, turning occasionally. Remove the beef from the pan, setting it aside until cool enough to handle. Reserve the cooking liquid in the pan.

2. Make several slits along the top of the beef. Combine the salt, pepper, cloves, nutmeg, mace, marjoram, savory, thyme, and parsley, and rub the mixture into the slits and over the surface of the roast. Coat all over with the egg yolk.

3. Return the roast to the Dutch oven. Pour in the red wine and balsamic vinegar, stirring to combine with the cooking liquid. Cover and bring to a boil over medium-high heat. Reduce the heat, cover, and simmer for about 1 hour, until the roast is tender. Add the onion, cover again, and continue simmering for about 1 hour more, turning occasionally and stirring the gravy until the beef is fork-tender.

4. Transfer the roast to a cutting board, and cover loosely with aluminum foil. Stir the gravy, and bring back to a simmer. Add more salt and pepper, if necessary, and whisk in the butter, stirring until dissolved and the gravy is smooth.

5. To serve, cut the beef into thin slices, and arrange on a platter. Pour some of the gravy over the beef. Surround with boiled potatoes, and pour more gravy over the potatoes. Pour the remaining gravy into a sauceboat, and serve on the side. Garnish the roast and potatoes with orange slices, and send to the table.

This Chinese export porcelain platter, in the historic Society of the Cincinnati pattern, was routinely used at Mount Vernon for serving large portions of meat. Washington was the first president general of the society, a veterans' organization founded by French and American officers who had served in the Revolutionary War.

To Make Force-Meat Balls

—— ◆ ——

"Now you are to observe that Force-Meat Balls are a great addition to all Made-Dishes," wrote Hannah Glasse. Roll "them in little round Balls, and some in little long Balls . . . and fry them Brown."[6] Forcemeat was used in a number of ways: baked in a crust; as a filling; or as a garnish for made dishes. It was also used as a stuffing, as in Veal Olives (page 143). (For a definition of forcemeat, see Forced Beef Tenderloin [page 139]. For "made dishes," see Rump of Beef to Stew [page 140]).

This recipe makes quite a bit of forcemeat, but if desired, it can be prepared ahead and frozen in 1-cup portions for later use.

Makes about 6½ cups of forcemeat

2 pounds ground veal
1 pound ground pork
2 teaspoons dried thyme
1½ teaspoons dried marjoram
1 teaspoon dried savory
2 tablespoons finely chopped fresh parsley
½ teaspoon ground nutmeg
½ teaspoon ground mace
1 teaspoon freshly grated lemon zest
2 teaspoons salt
½ teaspoon ground black pepper
2 large eggs, lightly beaten

Lard or vegetable oil for frying
All-purpose flour for dredging
Parsley sprigs for serving

1. Combine the veal and pork well. Add the thyme, marjoram, savory, parsley, nutmeg, mace, lemon zest, salt, and pepper, and blend into the meat thoroughly. Add the eggs, and mix well.

2. Shape the forcemeat into small balls and cigar-shaped pieces by hand.

3. Melt the lard in a large saucepan over medium-high heat. (It should measure about 1 inch deep.) Dredge the forcemeat pieces in flour, and then cook in the hot lard, turning once or twice until well browned and cooked through. Drain well on paper towels.

4. Serve the forcemeat balls on a bed of parsley sprigs.

Savoury Patties

—— ◆ ——

This modern recipe for meat-filled tarts—also called patties—evolved from a combination of several historic recipes of the Colonial and early-Federal periods. Patties were baked and generally served as side dishes. In her recipe, Hannah Glasse asserted that five of the tarts "will be a dish."[7]

Glasse offered a decorative approach to the pastry shells as an alternative to the simple, filled patties. "Cut some long narrow bits of paste and bake them . . . for handles," she wrote, and after the baked shells have been filled with the hot meat mixture, "set the handles across the patties; they will look like baskets if you have nicely inched the walls of the patties."[8]

Serves 6 to 8

1 pound ground chicken
1 pound ground pork
8 ounces ground beef
1 medium onion, peeled and finely chopped
¾ teaspoon ground black pepper
½ teaspoon ground nutmeg
2 teaspoons dried thyme
1½ tablespoons finely chopped fresh parsley
1 teaspoon salt
2 tablespoons unsalted butter, softened
3 tablespoons all-purpose flour
1 cup chicken broth (preferably homemade)
½ cup heavy cream
1 recipe Common Pie Crust (page 171), chilled

Fresh parsley sprigs for garnish

1. Combine the chicken, pork, beef, and onion, mixing them together thoroughly. Heat a skillet over medium-high heat. Add the meat mixture and cook, stirring and breaking the meat apart, until it is browned and thoroughly cooked. Drain the excess fat from the pan, and return to medium heat. Add the pepper, nutmeg, thyme, parsley, and salt, stirring until well blended.

2. Mix the butter and flour to form a paste. Blend into the browned meat, stir in the broth, and bring to a simmer over medium heat. Stir constantly until the liquid is smooth and has thickened. Add the cream, and blend together well. Reduce the heat, cover, and simmer for about 30 minutes, stirring occasionally, until thoroughly cooked. Set aside to cool to room temperature.

3. Preheat the oven to 350°F. Grease a 12-cup patty-pan tin or muffin pan with lard or vegetable shortening.

4. Roll out the pie dough on a lightly floured surface to ¼ inch thick. Using a 3-inch round cookie cutter, cut the dough into about 24 circles. Fit half the circles into the cups of the prepared tin or pan.

5. Divide the meat mixture among the prepared dough cups. Cover with the remaining dough circles, tucking each one into the sides of the cups and around the meat mixture. Poke a small hole in the center of each top crust.

6. Bake the patties for 30 to 35 minutes, or until the crusts are lightly browned.

7. Serve the patties on a platter garnished with parsley sprigs.

Veal Olives

Veal olives are "a seventeenth-century variant of the so-called beef or mutton olives" that were stuffed, rolled up, and tied with string to be roasted on a spit or gridiron.[9] Hannah Glasse suggested a lemon garnish for this recipe, which likely could have been a side dish or corner dish for a first or second course.[10]

Serves 6 to 8

2 pounds veal scaloppini
½ recipe Mrs. Glasse's Force-Meat Balls (page 142)
1 cup fresh breadcrumbs
½ teaspoon ground nutmeg
½ teaspoon salt
¼ teaspoon ground black pepper
1 large egg, lightly beaten
4 tablespoons unsalted butter, plus more as needed
8 ounces white button mushrooms, sliced
2 to 3 cups chicken stock (preferably homemade)

Browned bacon strips for serving
Lemon slices for garnish

1. Spread each piece of veal with about 2 tablespoons of forcemeat. Roll the slices, beginning at the long sides, and tie firmly with kitchen string, making "olives."

2. Combine breadcrumbs with nutmeg, salt, and pepper.

3. Coat the veal olives on all sides with the beaten egg, then roll in the breadcrumbs, coating them well.

4. Melt butter over medium heat. Sauté veal olives on all sides until well browned, adding more butter, if necessary.

5. Stir in the mushrooms, and then pour in 2 cups of the chicken stock, stirring to blend with the butter in the pan. Cover and simmer for 20 to 30 minutes, turning the olives occasionally, until the veal is fully cooked.

6. To serve, place the veal olives on a platter, and spoon the sauce over the top. Break the bacon strips into pieces, sprinkle over the veal, and garnish with lemon slices.

LEFT:
In 1784 the Marquis de Lafayette sent the Washingtons a shipment of tableware that included a set of eight silver-plate neoclassical-style "Bottle Sliders" (wine coasters), of which this is one.

To Make Scotch Collops

In this recipe, E. Smith instructed the cook to "hack" thin slices of veal fillets and, after seasoning them, to "lay them in a pewter dish . . . and let them lie till you want them."[11] By using the term *hack* in her directions, Smith was describing scotching, which Samuel Johnson's *Dictionary of the English Language* defines as "cut with shallow incisions."[12] The cubed steaks we know today can be considered a modern version of the scotched meat of the eighteenth century.

The *Oxford English Dictionary* notes that the word *collop* is of obscure derivation, perhaps connected with coal. In early Britain, the term meant a rasher of bacon that was to be fried, generally with eggs, but later it came to mean just a slice of meat. Hannah Glasse's scotch collops recipe illustrates this development in the meaning of the word. Although collop seems to have become confused with *scallop*, there is no association between the two.[13] Johnson's dictionary defined it as a "rasher boiled upon the coals."[14]

This miniature portrait of General George Washington in profile (ca. 1800, after an original by James Sharples) descended in the family of Martha Washington.

Serves 6 to 8

2½ to 3 pounds veal scaloppini
Salt
Ground white pepper
6 to 8 tablespoons unsalted butter, divided
½ teaspoon ground nutmeg
1½ teaspoons freshly grated lemon zest
3 large egg yolks, lightly beaten
All-purpose flour, as needed
2 cups chicken broth
About 4 ounces white button mushrooms, sliced
    (about 1 cup)
2 oranges

1. Lightly season the scaloppini with salt and pepper.
2. Melt 3 tablespoons of the butter, and combine with the nutmeg, lemon zest, and ¼ to ½ teaspoon of salt. Mix with the egg yolks, stirring together until well mixed.
3. Dip the scaloppini in the mixture, coating both sides, and then dredge both sides in flour. Put the scaloppini on waxed paper, and leave it to set at room temperature for 10 to 15 minutes.
4. Melt another 2 tablespoons of the butter in a large sauté pan. Add the scaloppini, and cook until browned on both sides—2 to 3 minutes per side—adding another 1 or 2 tablespoons of butter, if necessary. Remove the scaloppini from the pan, cover loosely with aluminum foil, and set aside to keep warm.
5. Sprinkle about 1½ tablespoons of flour in the sauté pan, stirring up any browned bits on the bottom of the pan. Stir in the chicken broth, and bring to a boil. Add the mushrooms and cook for about 5 minutes, stirring frequently.
6. Return the scaloppini to the pan, turning to coat on both sides with the sauce. Cover and continue to cook until the scaloppini and mushrooms are cooked through.
7. To serve, place the scaloppini and mushrooms on a platter and surround with the sauce. Squeeze the juice of 1 of the oranges over the scaloppini. Cut the second orange into quarters or slices, and set around the platter to garnish. Serve hot.

A serving of Scotch Collops, made with veal scaloppini, is covered in cooked mushrooms and served with asparagus ragout.

E. Smith's Roast Pork

Livestock of all kinds were raised on George Washington's outlying farms. His farm reports list hogs at Dogue Run and Muddy Hole, for instance; they generally were butchered in early December.

E. Smith, whose recipe is adapted here, recommended applesauce as an accompaniment.[15]

Serves 6 to 8

1 boneless pork loin (4 to 5 pounds)
Salt
Ground black pepper
1½ teaspoons dried marjoram
2 cups fresh breadcrumbs
½ teaspoon dried sage
2 teaspoons freshly grated lemon zest
¼ teaspoon ground nutmeg
¼ cup finely chopped fresh parsley
1 large egg
3 tablespoons unsalted butter, melted and cooled
About ⅓ cup lard or vegetable shortening, melted and
　　cooled, plus more as needed

Applesauce (page 168) for serving

1. Preheat the oven to 500°F. Set a rack in a roasting pan.
2. Rinse and dry the pork loin. Using a very sharp paring knife, carefully remove any silver skin and excess fat from the surface. Rub salt, pepper, and marjoram all over the loin.
3. Using the same paring knife or another very sharp knife, make 1½- to 2-inch-deep slits along surface of the loin, about 1½ inches apart, being careful not to cut all the way through the loin.
4. Combine the breadcrumbs with the sage, lemon zest, nutmeg, parsley, ½ teaspoon salt, and ¼ teaspoon pepper. Add the egg and butter, mixing together thoroughly. Using

your fingers, push the stuffing into the slits, packing loosely. (Any remaining stuffing can be pressed over the surface of the loin to create a delicious crusty topping.) Place the pork in the roasting pan. Carefully pour the lard over the meat.
5. Roast the pork for about 5 minutes. Then reduce the temperature to 400°F, and roast for another 30 minutes. Reduce the temperature to 350°F, and continue roasting, basting occasionally with the drippings or additional melted lard, for 2 to 2½ hours to an internal temperature of about 150°F. When the pork is done, the juices will run clear when it is pierced with a fork. Remove the loin to a carving board, cover loosely with aluminum foil, and set aside to rest for about 15 minutes before slicing.
6. Cut the loin into slices as desired, arrange on a platter, and serve with Applesauce.

Eliza Leslie's Collared Pork

This highly seasoned dish was usually served as part of the second course at the tables of the well-to-do. Collaring meat was "among the skills that the compleat housewife was expected" to know; it was likely a task Martha Washington would have overseen.[16]

This recipe is adapted from one by Philadelphian Eliza Leslie. She instructed the cook to "take the bone out of a leg of pork" and, after spreading on the filling "thick all over the meat," to "roll it up very tightly, and tie it down with tape."[17] Her explanation closely parallels Samuel Johnson's definition of collaring beef in his *Dictionary of the English Language*: "to roll it up, and bind it hard and close with a string or collar."[18]

Serves 6 to 8

1 boneless pork loin (5 pounds)
Salt
4 cups fresh breadcrumbs
    (preferably from a country-style loaf)
⅓ cup water
1 tablespoon dried sage
1 tablespoon dried marjoram
1½ teaspoons dried sweet basil
¾ teaspoon ground mace
¾ to 1 teaspoon ground cloves
½ teaspoon ground nutmeg
1 teaspoon dried thyme
1 teaspoon dried chervil
1 teaspoon dried winter savory
¼ teaspoon dried rosemary
1 teaspoon ground black pepper
½ cup (1 stick) unsalted butter, melted
1 large egg, lightly beaten
2 cups water
1 cup white wine
2 to 3 dried bay leaves

1. Preheat the oven to 375°F.

2. Cut the loin nearly in half lengthwise, being careful not to cut entirely through the meat. Trim the excess fat and silver skin from the surface, and then open the loin like a book so that it lies flat. Rub well with salt on both sides.

3. Moisten the breadcrumbs with the water. In a small bowl, combine the sage, marjoram, sweet basil, mace, cloves, nutmeg, thyme, chervil, winter savory, rosemary, pepper, and 1 teaspoon of salt. Mix into the moistened breadcrumbs, and then blend in the butter and egg, combining thoroughly. Spread thickly over opened surface of the pork.

4. Carefully roll up the stuffed loin, tucking in the stuffing and gently pulling the pork over it to enclose it as you go. Using kitchen twine, tie the rolled pork securely at 2-inch intervals. Place the loin in a large Dutch oven.

5. Combine the water and wine, and pour over the loin. Add the bay leaves. Cover the Dutch oven, and roast for 2 to 2½ hours to an internal temperature of about 150°F. When the pork is done, the juices will run clear when it is pierced with a fork. Remove the loin to a carving board, cover loosely with aluminum foil, and set aside to rest for about 15 minutes before slicing.

6. To serve, slice pieces of the loin on the diagonal, and arrange on a platter.

In 1757 Washington ordered and received from his London agent Richard Washington (no known relation) a large assortment of household goods that included this silver-handled knife and fork.

*Livestock, kept in abundance at Mount Vernon, furnished
the best meats for the Washingtons' table. Today, the estate still
abounds with a number of heritage breeds that would likely be
familiar to George Washington, including Ossabaw Island hogs (left),
Dominique chickens (above right), and Red Devon cows.*

To Roast a Ham or Gammon

Martha Washington took great pride in the hams produced at Mount Vernon. She supervised their curing and subsequent preparation for meals. Her grandson recalled that a "ham was boiled daily" for enjoyment at every meal.[19] In a July 1798 letter to William Hambly, an English merchant, George Washington wrote, "Being in grateful remembrance the very fine Cheeses you had the goodness to send me, Mrs. Washington prays your acceptance of half a dozen Hams of her own curing."[20]

Gammon is the English corruption of the northern French word *jambe*. In Samuel Johnson's *Dictionary of the English Language*, it is defined as the "buttock of an hog, salted and dried."[21] The word is interchangeable with *ham*, as reflected in the title of this Hannah Glasse recipe.[22]

Unfortunately, Mrs. Washington's recipe for roasting ham has not come down to us. Because she owned a copy of Glasse's cookbook, however, it is possible that this recipe was one she tried.

Serves 8 to 10

1 bone-in Virginia ham (country ham) (6 pounds)
4 cups dry white wine
4 to 6 cups fresh breadcrumbs
1 bunch fresh parsley, stemmed and minced

1. Soak and scrub the ham according to the method suggested on the package or by your butcher. Put it in a large pot, and add enough water to cover it completely. Bring to a simmer, and cook for 2 to 2½ hours (20 to 25 minutes per pound). Add water as needed to keep the ham covered. When thoroughly cooked, remove it from the pot and cool slightly until it can be easily handled. Cut off the skin, and trim the fat to ¼ inch thick.

2. Place the ham in a large pan or ceramic bowl, and pour the wine over it. Set it in the refrigerator, and let it steep for 8 to 9 hours, turning every 2 hours. Drain thoroughly, reserving the wine.

3. Preheat the oven to 400°F. Set a rack in a large roasting pan.

4. Wrap the ham in parchment paper, secure with butcher's or kitchen twine, and place in the roasting pan. Roast for 35 to 45 minutes, basting every 15 minutes with about ½ cup of the reserved wine, until the ham is heated through.

5. Remove the ham from the parchment paper, and cover the top and sides with breadcrumbs and parsley. Return to the oven, and roast for 15 to 20 minutes, or until well browned.

6. To serve, place the ham on a platter, and cut it into thin slices.

The estate inventory taken after George Washington's death listed eight knife cases. This handsome example holds forty-six pieces of cutlery. It likely included three sets of twelve knives and forks for the first course and desserts, one carving knife and fork, seven serving implements, and a marrow scoop or skewer. Diners were given fresh cutlery at the start of each course, requiring multiple sets for each place setting.

To Fry a Loin of Lamb

Joshua Brookes, an English businessman who dined at Mount Vernon is February 1799, noted that mutton chops were among the dishes he was served.[23] Because mutton has a strong flavor, I have chosen a lamb chop recipe by Hannah Glasse that will be more agreeable to modern palates.[24]

Serves 6 to 8

3 large egg yolks
6 to 8 lamb chops
Salt
Ground black pepper
3 cups fresh breadcrumbs
2 tablespoons minced fresh parsley
2 teaspoons dried thyme
2 teaspoons dried marjoram
2 teaspoons dried winter savory
1 tablespoon freshly grated lemon zest
3 tablespoons unsalted butter
1 tablespoon olive oil

Fried parsley for garnish (see Note, above right)

1. Whisk the egg yolks until light and foamy. Lightly season the lamb chops with salt and pepper, and then coat with the yolks. Combine the breadcrumbs with the parsley, thyme, marjoram, winter savory, and lemon zest. Dredge the lamb chops on both sides in the breadcrumbs, pressing them into the chops. Let them sit at room temperature for 15 to 20 minutes.
2. Heat the butter and oil in a skillet over medium-high heat. Place the lamb chops in the skillet, reduce the heat to medium, and cook on each side for about 5 minutes, or until lightly browned.
3. Arrange the lamb chops on a serving platter, garnish with fried parsley, and serve.

NOTE: To fry parsley, rinse and thoroughly dry about 4 fresh parsley sprigs. Melt enough lard or vegetable shortening in a frying pan to measure 2 to 3 inches deep, and heat until sizzling hot. The fat will appear to shimmer on the surface when it is ready. Carefully place the parsley sprigs in the hot fat (they will spatter a bit as they hit the oil), and fry briefly—not more than 30 seconds. Lift out of the oil, using tongs or a wire strainer, and drain thoroughly on paper towels. The parsley will be crisp and bright green, an attractive garnish for many meat and fish dishes.

RIGHT:
This silver caster, made by London silversmith Samuel Wood in 1736 and engraved with the Washington family crest (a winged griffin), was used at the dining table to hold and dispense salt, pepper, sugar, and mustard powder.

This modern adaptation of Hannah Glasse's fried loin of lamb (lamb chops) is encrusted in a rich and flavorful coating of herbs and breadcrumbs and topped with sprigs of fried parsley.

This modern adaptation of the classic Yorkshire Christmas Pie is a rich and hearty layering of poultry, bacon, and fresh vegetables, encased in a pastry shell—a festive and delicious addition to any holiday gathering.

Yorkshire Christmas Pie

A celebrated Yuletide tradition in England, Christmas pie was a sizable pastry filled with boned, buttered, and highly spiced game and poultry that was baked in an elaborately decorated standing crust. A French visitor to England in 1717 described that country's Christmas festivities: "[E]very family . . . makes a famous pye, which they call Christmas Pye. It is . . . a most learned mixture of neat's tongues, chicken, eggs, sugar, raisins, lemon and orange peel, and various kinds of spicery, &c."[25]

The pie appears to have been a Christmas custom in the Washington household as well, mentioned in letters as the season approached. For example, in November 1786, David Humphreys, a former military aide to the general, expressed his disappointment that he could not be at the estate for the holidays and thus would "not have the felicity of eating Christmas Pie at Mount Vernon."[26] In his post–Christmas reply, Washington voiced regret that Humphreys had not been with them to "aid in the Attack of Christmas Pyes . . . on which all the company . . . were hardly able to make an impression."[27]

A January 1770 article in England's *Newcastle Chronicle* noted that one Christmas pie being shipped to London "was nine feet in circumference at bottom, weighed about twelve stone [168 pounds], and will take two men to present it at table. It was neatly fitted with a case, and four wheels to facilitate its use to every guest that inclines to partake of its contents at table."[28] One can assume that the Washingtons' pies were smaller than that and that they were likely prepared according to Hannah Glasse's recipe in *The Art of Cookery.*[29]

Our analysis of various Christmas pie recipes indicates that the preparation can be lengthy, labor intensive, and difficult; given the poultry boning and other preliminary steps involved, it can require at least two days to put together.

Chef Mike Lund, formerly of the Inn at Little Washington in Washington, Virginia, developed the pie for this book, working closely from the old recipes. He recognized that such a version would need considerable alteration in order to be appealing to contemporary palates. Noting that most such recipes he researched called for heavy amounts of mace and cloves, he decided to season the dish more delicately, using fresh herbs that included winter savory, thyme, sage, and parsley. Lund also found that period recipes called for a crust that was essentially just a cooking vessel, not a pastry to be eaten. So he developed an edible crust, using milk instead of water, which resulted in a tender, flaky pastry. His recipe for a delectable Yorkshire Christmas pie follows.

Serves 8 to 10

PASTRY

3 cups all-purpose flour
3 teaspoons salt
⅔ cup lard or vegetable shortening
¼ cup whole milk

FILLING

1 whole turkey breast (about 4 pounds), skin on and boned
1 whole chicken (about 3 pounds), skin on and boned, or 4 chicken breasts (about 6 ounces each), skin on and boned
Salt
Ground black pepper
2 to 4 tablespoons vegetable oil
2 large carrots, peeled and diced
1 medium onion, peeled and diced
3 ribs celery, diced
½ teaspoon ground cloves
¼ cup dry white wine

Glass rinsers, like finger bowls (page 139), were essential to genteel dining in the eighteenth century. These deep glasses were placed around the table and filled with water or ice for washing and chilling one's glass between courses or wines. George Washington's choice of an opaque "Bristol Blue" glass was as practical as it was elegant, for it masked the bowls' often dirty contents.

ASSEMBLY

2 tablespoons chopped fresh parsley

2 tablespoons chopped fresh winter savory

2 tablespoons chopped fresh thyme

About 1 pound thinly sliced bacon

1 large egg, lightly beaten

GRAVY

1 tablespoon unsalted butter

1 tablespoon all-purpose flour

2 cups chicken stock

2 sprigs fresh parsley

2 sprigs fresh thyme

4 leaves fresh sage

1. To make the pastry, sift the flour and salt into a large mixing bowl.

2. Melt the lard in the milk, bring to a boil, and pour into the flour. With a wooden spoon, mix together quickly to form a dough; it will be quite firm, somewhat like Play-Doh. Turn the dough out onto a lightly floured work surface, and knead until smooth. Cover loosely with plastic wrap, and let it rest on the work surface at room temperature for 20 minutes.

3. To make the filling, season the turkey and chicken all over with salt and pepper. In a large sauté pan over medium-high heat, heat 2 tablespoons of the vegetable oil. Put the turkey breast in the pan, skin-side-down, and cook until browned. Remove from the pan, and set aside. Put the chicken in the hot pan, skin-side-down, and cook until browned. Remove from the pan, and set aside along with the turkey.

4. Reduce the heat, and add about 2 more tablespoons of the vegetable oil to the pan, if necessary. Add the carrots, onion, and celery, and cook for about 5 minutes until softened, stirring frequently to keep from browning. Season with salt and pepper, and stir in the cloves. Add the

The table in the Mansion's large dining room, aglow with candlelight, is set with many of the Washingtons' favorite Christmas confections, including a marzipan hedgehog cake, plum pudding, a pyramid of candied crabapples, and a Twelfth Night cake covered with hard white icing and topped with molded swans.

wine, stirring to deglaze (to loosen the browned bits on the bottom of the pan), and simmer for about 5 minutes, until reduced by half. Transfer the vegetables to a bowl, and set aside to cool.

5. Preheat the oven to 400°F. Grease a 9-inch springform pan with vegetable shortening.

6. On a lightly floured work surface, roll two-thirds of the pastry into a circle about ¼ inch thick. Line the greased pan with the pastry, allowing it to hang about ½ inch over the sides.

7. To assemble the pie, sprinkle the bottom and sides of the pastry with about one-third of the parsley, winter savory, and thyme. Line the bottom and sides of the pastry with about one-third of the bacon. Spread one-third of the vegetable mixture on top of the bacon.

8. Lay the turkey breast, skin-side-up, on top of the vegetables. It may be necessary to trim the turkey to fit, using the trimmings to fill in any gaps. Cover the turkey with another one-third of the vegetable mixture, sprinkle on another one-third of the herbs, and cover with a thin, even layer of about another one-third of the bacon.

9. Arrange the chicken, skin-side-up, on top of the bacon, again trimming to fit, if necessary. Cover the chicken with the final one-third of the vegetables, herbs, and a thin, even layer of bacon.

10. Roll out the final one-third of the dough on a lightly floured work surface to form a circle about 9 inches in diameter. Brush the ½-inch overhang with beaten egg, drape the pastry circle over the top of the filled pan, and fold the ½-inch overhang over the edges of the pastry circle to seal together. Cut out any dough scraps to create decorative toppings, such as leaves, stars, or trees. Brush the top lightly with the beaten egg.

11. Set the pie on a baking sheet, and bake for 30 minutes. Cover loosely with aluminum foil, and continue baking for about another hour. Then, check the temperature every 10 minutes or so (piercing an instant-read thermometer through the crust and into the pie) until the internal temperature reaches 155°F. Remove from the oven, and set the pie on a wire rack to allow the temperature to rise to 165°F. Cool for 1 hour before carefully releasing it from the pan.

12. While the pie cools, make the gravy. Melt the butter in a small saucepan over medium heat. Whisk in the flour until incorporated to make a blond (light-colored) roux (thickening paste). Slowly whisk in the chicken stock and simmer for 2 to 3 minutes, until thickened. Remove from the heat, add the parsley, thyme, and sage, and allow the herbs to steep for 15 minutes. The gravy can also be prepared ahead of time and reheated just before serving.

13. To serve, set the cooled pie on a platter. At the table, cut a small hole in the top of the crust, and carefully pour in the hot gravy. Slice into wedges.

To Fricassee Chicken

Elizabeth Raffald's fricassee is one of the "made dishes" enjoyed in the eighteenth century. Her clear directions included combining the ingredients and stewing them "together till your chickens are tender." Regarding the gravy, she cautioned that once the egg yolks and cream are added to the rest of the mixture, the cook should "shake it over the fire, but do not let it boil"—a helpful warning to bear in mind even today.[30]

Serves 6 to 8

5 pounds bone-in chicken breasts and thighs, skinned
Salt
Ground black pepper
2 to 3 cups chicken broth
5 tablespoons unsalted butter, softened and divided
½ lemon, halved
2 teaspoons dried marjoram
½ teaspoon ground mace
½ teaspoon ground nutmeg
3 sprigs fresh lemon thyme
1 large onion
3 cloves
2 teaspoons anchovy paste

Fresh, tender chicken is cooked to perfection in broth, cream, and herbs. This modern version of Elizabeth Raffald's chicken fricassee is served on a plate in the Society of the Cincinnati pattern by Mottahedeh.

¼ cup dry white wine

4 tablespoons all-purpose flour

3 large egg yolks, beaten until thick and lemon colored

½ cup heavy cream

1. Season the chicken with salt and pepper, and place in a large Dutch oven. Pour in 2 cups of the broth. Add 2 tablespoons of the butter, the lemon, marjoram, mace, nutmeg, and lemon thyme sprigs. Pierce the onion with the cloves, and add to the pan along with the anchovy paste and the wine.

2. Cover and bring to a boil over medium-high heat. Stir to blend the ingredients, reduce the heat to low, cover, and simmer for 30 to 40 minutes, until the chicken is tender, adding more broth, if necessary.

3. Preheat the oven to 200°F.

4. Transfer the chicken to a deep serving platter, cover loosely with aluminum foil, and set aside in the warm oven. Strain the broth, discarding the solids, and reserve 2 cups. (Freeze any remaining broth for later use for up to 6 months.) Return the strained broth to the Dutch oven, and bring back to a simmer over low heat.

5. Combine the remaining 3 tablespoons of butter with the flour in a small bowl. Mix in a little of the hot broth, and then gradually stir it back into the simmering broth. Blend in thoroughly and simmer for about 2 minutes, until the broth has thickened slightly.

6. Mix the egg yolks with the cream, stirring to combine thoroughly. Blend into the broth gradually. Continue to cook, and stir until the broth simmers. Do not let it boil, or the egg yolks will curdle. Season with additional salt and pepper, if necessary.

7. Place the chicken in the thickened sauce, coating it well.

8. Return the chicken to the deep serving platter, and spoon some of the sauce around it. Pour the remaining sauce into a sauceboat to accompany the dish.

To Roast Ducks

———•———

George Washington Parke Custis, Martha Washington's grandson, described a visit to nearby Alexandria that occurred late in George Washington's life. While dining at Gatsby's City Hotel, the proprietor informed Washington "that there was good store of canvass-back ducks in the larder." "Very good, sir," he replied, "give us some of them, with a chafing-dish, some hominy, and a bottle of good Madeira, and we shall not complain."[31] Washington's diaries contain many references to duck hunting. For example, on February 24, 1768, he "Went a ducking between breakfast & dinner & killd 2 Mallards & 5 bald faces."[32]

Although canvasback ducks are rarely to be had these days, the Washingtons would surely have recognized this adaptation of a recipe by Elizabeth Raffald.[33] Mushroom catchup, which is called for here, can be ordered online or found in specialty stores.

Serves 4

1 domestic duck (4½ pounds)

Water as needed

Salt

Ground black pepper

2 large fresh sage sprigs

1 medium onion, peeled and quartered

All-purpose flour for sprinkling

3 to 4 tablespoons unsalted butter, melted

¼ teaspoon ground mace

2 tablespoons mushroom catchup

1 tablespoon fresh lemon juice

2 to 4 tablespoons Brown Flour (page 168)

Onion Sauce (page 165) for serving

1. Preheat the oven to 475°F. Set a rack in a medium roasting pan.

2. Remove the gizzards (giblets) from the duck, and put them in a saucepan. Add enough water just to cover, and set aside. Rinse the duck thoroughly, and pat it dry with paper towels.

3. Season the duck with salt and pepper, rubbing them into the skin as well as in the cavity. Tuck the sage sprigs and onion into the cavity.

4. Sprinkle the duck with flour, patting over the skin. Brush all over with the melted butter.

5. Place the duck in the roasting pan. Put it in the oven, and immediately reduce the temperature to 350°F. Roast the duck for about 1½ hours, pricking the skin every 20 minutes to drain the excess fat, until an instant-read thermometer inserted in the thigh registers 180°F.

6. Meanwhile, complete the sauce. Bring the gizzards (giblets) to a boil. Cover and simmer briskly for about 20 minutes, until they are cooked through. Remove and discard the gizzards. Return the broth to the heat, and stir in the mace, catchup, lemon juice, and ¼ teaspoon of black pepper. Continue simmering about 5 minutes more on very low heat, until the flavors are well blended.

7. When the duck is done, drain the juices into the roasting pan, transfer the duck to a deep serving platter, and cover loosely with aluminum foil. Skim as much fat off the juices as possible, and pour them into the simmering broth. Whisk in 2 tablespoons of the Brown Flour, and stir until thickened. Add 1 to 2 tablespoons more of the flour, if necessary.

8. To serve, pour the sauce around the duck, and send to the table. Accompany with Onion Sauce in a separate gravy boat.

To Dress Fish

———•◆•———

George Washington's love of fish is legendary. Living along two of Virginia's major rivers assured him easy access to many varieties. In fact, the sole duty of a Washington slave known as Father Jack was to provide fish for the table when the family was at Mount Vernon. According to Martha Washington's grandson, George Washington Parke Custis, the cook "required" the fish to be available at a specific time, "so that they might be served smoking on the board precisely at three o'clock."[34]

Hannah Glasse suggested that a sauce "according to your fancy" should accompany this dish.[35] Try it, for example, with melted butter sauce or remoulade (pages 164 and 165).

Serves 6 to 8

6 to 8 freshwater trout (about 8 ounces each), cleaned and butterflied
Salt
Ground black pepper
All-purpose flour for dredging
2 tablespoons lard or vegetable shortening
4 tablespoons unsalted butter

1. Lightly season the trout on both sides with salt and pepper. Dredge well on both sides in the flour.

2. In a frying pan over medium-high heat, melt the lard and butter. When the pan sizzles, reduce the heat to medium. Add the trout fillets, flesh-sides-down, and cook for about 3 minutes. Carefully turn the fillets, and cook about 3 more minutes until lightly browned. Remove from the pan, and drain thoroughly on paper towels.

3. Transfer the fillets to a platter, and serve immediately.

LEFT: *An engraving of Elizabeth Raffald (1733–1781) from her hugely successful cookbook,* The Experienced English House-keeper. *In an age when many women writers published anonymously, Raffald used her name and image, finally selling copyright to her publisher for £1400.*

RIGHT: *Mary Randolph (1762–1828), was the author of* The Virginia House-Wife *(1824), one of the most influential housekeeping and cooking books of the nineteenth century. The book went through many editions, well into the 1860s. This fine profile portrait in chalk and pencil was done by Charles Balthazar Julien Févret de Saint-Mémin.*

To Dress a Salt Cod

Of all the fish Washington enjoyed, salt fish ranked highest. The general is "exceedingly fond of" them, wrote General Robert Howe of North Carolina in a June 1782 request "for as much fish as would serve a pretty large company for dinner."[36]

The egg sauce Mary Randolph added to her recipe became fashionable during the eighteenth century.[37] The ingredients are simple—just butter and finely chopped eggs, with a little seasoning to accent the flavor. The following recipe is enhanced with cream, plus a bit of cayenne pepper to add color.

Serves 6

1 pound dried salt cod
4 tablespoons unsalted butter
¾ cup heavy cream
¼ teaspoon ground white pepper
4 large hardboiled eggs, peeled, with yolks and whites
    separated
Salt
Cayenne pepper as needed (optional)

1. Put the cod in a large glass or ceramic bowl, cover with cold water, and set in the refrigerator to soak and soften for at least 8 hours, or overnight.

2. When you are ready to cook the cod, drain it thoroughly, place in a large heavy-bottomed saucepan, and pour in enough water to cover it. Set the cod over very low heat and cook, barely simmering, for about 8 minutes. Do not let the water boil. Drain and repeat the procedure two more times, until most of the salt is extracted from the flesh.

3. Remove the cod, and rinse out the saucepan. Return the cod to the pan, and again pour in just enough water to cover it. Bring to a gentle simmer over low heat, and cook for 35 to 40 minutes, until the cod is easily flaked into pieces. Again, do not let the water boil. Carefully lift out the cod with a strainer, and cool just until it can be easily handled. Using a fork, flake the cod into pieces and set aside.

4. Melt the butter in a saucepan. Add the cream and white pepper. Bring to a gentle simmer over very low heat, and cook until it thickens slightly, stirring often. Fold in the cod, and continue simmering for about 3 minutes until heated through.

5. Discard 2 of the hardboiled egg whites, or reserve for another use. Finely chop the remaining 2 egg whites and 2 of the egg yolks, and stir into the sauced cod. Season with salt, if necessary.

6. Pour the cod into a serving dish. Break the 2 remaining egg yolks into small bits, and scatter over the top. Dust on a little cayenne, if desired.

A Ragoo of Oysters

Washington's cash accounts indicated that he often purchased bushels of oysters to be prepared for his family's table.

Hannah Glasse's "ragoo" (ragout) can be served as a starter or as a main course. The combination of spices with fresh parsley creates a flavorsome dish.[38]

OPPOSITE:
Fish from the Potomac River were not only a major source of food for Mount Vernon's residents and guests, but also provided substantial commercial income. In the spring of 1798, Washington's enslaved fishermen reportedly caught one hundred thousand herring with a single draw of the net, an enterprise suggested by John Gadsby Chapman's 1830s Potomac River scene Distant View of Mount Vernon.

LEFT:
George Washington's tackle box—possibly ordered from London in 1762—provides a rare glimpse of eighteenth-century fishing gear: hand-wrought iron hooks, horsehair and silk lines, and wax for preparing the lines. Washington caught catfish in the Ohio Country and trout and perch in Philadelphia during the recess of the Constitutional Convention in the summer of 1787.

Serves 6 to 8

BATTER

3 large eggs

1 tablespoon finely grated lemon zest

½ teaspoon ground nutmeg

½ teaspoon ground mace

1 tablespoon minced fresh parsley

1½ teaspoons salt

¼ teaspoon ground black pepper

4 tablespoons all-purpose flour

1½ pints fresh shucked oysters in their liquor

6 tablespoons unsalted butter, divided

3 tablespoons lard or vegetable shortening, plus more
as needed

5 tablespoons all-purpose flour

6 tablespoons dry white wine

1 cup chicken broth

¼ teaspoon ground nutmeg

Salt

Browned buttered breadcrumbs for garnish

1. Preheat the oven to 200°F.

2. To make the batter, beat the eggs until frothy. Blend
in the lemon zest, nutmeg, mace, parsley, salt, and pepper. Whisk in the flour until all ingredients are thoroughly
mixed. Cover and set aside.

3. Put the oysters in a strainer set over a bowl, and set
aside to drain, reserving the liquor.

4. Melt 3 tablespoons of the butter and the lard in a large
frying pan over medium heat. Dip the oysters one by one
in the batter, and sauté on both sides until lightly browned.
Drain the oysters on paper towels, and set aside in the oven
to keep warm.

5. Melt the remaining 3 tablespoons of butter in a saucepan over low heat. Stir in the flour, blending in well and
stirring until lightly browned. Gradually add the wine,
chicken broth, nutmeg, and reserved oyster liquor. Whisk
constantly, until the sauce bubbles and thickens slightly.
Season with salt, if necessary.

6. To serve, place the oysters in a bowl, pour the sauce on
top, and garnish with breadcrumbs.

To Dress Crab

———◆———

Hannah Glasse's only recommendation for serving this
stewed crab was to "serve it up on a plate."[39] It can also easily be combined with rice or pasta and baked as a casserole.

Serves 6 to 8

1 cup dry white wine

1½ pounds fresh lump crabmeat

¼ teaspoon ground nutmeg

¼ teaspoon ground black pepper

½ teaspoon salt

3 tablespoons unsalted butter

2½ cups fresh breadcrumbs

2 large egg yolks

1 tablespoon apple cider vinegar

1. Bring the wine to a simmer over medium heat. Stir
in the crabmeat, nutmeg, pepper, and salt, blending all
together well. Reduce the heat to low, cover, and simmer
gently for 5 to 7 minutes, stirring occasionally, until the
wine has reduced slightly.

2. Melt the butter in a saucepan over medium heat. Stir in
the breadcrumbs, and cook until lightly browned. Add to
the crabmeat, and stir to blend.

3. Combine the egg yolks and vinegar. Blend into the crab
mixture and cook for about 3 minutes, stirring frequently.
Season with additional salt and pepper, if necessary.

4. To serve, spoon onto a platter or into individual cups.

Fresh crab from the Chesapeake Bay was one of Martha Washington's favorites. This modern adaptation of Hannah Glasse's recipe for dressed crab is baked with wine and breadcrumbs.

SAUCES

Flavorful sauces, usually made with drippings or broth left over from cooked foods, complemented many eighteenth-century entrees. They were combined with herbs and spices, and often slightly thickened with egg yolks or a small amount of softened butter and flour that was worked into a paste and then stirred into the broth. The finished sauces were either poured directly over the dishes before being sent to the table or were served in sauceboats to join the entrees in the first course.

Sweet sauces were generally meant to accompany a variety of desserts. Boiled custard was especially enjoyed as a complement to baked desserts, such as bread pudding and apple pie.

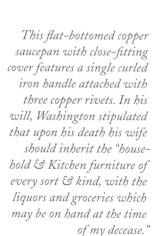

This flat-bottomed copper saucepan with close-fitting cover features a single curled iron handle attached with three copper rivets. In his will, Washington stipulated that upon his death his wife should inherit the "household & Kitchen furniture of every sort & kind, with the liquors and groceries which may be on hand at the time of my decease."

To Melt Butter

"A great variety of delicious sauces can be made, by adding different herbs," wrote Mary Randolph in her directions for this basic butter sauce. She recommended parsley, chervil, cress, and tarragon, among others herbs, and assured her readers that making this slightly thickened, elegant butter sauce is a "simple . . . process."[1] The sauce can be served as an accompaniment to various fish, poultry, and beef dishes.

Makes ⅔ to 1 cup

½ cup unsalted butter, softened
2 teaspoons all-purpose flour
1 to 2 tablespoons water
½ teaspoon salt
½ cup fresh stemmed herbs, such as parsley, chervil,
   tarragon, cress, or lemongrass (optional)

1. In the top of a double boiler, combine the butter and flour. Set over boiling water, and stir until the butter is melted. Add the salt and 1 tablespoon of water and cook, stirring constantly, until the sauce begins to bubble.

2. If using the herbs, parboil them for about 3 to 4 minutes. Then drain, dry thoroughly, and mince before adding to the basic sauce. Add the second tablespoon of water if flavoring the sauce with herbs.

3. Remove the sauce from the heat, pour into a sauceboat, and serve warm. The sauce can also be cooled, covered with plastic wrap, and stored in the refrigerator for up to 2 days. Warm slowly over low heat to serve.

To Make Onion Sauce

In *The Experienced English House-keeper*, Elizabeth Raffald recommended serving this sauce as an accompaniment to Roast Duck (page 157).[2] It can also be used for other poultry or for mild-flavored fish, such as flounder. Similar onion sauces can be found in many old cookbooks. In fact, Mary Randolph copied Raffald's recipe verbatim in her own book, *The Virginia House-Wife*.[3]

Makes 2 to 3 cups

4 large onions, peeled and quartered
5 tablespoons unsalted butter, softened
½ teaspoon salt
¼ teaspoon ground black pepper
¼ cup heavy cream

1. Cover the onions with water, and bring to a boil over high heat. Reduce the heat to low, and simmer for 10 minutes. Drain in a colander, repeat the process twice more, and then drain the onions thoroughly. Set aside to cool until they can be handled easily, and chop them finely. (You should have about 4 cups.)
2. Melt the butter in a saucepan over medium-low heat. Stir in the onions, and bring to a simmer. Add the salt and pepper and cook for 5 to 10 minutes, stirring frequently.
3. Stir in the cream, blending together thoroughly. Bring the sauce back to a simmer, and continue to cook for 5 to 10 minutes, stirring frequently, until the cream is slightly reduced.
4. Season with additional salt and pepper, if necessary, and pour the sauce into a sauceboat.

A Particular Sauce Called Ramolade

The following recipe for ramolade—or rémoulade, as we know it today—is adapted from *The Lady's Companion*, a mid-eighteenth-century cookbook published in London. Martha Washington's younger sister Anna Maria (Nancy) Dandridge Bassett had a copy of it at Mount Vernon. This sauce, featured with other fish sauces in *The Lady's Companion*, is thinner and darker than today's bottled rémoulades, which are thickened with mayonnaise. The anonymous author recommended the sauce as "being proper for several sorts of Fish cut into Fillets," and also suggested that it be "turn'd over" the dressed fish "when they are to be served up cold."[4]

This piquant rémoulade makes a delicious accompaniment to various fish dishes, such as Hannah Glasse's To Dress Fish (page 158).

Makes about 1½ cups

¼ cup balsamic vinegar
¾ cup plus 2 tablespoons olive oil
½ teaspoon salt
⅛ teaspoon ground black pepper
⅛ teaspoon ground nutmeg
¼ cup minced fresh parsley
2 to 3 green onions, trimmed and chopped
4 teaspoons capers, drained and chopped
1 to 2 teaspoons anchovy paste (optional)

1. Combine the vinegar with ¼ cup of the olive oil. Gradually add the remaining oil, whisking until the sauce is emulsified and creamy.
2. Add the salt, pepper, and nutmeg, combining well.
3. Stir in the parsley, onions, capers, and anchovy paste, if desired.
4. Serve the rémoulade chilled or at room temperature. The sauce can be stored in an airtight container (preferably a glass jar) for up to a week.

Mushroom Sauce

In *The Virginia House-Wife*, Mary Randolph recommended this as a "very good sauce for white fowls of all kinds."[5]

Makes 3 to 3½ cups

6 tablespoons unsalted butter
1 pound fresh mushrooms (preferably cremini), rinsed, stemmed, and cut into thick slices (about 6 cups)
1¼ teaspoons salt
¾ teaspoon ground mace
2 cups heavy cream
2 large egg yolks, lightly beaten
4 teaspoons fresh lemon juice

1. Melt the butter over medium heat. Stir in the mushrooms, salt, and mace. Reduce the heat, cover, and simmer for 20 to 25 minutes, stirring occasionally until the mushrooms are very tender.
2. Combine the cream with the egg yolks. Gradually blend into the mushrooms, stirring continuously over medium-low heat, until the sauce just reaches the boiling point and begins to thicken. Watch carefully, as the sauce scorches easily.
3. Stir in the lemon juice, continuing to stir until heated through.
4. Pour the sauce into a sauceboat, and serve hot.

Mrs. Taylor's Sallad Dressing

This simple vinaigrette harkens back to a late-seventeenth-century recipe by John Evelyn. Beginning with a "Sallet-Oyl" that is "smooth, light, and pleasant upon the tongue," Evelyn went on to recommend the "best Wine Vinegar . . . the brightest Bay grey-Salt," and all other ingredients of the finest quality, from sugar to mustard and other seasonings, and even notes the type of container in which the salad is to be served.[6]

The following vinaigrette from E. Taylor's *The Lady's, Housewife's, and Cookmaid's Assistant* is delicious when drizzled over a variety of fresh salad greens.[7]

Makes about 1¼ cups

2 large hardboiled-egg yolks
¼ teaspoon salt
2 rounded teaspoons Dijon mustard
¼ cup balsamic vinegar
1 cup olive oil

1. With a fork, mash the egg yolks. Add the salt and mustard, stirring together until completely blended. Stir in the vinegar, mixing well.
2. Gradually add the olive oil, a small amount at a time, whisking continuously to emulsify the dressing.
3. Cover and refrigerate the dressing until ready to use. Store in an airtight container in the refrigerator for up to 3 weeks.

OPPOSITE:

An illustration of a variety of mushrooms from the Taalryk *register (ca. 1748), published by German apothecary and botanist Johann Wilhelm Weimann.*

RIGHT:

This French porcelain butter dish from the Angoulême factory matched Washington's preference for neat and plain, while offering his guests fashionable French porcelain that may also have subtly referred to the white-marble statuary and republican ideals of ancient Greece.

N. 524

Brown Flour

—◆—

"There should always be a supply of brown flour kept in readiness to thicken brown gravies," Mary Randolph wrote in her 1824 cookbook, *The Virginia House-Wife*.[8] Indeed, this simple ingredient is one to have on hand in modern kitchens as well.

This flour adds a nuttiness and depth to a variety of red-meat-based sauces. Use it to thicken these sauces as you would all-purpose flour.

Makes 1 cup

1 cup all-purpose flour

1. Put the flour in a skillet (preferably cast iron) over medium-high heat. Stir continuously until the flour is a dark golden brown. Watch carefully, as it burns easily.

2. Remove from the heat, and immediately transfer to a bowl to stop it from browning. Cool to room temperature, and store in an airtight glass jar in a cool, dry cupboard.

A charming engraving of Martha Washington done in 1834 by J. B. Longacre, after a circa 1791 painted portrait miniature by Scottish artist Archibald Robertson.

Applesauce

—◆—

Mentions of the importance of apples are abundant in Washington's papers. For example, on February 1, 1796, he noted, "For every acre . . . an Apple tree of good grafted fruit is to be planted on the premises."[9]

The recipe here is adapted from one in Hannah Glasse's *The Art of Cookery*.[10] This sauce is delicious with a variety of dishes, but it pairs particularly well with E. Smith's Roast Pork (page 146).

Makes 3 or 4 cups

2½ pounds tart cooking apples, such as Granny Smith, or heirloom apples such as Newtown (Albemarle) Pippin, peeled, cored, and cut into thick slices
2 to 3 teaspoons freshly grated lemon zest
Water as needed
3 tablespoons unsalted butter, softened
¾ to 1 cup sugar
½ teaspoon ground nutmeg

1. Put the apples in a saucepan over low heat. Add the lemon zest and about ½ cup of water. Cover and cook the apples, stirring often and adding more water if the fruit seems too dry. Add only enough, however, to prevent the apples from sticking to the pan. Cook for about 20 minutes, until the apples are very soft. Remove from the heat, and mash the apples roughly.

2. Blend in the butter. Add ¾ cup of the sugar, stirring in more as needed, and then add the nutmeg.

3. Serve the applesauce warm or at room temperature. It can be cooled completely and stored in an airtight container in the refrigerator for up to 3 days.

Boiled Custard

This rich dessert sauce is adapted from a recipe by nineteenth-century cookbook author Hannah Mary Bouvier Peterson.[11] Other recipes for boiled custard can be found in contemporary cookbooks, indicating that its popularity has not lessened over time. It can be served with desserts such as apple pie (page 172) and bread pudding (page 176).

Makes about 6 cups

1 quart half-and-half
¾ cup sugar
6 large eggs, well beaten
2 teaspoons rose water

1. In a saucepan, combine the half-and-half with the sugar. Set over medium heat, and stir until the sugar is dissolved and the milk is scalding (just below the boiling point). Remove from the heat.
2. Whisk ½ cup of the hot cream into the eggs. Reduce the heat to low, and blend the egg-and-cream mixture into the hot cream, stirring constantly to prevent the eggs from curdling. Continue stirring until the custard thickens enough to coat the back of a spoon.
3. Remove the custard from the heat, and stir in the rose water. Pour the custard into a pitcher, and set aside to cool to room temperature. Store in an airtight container in the refrigerator for up to 4 days. Warm slightly before serving.

Fairy Butter

This simple dessert sauce makes a tasty accompaniment to gingerbread—either dotted onto the surface before serving or passed around at the table. The recipe here is adapted from one by Elizabeth Raffald in which she suggested letting the sauce "stand two or three hours" before rubbing it "through a cullendar upon a plate; it looks very pretty."[12] Maria Rundell included this recipe under the title Orange Butter in her 1808 cookbook, *A New System of Domestic Cookery*, noting that it pairs well with "sweet biscuits."[13]

Makes 1 cup

4 large hardboiled-egg yolks
5 teaspoons orange-flower water
4 to 6 tablespoons sugar (preferably superfine)
½ cup (1 stick) unsalted butter, softened

1. Mash the egg yolks with the orange-flower water. Add the sugar, and mix to a smooth paste.
2. Work in the butter until the mixture is smooth, and set aside in a cool place for 2 to 3 hours.
3. Press the butter through a strainer into a small serving bowl. Store in an airtight container in the refrigerator for up to 3 days.

In 1757 George Washington received from London a "Compleat sett Fine Image China," which included this sugar bowl. He drew on credit earned from his tobacco shipments to England to purchase such commodities as tea, Chinese porcelain, and sugar.

The flavors of tart cherries and sweet red currants are presented in a classic flaky pie crust.

PIES, PUDDINGS,
FRITTERS & PANCAKES

Eighteenth-century Virginians delighted in sweets of all kinds, pies being among their favorites. Numerous guests left accounts referring to pies and puddings they enjoyed at the Washingtons' table.

Period cookbooks offer a great many recipes for pie and tart crusts. Hannah Glasse's *The Art of Cookery*, for example, includes no fewer than nine such recipes. Among these are a dripping crust, a standing crust, a crust for custards, and two crusts especially for tarts. These recipes provide detailed methods of preparation and even suggest using specific tools. Writing about tart pastes, for instance, Glasse instructed the reader to "mix [the ingredients] well together" and then to "beat well with a rolling pin."[1]

Similarly, in her *Seventy-five Receipts for Pastry, Cakes, and Sweet-meats*, Eliza Leslie provided meticulous instructions for preparing fruit pies. "Apples should be cut into very thin slices," she wrote, "and are much improved by a little lemon peel. Sweet apples are not good for pies, as they are very insipid when baked." Cherries, she added, should be stoned, as should peaches and plums, and she cautioned that red cherries should only be used for pies. Leslie further noted that "[f]ruit pies for family use, are generally made with common paste," and this is the very one we rely upon in the recipes that follow.[2]

Common Pie Crust

———◆———

Eliza Leslie recommended familiar ingredients and techniques in her recipe for pie crust. "This paste will do for family use, when covered pies are wanted," she wrote, and "should always be eaten fresh."[3]

Makes enough for one double-crust 9- or 10-inch pie

2½ cups all-purpose flour
1 teaspoon salt
½ cup (1 stick) unsalted butter, chilled and cut into
    pea-size pieces
¼ cup lard or vegetable shortening, chilled
5 to 6 tablespoons ice water

1. Sift the flour and salt together.
2. With a pastry blender or by hand, work the butter and lard into the flour until the mixture is well combined and resembles coarse breadcrumbs.
3. Blend in about 5 tablespoons of water, mixing until the dough comes together. Add up to 1 more tablespoon of water, if needed.
4. Divide the dough in half, and shape into disks. Wrap individually in waxed paper, and refrigerate for at least 2 and up to 24 hours. Wrapped disks can be sealed in a plastic bag and frozen for later use.

To Make an Apple Pie

Apple pie seems to have been a favorite of George Washington. In an August 1779 letter from West Point inviting friends to dine with him, he noted that they might be treated to an apple pie. "[The cook] has had the surprizing luck to discover that apples will make pyes," the general wrote.[4]

Apple trees grew in abundance at Mount Vernon, with Newtown (Albemarle) Pippins being among the most popular there. When fresh apples were not available, the fruit was ordered by the barrel to be stored for winter use.

This apple pie recipe from Hannah Glasse requires a bit more time than standard ones of today, but the end result is more than satisfying. Glasse instructed that the apple peels and cores should be boiled with mace "till it is very good." The liquid is then to be strained and reduced prior to being poured over and around the apples in the crust before baking. Although this recipe does not call for any accompaniment, another of her apple pie recipes suggests clotted cream. Both recipes recommend that the pie be sent to the table cold.[5]

Makes one 9- or 10-inch double-crust pie

1 recipe Common Pie Crust (page 171)
Juice and zest of 1 lemon
5 to 7 tart apples, such as Newtown (Albemarle) Pippin or Granny Smith, peeled, cored, and cut into ½-inch-thick slices; peels and cores reserved
About 3 cups water
½ teaspoon ground mace
1⅔ cups sugar, divided
6 cloves
4 tablespoons unsalted butter, chilled and diced into small pieces

1. Preheat the oven to 400°F.
2. On a lightly floured surface, roll the pie-crust dough into a circle about ¼ inch thick, and place in a lightly greased pie pan, gently pressing it into the pan. Set aside in the refrigerator.

3. Combine the lemon juice with about 3 cups of water in a large bowl, and add the apple slices to prevent them from darkening. Cover and set aside.
4. Cover the reserved apple peels and cores with water, add the mace, and bring to a boil. Reduce the heat, cover, and simmer for 10 to 15 minutes. Strain and reserve the liquid. Discard the peels and cores, and return the liquid to the heat. Add 1 cup of the sugar and bring to a boil, stirring until the sugar is dissolved. Boil uncovered for about 15 minutes, or until the liquid is reduced by half. Remove from the heat, and set aside to cool.
5. Thoroughly drain the apples from the acidulated water. Put one layer of the apples in the prepared pie shell. Dot with cloves, and sprinkle with ⅓ cup of the sugar. Add another layer of apples, packing them densely and piling them high. Sprinkle with the remaining ⅓ cup of sugar. Carefully pour 2 cups of the reserved apple liquid over and around the apples.
6. Put on the top crust, tucking it in and around the edges of the bottom crust, folding the bottom edges up over the top piece of dough and then pinching together to seal. Cut several slits in the top crust, and dot with butter.
7. Bake for 40 to 45 minutes, or until the crust is golden brown and the juices are thick and bubbly. Remove the pie to a wire rack, and cool thoroughly before slicing.

RIGHT:
This waste bowl is from a tea and coffee service presented to Martha Washington in 1793 by the Comte de Custine-Sarreck, a French officer who served with General Washington during the Revolutionary War. The service was specifically made for the Washingtons at his Niderviller porcelain factory, each piece incorporating a stunning array of gilded and enameled borders and George Washington's monogram.

To Make a Cherry Pie

Although cherries were preserved or dried for use at Mount Vernon, visitors are not known to have mentioned them. Many varieties of the fruit were grown on the estate, including the Morello cherries suggested in this Hannah Glasse recipe, which the Washingtons' cooks might have used.[6] Both fresh and jarred cherries work well here. If using fresh ones, set the pitted fruit aside for at least two hours so that the cherries can release their juices. Glasse suggested adding red currants to the basic recipe. Because fresh currants are often difficult to find, currant jam is offered here as an alternative.

Makes one 10-inch double-crust pie

1 recipe **Common Pie Crust** (page 171)
1 cup red currant jam
5 cups fresh sour cherries, preferably Morello, pitted,
    or 3 jars (1 pound, 9 ounces each) preserved Morello
    cherries, drained with about ¼ cup of juice reserved
4 tablespoons arrowroot
About 1 cup sugar, plus more for sprinkling over crust
    (optional)
⅛ teaspoon salt
1 tablespoon butter, chilled and diced

1. Preheat the oven to 400°F.
2. On a lightly floured surface, roll the pie-crust dough into a circle about ¼ inch thick and place in a lightly greased pie pan, gently pressing it into the pan. Set aside in the refrigerator.
3. Heat the red currant jam, stirring until it begins to soften, about 2 minutes. Stir into the cherries, mixing together well. Combine the sugar and salt, and stir into the cherry and jam mixture to dissolve. Taste the mixture, and add more sugar if it seems too tart.
4. Combine the arrowroot with half of the reserved juice, and then blend in the remainder. Add to the cherries, and mix until well combined.

5. Pour the cherries into the prepared pie shell. Dot the butter over the filling. Place the top crust over the filling, folding the bottom edges up over the top piece of dough and then pinching together to seal. If desired, sprinkle additional sugar over the top.
6. Bake for 20 minutes. Then reduce the temperature to 375°F, and bake for another 25 to 30 minutes, or until the filling is bubbly and the crust is golden brown.
7. Remove from the oven, and set on a rack to cool thoroughly before slicing. The juices will thicken as the pie cools.

Fresh red currants from the Mount Vernon garden are a featured ingredient in Hannah Glasse's recipe for cherry pie.

Apple fritters are battered and fried to perfection, sprinkled with sugar, and sent to the table in a creamware bowl.

Apple Fritters

Early physicians cautioned that fritters were bad for one's stomach, possibly contributing to indigestion. That warning was no obstacle to those who long enjoyed these fried pastries. A thin egg batter envelops a wide selection of foodstuffs that includes thinly sliced vegetables and fruit. Apple fritters were the most popular, generally appearing on menus as part of a second course.[7]

This rendition combines two recipes from the "Booke of Cookery," a manuscript possibly dating to the seventeenth century that came to Martha Washington during her first marriage, to Daniel Parke Custis.[8] An heirloom apple variety, such as the Newtown (Albemarle) Pippin, which was grown and enjoyed at Mount Vernon, is suggested.

Makes 40 to 48 fritters

¾ cup dark ale

2 tablespoons dry sherry

1½ cups sifted all-purpose flour

½ teaspoon salt

½ teaspoon ground mace

¼ teaspoon ground nutmeg

¼ teaspoon ground cloves

3 large eggs, separated

5 to 6 medium apples, peeled, cored, and cut into
   ½-inch-thick slices

Lard or vegetable oil for frying
Cinnamon sugar for sprinkling

1. Combine the ale and sherry in a small saucepan set over medium-low heat. Warm slightly and set aside.
2. Sift together the flour, salt, mace, nutmeg, and cloves.
3. Whisk the egg yolks until smooth. Pour into the flour, and stir until well combined. The mixture will be dry and crumbly. Gradually add the ale and sherry, blending in each addition well before adding the next. The batter will be somewhat lumpy. Cover and refrigerate for at least 2 hours, or as long as overnight, to allow the batter to rest.

4. While the batter is resting, lay a sheet of waxed paper on a large baking sheet, set a wire rack on top, and cover with a clean dishtowel. Place beside the stove.

5. To finish the fritters, remove the batter from the refrigerator, and whisk until smooth. Beat 2 of the egg whites (reserving or discarding the third egg white) to stiff peaks. Gently fold into the chilled batter in two additions until thoroughly incorporated.

6. Over medium-high heat, melt enough lard in a deep frying pan to measure 2 to 3 inches, and heat to 375°F. Use a thermometer to determine the correct temperature, or test by dropping a bit of the batter into the hot lard. If the lard sizzles, it is hot enough to fry the fritters. Dip the apple slices, a few at a time, in the batter, coating well on both sides. Carefully drop into the hot oil and fry for 3 to 5 minutes, turning once to lightly brown on both sides. Remove and drain well on the towel-covered rack.

7. To serve, sprinkle the warm fritters generously with cinnamon sugar.

Martha Washington is the subject of this circa 1790 miniature portrait, after John Ramage. It is framed in the same locket with a portrait of her son, John Parke (Jacky) Custis, by Charles Willson Peale.

To Make a Baked Bread Pudding

Bread pudding recipes found in old cookbooks offer numerous preparation suggestions. Many bread puddings are boiled, while others are baked in a crust. Ingredients for seasoning vary; they include grated lemon zest, rose water, vinegar combined with butter, raisins, or currants and such spices as ginger, nutmeg, and cinnamon.

This baked, firm-textured bread pudding is primarily based on a Hannah Glasse recipe, with variations drawn from other sources.[9]

Serves 6 to 8

2 cups half-and-half
3 sticks cinnamon, broken into pieces
3 teaspoons finely grated lemon zest
¼ cup (½ stick) unsalted butter, softened
4 cups breadcrumbs (grated from stale bread)
½ cup currants
½ cup sugar
½ teaspoon salt
¼ teaspoon ground nutmeg
¼ teaspoon ground ginger
2 large eggs, lightly beaten

Boiled Custard or Fairy Butter (both page 169) for serving
  (optional)

RIGHT:
A one-quart Chinese export porcelain or Mandarin-pattern mug, probably one of four sent to Mount Vernon from London in 1766.

1. Preheat the oven to 350°F. Butter a 1½- to 2-quart baking dish.
2. In a saucepan, combine the half-and-half with the cinnamon sticks and lemon zest. Scald (bring just below the boil) over medium heat, whisking constantly. Do not let the milk boil. Remove from the heat, stir in the butter, and set aside to cool to room temperature. Stir occasionally.
3. Combine the breadcrumbs with the currants in a large bowl. Add the sugar, salt, nutmeg, and ginger, and combine well.
4. When the milk has cooled, strain and discard the cinnamon sticks. Whisk in the eggs. Pour into the breadcrumb mixture, and combine thoroughly.
5. Pour into the prepared baking dish and bake for 45 to 60 minutes, or until a knife inserted in the center comes out clean. Set aside to cool to room temperature before serving.
6. Serve slices of the bread pudding with Boiled Custard or Fairy Butter, if desired.

One of many traditional table-setting diagrams found in The Complete Practical Cook, *a popular book by Charles Carter published in England in 1730. Diagrams such as this one guided the proper setting of an elaborate table with many courses.*

This delicate Quire of Paper Pancakes is sprinkled with sugar, covered with stewed fruit, and served on a color-ful Duke of Gloucester plate by Mottahedeh.

A Quire of Paper Pancakes

This delicate dessert pancake recipe from Hannah Glasse was very fashionable during the eighteenth century and might have been found on the Washingtons' table as part of a second course.

Quire is a Middle English term meaning twenty-four or twenty-five sheets of paper of the same size and stock. It is used here to help the cook visualize the desired paper-thinness of the pancake. "[B]utter the Pan for the first Pancake; let them run as thin as possible," Glasse instructed. Her words were repeated verbatim in a Mary Randolph recipe written some seventy-five years later.[10]

Makes 18 to 20 pancakes

¾ cup sifted all-purpose flour
10 tablespoons sugar, plus more for sprinkling over
    pancakes
1 teaspoon ground nutmeg
3 large egg yolks
1½ cups heavy cream, plus more as needed
6 tablespoons unsalted butter, melted and cooled,
    plus more for frying
5 tablespoons sherry
1 teaspoon orange-flower water

Stewed fruit or preserves for serving (optional)
Lightly whipped cream for serving (optional)

1. Sift together the flour, sugar, and nutmeg.
2. Beat the egg yolks until smooth and lemon colored. Combine with the cream and melted butter, mixing together well. Gradually add to the flour mixture, blending thoroughly. Stir in the sherry and orange-flower water. Cover and refrigerate for at least 2 hours, or as long as overnight.
3. Preheat the oven to 200°F.
4. When ready to cook the pancakes, melt about 1 teaspoon of butter in a small sauté pan set over medium to medium-low heat. Make a small test pancake to ensure that the pan is the right temperature and that the batter has the right consistency. The batter can be thinned with a little milk or cream, if necessary; it should have the consistency of pudding, falling in splats from a spoon.
5. Prepare one pancake at a time, using a scant ¼ cup of batter per pancake. Pour the batter into the hot pan, tilting it so the batter can run evenly over the bottom. Cook until slightly puffy and pale yellow, 1½ to 2 minutes, until set.
6. Slide the pancake onto a plate, and sprinkle with sugar. Set aside in the oven to keep warm while preparing the rest of the pancakes, stacking and sprinkling sugar over each one.
7. Serve the pancakes plain in a stack, or serve them one at a time filled with stewed fruit or preserves, rolled (if desired), and topped with lightly whipped cream.

These English silver-plate cream and sugar pails and ladle bear the Washington family crest, a winged griffin. The cream pail still has its original cobalt-blue glass liner. Both pails were used when serving tea.

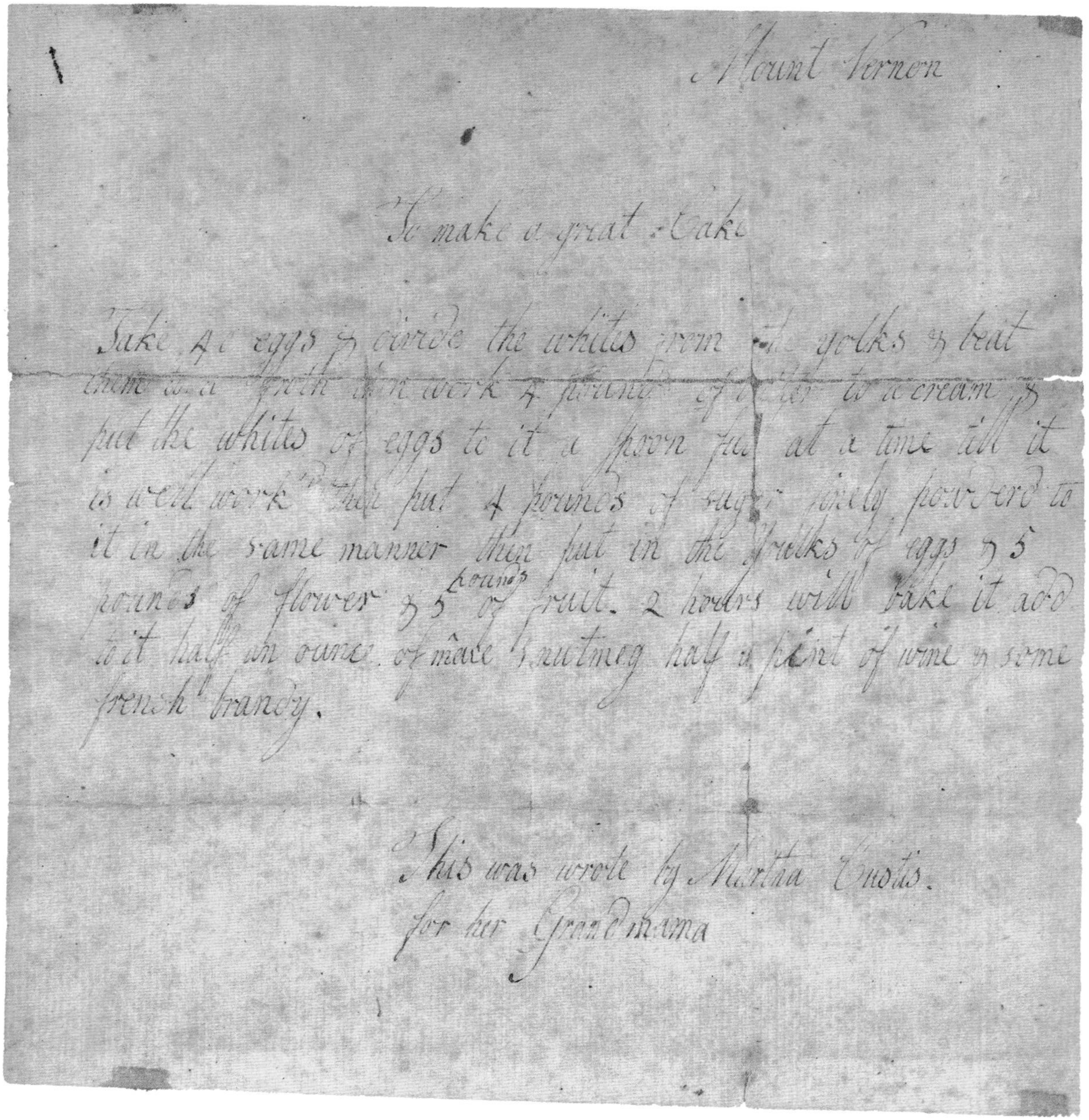

Mount Vernon

To make a great Cake

Take 4c eggs & divide the whites from the yolks & beat
them to a froth then work 4 pounds of butter to a cream &
put the whites of eggs to it a spoon full at a time till it
is well work'd then put 4 pounds of sugar finely powdered to
it in the same manner then put in the yolks of eggs & 5
pounds of flower & 5 pounds of fruit. 2 hours will bake it add
to it half an ounce of mace & nutmeg half a pint of wine & some
french brandy.

This was wrote by Martha Custis.
for her Grandmama

*Martha Washington's original
recipe To Make a Great Cake
was so popular that she asked
her granddaughter Martha
Parke Custis to write it out
for other family members. See
page 187 for the modern adaptation of this classic recipe.*

CAKES & SMALL CONFECTIONS

In the Washington household, cakes were part of the festive displays included in a second course at dinner and were served at tea and at the popular levées Mrs. Washington hosted during her husband's presidential years.

Cake making was one of the domestic accomplishments expected of gentry women, and although slave cooks carried out the tedious, more difficult preparations, the mistress of the house directed the operation, often doing the icing and decorating herself.

Detailed instructions for baking cakes are found in several early cookbooks, illustrating techniques that produced elegant and delicious results. One recipe comes from Elizabeth Raffald, an important eighteenth-century cookbook author whose work is often overshadowed by that of the better-known Hannah Glasse. Raffald's directions in *The Experienced English House-keeper* are clear: "When you make any kind of cakes, be sure that you get the things ready before you begin," she wrote, "then beat your eggs well . . . [or] your cakes will not be light."[1] Glasse recommended that when butter was used, it should be beaten to a "fine cream" before adding sugar "with your hands." Raffald cautioned her reader, above all, to "follow the directions of your receipt . . . [for] the management must be left to the maker's care."[2]

The selection of recipes for cakes and other baked confections that follows is representative of ones that were known and enjoyed in the Washingtons' day. Note that the only leavening agents employed are eggs or yeast, as was the case during that period. All ingredients should be at room temperature when preparation begins, and eggs should be well beaten in the batters to ensure a good rise.

Pound Cake

———◆———

The name *pound cake* stems from the fact that early recipes called for one pound apiece of butter, sugar, flour, and eggs. Mary Randolph's recipe is a delicious version of this classic treat.[3]

Makes one 10-inch Bundt cake

2 cups (4 sticks) unsalted butter
2 cups sugar
6 large eggs
3½ cups sifted all-purpose flour
1½ teaspoons ground nutmeg
1 teaspoon freshly grated lemon zest
¼ cup brandy

Boiled Custard (page 169) for serving (optional)

1. Preheat the oven to 350°F. Grease a 10-inch Bundt pan with vegetable shortening.
2. In the bowl of an electric mixer, or in a large bowl, beating by hand, cream the butter until it is light and fluffy. Add the sugar gradually while continuing to beat.
3. Add the eggs, one at a time, beating in each one thoroughly before adding the next.
4. Sift the flour with the nutmeg, and gradually add to the butter and sugar, mixing in each addition thoroughly before adding the next one.
5. Add the lemon zest and brandy, mixing until thoroughly combined.
6. Pour the batter into the prepared pan. Bake for 45 to 50 minutes, or until a wooden skewer inserted in the center

comes out clean. Cool the cake in the pan for about 10 minutes. Turn the cake out onto the rack, and allow it to cool completely before slicing.

7. Serve with Boiled Custard, if desired.

Queen Cakes

———— ◆ ————

This recipe for a little cake enjoyed at tea or on festive occasions is based on Hannah Glasse's version.[4] Traditionally, queen cakes were baked in "little fluted tin moulds in fancy shapes,"[5] but mini-muffin pans lined with paper baking cups are more often used today.

The origin of this confection's name is unknown.

Makes 5 dozen cakes

3 large eggs, separated
1 cup (2 sticks) unsalted butter, softened
1¼ cups, plus 2 tablespoons sugar
1¾ cups, plus 2 tablespoons all-purpose flour, sifted
½ teaspoon ground nutmeg
¾ teaspoon ground mace
2 teaspoons ground cinnamon
¾ cup currants
Sanding sugar for sprinkling

1. Preheat the oven to 375°F. Grease five 12-cup mini-muffin pans with vegetable shortening.

2. In the bowl of an electric mixer, or in a large bowl whisking by hand, whip the egg whites to stiff peaks. Pour into a separate bowl, and set aside. Put the egg yolks in the same bowl, and whip or whisk by hand until light and frothy. Set aside.

3. In the bowl of an electric mixer, beat the butter until creamy. Gradually add the sugar, beating in each addition thoroughly before adding the next. With the mixer on the lowest speed, add the whipped egg whites, blending thoroughly. Beat in the egg yolks until well combined.

4. Sift the flour with the nutmeg, mace, and cinnamon. Reserve 2 tablespoons. Gradually add the remainder to the creamed mixture, blending in each addition well before adding the next.

5. Add the reserved 2 tablespoons of spiced flour to the currants and mix. Gently fold into the batter until well combined.

6. Spoon the batter into the prepared pans, filling each cup about two-thirds full. Sprinkle the tops with sanding sugar.

7. Bake the cakes for 12 to 14 minutes, or until a wooden skewer inserted in their centers comes out clean and the tops spring back when lightly touched. Set the cakes on wire racks for 5 to 6 minutes before carefully removing them from the pans to cool thoroughly.

RIGHT:
A colorful Chinese porcelain tea caddy in the Tobacco Leaf pattern, a popular design among Virginia gentry.

****

182 DINING WITH THE WASHINGTONS

Chocolate Puffs

———— ◆ ————

Meringues were introduced to England from France in the early eighteenth century, and were quickly added to the array of sweets to be found there.[6] Chocolate puffs (meringues, really), so called because of their light and delicate appearance, should be made in dry weather, as high humidity will cause them to soften and become sticky.

This recipe combines preparation instructions from Mary Kettilby and Elizabeth Raffald.[7]

Makes 2½ to 3 dozen puffs

3 large egg whites at room temperature
¾ cup superfine sugar
4 tablespoons sifted Dutch-process cocoa

1. Preheat the oven to 200°F. Line baking sheets with parchment paper.
2. In the bowl of an electric mixer, beat the egg whites at medium speed until frothy.
3. Increase the speed to high and gradually add the sugar, about 1 tablespoon at a time, mixing until the sugar is dissolved and the egg whites hold stiff peaks.
4. Reduce the mixing speed to medium low and gradually add the cocoa, beating in each addition until well combined.
5. Drop the meringue in rounded tablespoons about 1½ inches apart on the prepared baking sheets, and bake for 2 hours, or until puffed and firm. Turn off the heat, and let the puffs dry further in the oven for at least 2 more hours, or until they are cooled and crisp.
6. Store the puffs in a covered tin for up to 3 days.

Shrewsbury Cakes

———— ◆ ————

These crisp, buttery cookies, of which many varieties exist, have been known in England since at least the 1500s. They can be flavored with spices such as nutmeg and cinnamon. Although their taste is similar to that of shortbread, they are rolled thin and cut into rounds. The late food historian Alan Davidson wrote that Shrewsbury cakes "always appear to have been known for their crisp, brittle texture."[8]

This recipe is based on the one found in Hannah Glasse's cookbook. Serve Shrewsbury cakes within a day of baking to ensure they maintain that characteristic crispness.

Makes about 4 dozen cakes

1 cup (2 sticks) unsalted butter, softened
3½ cups sifted all-purpose flour
1 cup sugar, plus more for sprinkling
2 large eggs, lightly beaten
1 tablespoon rose water
2 tablespoons heavy cream

1. In the bowl of an electric mixer, or in a large bowl beating by hand, cream the butter until light and fluffy.
2. Stir together the flour and sugar. Add to the butter gradually, mixing together well.
3. Stir together the eggs, rose water, and cream. Gradually add to the butter mixture, blending until smooth. Wrap the dough in waxed paper or plastic wrap, and refrigerate for at least 1 hour.
4. Preheat the oven to 375°F. Grease baking sheets with vegetable shortening.
5. Turn the dough out onto a lightly floured surface. Roll ¼ inch thick and cut into 3-inch rounds, or other desired shapes. Sprinkle with additional sugar.
6. Place the cakes on the prepared baking sheets, and bake for 8 to 10 minutes, or until crisp and slightly browned around the edges. Immediately transfer onto a wire rack, and set aside to cool.
7. Store in an airtight container for up to 2 days.

Lafayette Gingerbread

— ◆ —

Early cookbooks, published and unpublished alike, provide numerous recipes for soft gingerbread cake and crisp gingerbread cookies. Although we have no gingerbread recipes directly associated with Martha Washington, the spicy treat doubtless was enjoyed in the Washington household. In March 1759, for instance, an invoice for forty-nine pounds of "Cenemont [cinnamon] Gingerbread" arrived at Mount Vernon, billed to the estate of Martha's first husband, Daniel Parke Custis, who had died two years earlier. Her new husband, George Washington, promptly paid the bill. References to subsequent purchases of gingerbread over the years are documented as well.[9]

Gingerbread recipes are found in several relatives' manuscripts, from those in the Custis family's "Booke of Cookery," which may date back to the seventeenth century, up to the mid-nineteenth-century recipes compiled by Martha Washington's great-granddaughter Mary Anna Randolph Custis Lee (Mrs. Robert E. Lee).[10]

One of the better-known family-connected gingerbread recipes is attributed to George Washington's mother, Mary Ball Washington, who is said to have served it to the Marquis de Lafayette when he visited her in Fredericksburg toward the end of her life; it came to be called Lafayette Gingerbread, in honor of the beloved French general. That recipe calls for orange juice and orange zest, ingredients that are substituted for the lemon used in Eliza Leslie's recipe, from which the one here is adapted.[11]

This gingerbread is delicious on its own, but it can also be served with orange-scented Fairy Butter (page 169) spread on top.

Makes one 9-inch-square cake

½ cup (1 stick) unsalted butter, softened
½ cup plus 2 tablespoons packed dark brown sugar
1 cup molasses
Scant 2¾ cups sifted all-purpose flour

1 tablespoon ground ginger
1 teaspoon ground cinnamon
½ teaspoon ground cloves
¼ teaspoon ground allspice
2 large eggs, plus 2 large egg whites, lightly beaten
¼ cup fresh orange juice
1 tablespoon freshly grated orange zest

Fairy Butter for serving (optional)

1. Preheat the oven to 350°F. Butter a 9-inch-square cake pan.

2. In the bowl of an electric mixer, or in a large bowl beating by hand, combine the butter and brown sugar and beat until light and fluffy. Add the molasses, and continue to beat until well combined.

3. Sift the flour with the ginger, cinnamon, cloves, and allspice.

4. Alternately add the eggs and flour to the butter mixture, beating very well after each addition.

5. Add the orange juice and zest, and continue beating for several minutes until the batter is smooth and light.

6. Pour the batter into the prepared pan, and bake for 35 to 45 minutes, or until a wooden skewer inserted in the center comes out clean. Set the cake on a rack to cool completely in the pan before slicing.

7. Serve squares of the cake spread with Fairy Butter, if desired.

OPPOSITE:
Detail of John Vanderlyn's painting Washington and Lafayette at the Battle of Brandywine *(ca. 1825).*

RIGHT:
A teapot from the celebrated service bearing the insignia of the Society of the Cincinnati, sent to George Washington, the society's first president general, by his wartime comrade Henry (Light-Horse Harry) Lee.

Mary Randolph's Chocolate Cakes are actually a type of shortbread cookie and contain no chocolate, but they are delicious—especially when eaten, as directed, dipped in Chocolate Cream (see recipe on page 210).

Chocolate Cakes

— ·◆· —

The name of this recipe, which comes from Mary Randolph's *The Virginia House-Wife*, can be misleading, as it contains no chocolate. Instead, these are very crisp, thin cookies that are to be dipped in Chocolate Cream (page 210). Randolph provided a guideline for presenting the cakes: "[P]ut them in the plate in rows to checker each other, and serve them to eat with chocolate."[12]

Randolph's directions call for making the little cakes on a griddle. For ease of preparation, oven-baking directions are provided here.

Makes 5 to 6 dozen cakes

1¾ cups loosely packed dark brown sugar
Scant 3¾ cups all-purpose flour
½ cup (1 stick) unsalted butter
¾ cup whole milk

1. Add the brown sugar to the flour, and mix together until well combined.
2. Heat the butter and milk together over medium-low heat, stirring until the milk is very warm and the butter begins to melt. Remove from the heat, and set aside to cool to lukewarm.
3. By hand, work the butter and milk into the flour and sugar, kneading until well combined. Continue to knead until the ingredients are thoroughly incorporated and the dough is smooth. Shape into a ball, wrap in plastic wrap, and refrigerate for at least 1 hour.
4. Position a rack in the upper third of the oven. Preheat the oven to 375°F. Grease large baking sheets with vegetable shortening.
5. Divide the dough into thirds, and roll out on a lightly floured surface to about ¼ inch thick. Cut into 1-by-3-inch strips, and place 1 to 1½ inches apart on the prepared baking sheets.

6. Bake the cakes for 8 to 9 minutes, or until they are lightly browned on the bottoms. With a spatula, immediately transfer them to wire racks and cool completely.
7. Store the cakes for up to 3 days in airtight containers.

To Make a Great Cake

— ·◆· —

This is one of the few surviving recipes directly associated with Mrs. Washington. It was so well liked that she had her granddaughter Martha Parke Custis copy it down for use by other members of the family. Great cake likely would have been served as part of a grand Christmas dinner or Twelfth Night party. It might also have been served at tea.

Martha Washington's recipe, like many others of its time, is vague regarding certain ingredients as well as method of preparation. For that reason, we drew upon related period recipes, besides Mrs. Washington's, to develop a great cake resembling the one her family knew. Sources included the original Custis family recipe, Hannah Glasse's Rich Cake, and Elizabeth Raffald's Bride Cake.[13] The result is a rich confection, laced with brandy and Madeira, that is similar to the fruitcakes we are familiar with today. Although this cake takes some time to prepare, it keeps well when wrapped in aluminum foil and stored in a covered cake tin.

Lacking baking soda or baking powder, eighteenth-century cooks relied on such leavening agents as liquid yeast and eggs, which often yielded cakes heavier and denser than the light, soft ones we enjoy today. This cake is delicious if left plain, but it can become dry fairly quickly. For this reason, it is even better iced, as the sugary coating helps keep it moist. We don't know if Mrs. Washington iced her great cake, but provided here is a recipe for a sugar icing based on Elizabeth Raffald's version—a classic that is still prepared today.

Makes one 10-inch tube cake

1½ cups currants
⅓ cup chopped candied orange peel
⅓ cup chopped candied lemon peel
⅓ cup chopped candied citron
¾ cup Madeira, divided
¼ cup French brandy
3 cups all-purpose flour, sifted
½ cup slivered almonds
½ teaspoon ground nutmeg
½ teaspoon ground mace
¾ cup unsalted butter, softened
1½ cups sugar
3 large eggs, separated

Sugar Icing (recipe follows) (optional)

1. Combine the currants, orange and lemon peels, and citron in a large bowl. Add ½ cup of the Madeira, and stir to combine. Cover with plastic wrap, and set aside for at least 3 hours, or as long as overnight. Stir the remainder of the Madeira together with the brandy, cover, and set aside.

2. When ready to bake the cake, preheat the oven to 325°F. Grease and flour a 10-inch tube pan.

3. Drain the fruits in a large strainer set over a bowl, stirring occasionally to extract as much of the Madeira as possible. Add the strained Madeira to the set-aside Madeira and brandy.

4. Combine ¼ cup of the flour with the fruit, and mix well. Add the almonds, and set aside. Sift the remaining flour with the nutmeg and mace.

5. In the bowl of an electric mixer, cream the butter until it is light. Add the sugar, ½ cup at a time, beating for several minutes after adding each ingredient. Whisk the egg yolks until they are light and smooth, and add them to the butter and sugar. Continue to beat for several minutes, until the mixture is light and fluffy.

6. Alternately add the spiced flour, ½ cup at a time, and the Madeira and brandy, beating until smooth.

7. In a separate bowl, beat the egg whites to form stiff peaks. By hand, gently fold them into the batter, combining lightly until well blended. By hand, fold in the fruit in thirds, mixing until well combined.

8. Pour the batter into the prepared pan, smoothing the top with an offset spatula or the back of a spoon. Bake for about 1½ hours, or until a wooden skewer inserted in the center comes out clean. Set the cake on a wire rack to cool in the pan for 20 minutes. If serving the cake plain, turn it out of the pan to cool completely. If finishing it with icing, turn the warm cake out of the pan onto a baking sheet, and proceed with the icing.

9. To ice the cake, spread Sugar Icing generously onto the surface, piling it high and swirling it around the top and sides. Set in the turned-off warm oven, and let sit for at least 3 hours, or until the cake is cool and the icing has hardened. The icing will crumble when the cake is sliced.

Sugar Icing

———◆———

3 large egg whites at room temperature
1½ cups sugar
2 tablespoons rose water or orange-flower water

1. In the bowl of an electric mixer, start beating the egg whites on low speed, gradually adding 2 tablespoons of the sugar. After about 3 minutes, or when they just begin to form soft peaks, increase the speed to high and continue adding the sugar, 2 tablespoons at a time, beating until all the sugar is incorporated and the egg whites form soft peaks.

2. Add the rose water, and continue beating to form stiff peaks. Use immediately to ice the cake.

This modern adaptation of Martha Washington's Great Cake is based on several period recipes. Full of candied fruits and baked with Madeira and brandy, the delicious confection is shown here encased in a classic sugar icing.

CUSTARDS,
ICE CREAMS & FRUIT

British culinary historian C. Anne Wilson writes that eighteenth-century fare "was rich with butter and cream." Nowhere is this more evident than in the dozens of recipes found in early cookbooks for cream-based desserts.[1] These were fancy dishes that included creams, custards, blancmanges, jellies, and the like, arrayed on elegant salvers and epergnes (decorative centerpieces for serving sweets and fruits) as part of the second course.

Often, the mistress of the house herself fixed these elegant desserts; she would have learned to make them as part of her training in proper household skills. Nelly Custis once complained of a headache she developed from her efforts to create a dessert for some dinner guests. The headache was so severe, she wrote, that she missed her own party, having retreated to her room after taking medicine to relieve it.[2]

Very Good Custards

Ten china custard cups were listed in the inventory of the pantry taken after George Washington's death, perhaps part of an order from England he placed in 1761. Although custard is not specifically mentioned in Mount Vernon meal descriptions, the presence of such a set indicates that the dessert was frequently served on the Washingtons' table.

This recipe comes from Mary Kettilby's *A Collection of above Three Hundred Receipts in Cookery, Physick, and Surgery*, which was first published in 1714, preceding the better-known works of Hannah Glasse by three decades. Glasse appears to have "drawn on" Kettilby's book. In her preface, Kettilby assured readers that "the Desire of doing Good was

the sole Motive that at first engaged [her] in this Work."[3] It appears she gathered recipes from several sources, although they are not attributed. Five editions of Mary Kettilby's book were issued—the last one posthumously, in 1734.

Serves 8

4 cups heavy cream
¾ cup sugar
8 large egg yolks
2 teaspoons orange-flower water

1. Preheat the oven to 325°F.
2. Pour the heavy cream into a medium saucepan and scald (bring just below the boiling point) over medium heat.

OPPOSITE:
This pair of Chinese porcelain ice cream chillers, or iceries, was used for serving ice creams or custards and are shown in the Mansion's small dining room. Both the bowl-shaped lid and the deep outer vessel held ice, while a shallow inner bowl contained the ice cream.

LEFT:
Eleanor (Nelly) Parke Custis, was raised in the home of her grandparents, George and Martha Washington. She kept a housekeeping book that included a recipe for Rice Pancakes (see page 202).

Remove from the heat and add the sugar, stirring until it is completely dissolved.

3. Whisk the egg yolks in a medium bowl until slightly foamy. Slowly blend about ½ cup of the hot cream mixture into the egg yolks, whisking constantly. Pour the mixture into the hot cream, and stir in the orange-flower water. Set the pan over low heat and, stirring constantly, cook until the custard thickens just enough to coat the back of the spoon. In order to prevent the egg yolks from curdling, do not let the custard boil.

4. Remove the custard from the heat, and divide it among eight 4- to 6-ounce custard cups or ramekins. Carefully arrange the filled cups in a 13-by-9-by-2-inch baking dish. Pour enough boiling water into the dish to come about one-third of the way up the sides of the cups, being careful not to drip any water into the custards.

5. Bake the custards for 45 to 60 minutes, or until a knife inserted in the centers comes out clean. Remove the custards from the pan, and set on a wire rack to cool completely. Cover each custard with plastic wrap, and set in the refrigerator to chill for at least 8 hours, or overnight, before serving.

A covered, or custard cup of Chinese export porcelain (ca. 1790–1840). This cup would have been part of a large service and was likely used to serve custard when the Washingtons dined with their close friend Elizabeth Willing Powel of Philadelphia.

Blancmange

Blancmange (white food) was found on tables throughout western Europe during medieval times and the Renaissance, although it was then part of the first course and prepared in a very different form than the dessert we know today. According to the late food historian Alan Davidson, "the 14th- and 15th-century English *blancmangers* were made with shredded chicken breast, sugar, rice, and either ground almonds or almond milk," though he added that there were many variations to be found. Although there is speculation that blancmange originated in the Middle East, its provenance is uncertain.[4] By the eighteenth century, the dish had evolved into the sweet jellied dessert that would have been known to the Washingtons.

Included in the second course at dinner, blancmange was, according to Hannah Glasse, a "fine side dish." She suggested serving Stewed Pears (page 196) as an accompaniment.[5]

Serves 6 to 8

4 cups heavy cream
2 tablespoons unflavored powdered gelatin
¾ cup sugar
1 tablespoon rose water
2 teaspoons orange-flower water

Sugared grapes for garnish (optional)

1. In a saucepan over medium heat, warm the cream slightly.

2. Combine the gelatin with ½ cup of cream, and set aside for about 5 minutes to soften. Add to the warm cream and heat until it comes to a slight simmer, stirring constantly to dissolve the gelatin. Do not let the mixture boil.

3. Remove from the heat and add the sugar, stirring until it is dissolved. Set the custard aside to cool, stirring occasionally to prevent a skin from forming on the surface. When it is lukewarm, add the rose water and orange-flower water, combining well.

4. Rinse a 4- to 6-cup mold in cold water. Pour in the custard, cover, and refrigerate until firmly set, 6 to 8 hours.
5. When the blancmange is set, quickly dip the mold in very hot water and turn it into a serving dish. Cover and keep refrigerated until ready to serve.
6. Serve garnished with sugared grapes, if desired.

Snow and Cream

———◆———

This is a classic *oeufs à la neige* (snow eggs), served during the second course at dinner. Here, *snow* refers to the poached meringues, and *cream* is the custard in which they are floated. Elizabeth Raffald suggested snow and cream as "a pretty supper dish."[6]

Serves 6 to 8

3 large egg whites
6 tablespoons sugar
2½ cups whole milk

Cooled Boiled Custard (page 169) for serving

1. Beat the egg whites to soft peaks, gradually adding the sugar. Once all the sugar is incorporated, continue beating the meringue to stiff peaks.
2. Bring the milk to a simmer over medium-low heat. Using a tablespoon or soupspoon, shape the meringue into ovals and drop into the simmering milk. Poach gently for 4 to 5 minutes, turning once. The cooked meringues will be puffed and firm. Use a slotted spoon to remove the meringues from the milk, and set on paper towels to drain.
3. Pour the Boiled Custard into a serving bowl, and place the poached meringues on the surface. Cover and set in the refrigerator to chill for at least 2 hours before serving.

Peach Ice Cream

———◆———

Washington kept extensive records on planting and gardening at Mount Vernon. Orchards abounded, with peach and apple trees predominating. His diaries contain numerous details about the planting and fencing of peach trees, notes on their spring blooms and the ripening of the fruit, and descriptions of how slave women gathered the fruit for drying or for making peach brandy.

In early August 1767, Martha and George Washington traveled with their friends Sally and George Fairfax to what is now Berkeley Springs, West Virginia, where they settled in to enjoy the cool mountain air. The Washingtons' cook accompanied the party and "soon laid in" food supplies such as meats and various vegetables and fruits, including peaches.[7] The peaches could be eaten fresh or used to make ice cream—a welcome treat on an August day.

In her peach ice cream recipe, adapted here for the modern kitchen, Mary Randolph called for "fine soft peaches, perfectly ripe" that should be chopped "very small."[8]

Makes about 2 quarts

3 pounds fresh ripe peaches, peeled, pitted, thinly sliced
1¼ cups sugar, divided, plus more as needed
3 cups heavy cream
3 cups half-and-half

1. Stir together the peaches and ½ cup of the sugar. Set aside, stirring occasionally to dissolve the sugar.
2. Scald the cream (bring just below the boiling point), remove from the heat, and add the remaining ¾ cup sugar, stirring to dissolve. Blend in the half-and-half.
3. Coarsely mash the peaches, either by hand or in a food processor, and then combine with the cream and half-and-half, stirring well. Cover tightly with plastic wrap, and refrigerate for at least 3 hours.
4. When ready to freeze, stir the mixture and add more sugar, if desired. Freeze in an ice-cream machine according to the manufacturer's directions.

Raspberry Ice Cream, a sweet and refreshing treat from the eighteenth century.

Raspberry Ice Cream

Raspberries were a favorite among eighteenth-century Virginians, particularly in desserts. As the witty and socially prominent Virginian Anne Blair happily noted in a 1769 letter, "I am going to Dinner, after which we have a dessert of fine Raspberry's & cream."[9]

This flavorful dish is based on Mary Randolph's recipe. She observed that ice cream should be made "very sweet, for much of the sugar [taste] is lost in the operation of freezing."[10]

Makes about 1½ quarts

3 to 4 cups fresh or frozen raspberries
1¼ cups sugar, plus more as needed
1 recipe Boiled Custard (page 169), chilled

1. Press the raspberries through a sieve to remove the seeds. (If using frozen berries, thaw them first, and then press them.) Add the sugar, and stir to dissolve. Stir in the custard. Cover and set aside in the refrigerator to chill for at least 2 hours.
2. When ready to freeze, stir the raspberry custard and add additional sugar, if desired. Freeze in an ice-cream machine according to the manufacturer's directions.

Orange Fool

Made with such fruits as gooseberries, strawberries, and raspberries, fools have been popular desserts in Britain since at least the early seventeenth century. According to food historian C. Anne Wilson, they were served as part of the second course in the eighteenth century. Renowned food historian Alan Davidson wrote that "oranges were added to the list of fruits" used in fools during that period.[11]

This recipe is based on one by Hannah Glasse.[12]

Serves 6 to 8

4 large eggs
1 cup fresh orange juice
¾ cup sugar
¼ teaspoon ground cinnamon
⅛ teaspoon ground nutmeg
2 cups heavy cream
2 teaspoons unsalted butter, softened (optional)
2 oranges, peeled and segmented

1. Beat the eggs until light. Add the orange juice, and combine well. Blend in the sugar, cinnamon, and nutmeg.
2. Scald the cream (bring just below the boiling point) over medium to medium-low heat, stirring to prevent burning.
3. Very slowly, add ½ cup of the hot cream to the egg mixture, whisking steadily. When well blended, stir it into the hot cream. Cook over low heat, stirring constantly until it thickens enough to coat the back of a spoon. Do not let it boil, or the eggs will curdle. Remove from the heat, add the butter (if desired), and pour into a bowl. Set aside to cool, stirring occasionally.
4. Chop about half of the orange segments, and drain in a colander. Fold into the cooled custard, and pour into a serving dish. Cover with plastic wrap, and set aside in the refrigerator to chill for at least 2 hours before serving.
5. When ready to serve, top the fool with the remaining orange segments.

LEFT:
Raspberries still grow in Mount Vernon's lower garden.

Stewed Pears

The title of this Hannah Glasse recipe may confuse modern readers. Her directions specify baked, not stewed, pears, although they are to be baked in red wine or port if the recipe below is followed. Glasse noted that the fruit "will [also] be very good with water in the place of wine." As an alternative to baking, she suggested stewing the pears in a saucepan set over a low fire, using the same ingredients.[13]

When the pears are thinly sliced and prepared in this manner, they can be used as a filling for Glasse's Quire of Paper Pancakes (page 179). Whether we call them "stewed" or "baked," the pears in the following recipe are lovely paired with Glasse's Blancmange (page 192).

Serves 6 to 8

6 to 8 large ripe pears, peeled, halved lengthwise, and cored
1½ tablespoons freshly grated lemon zest
½ cup sugar
3 cloves
1 cup red wine or port

1. Preheat the oven to 350°F.
2. Arrange the pears in a single layer in a 9-by-13-by-2-inch baking dish. Sprinkle the lemon zest and sugar over the pear halves, and place the cloves in the dish. Pour the wine over the pears.
3. Cover the dish with aluminum foil, and bake for 25 to 35 minutes, or until the fruit is easily pierced with a skewer or paring knife, basting occasionally with the liquid. The pears should be tender but not soft enough to break into pieces.
4. Remove the pears from the oven, and set aside to cool completely in the baking dish before serving.

Compote of Apples

This recipe is adapted from Mary Randolph's version.[14] The apples, thinly sliced, can also be used as a filling for Quire of Paper Pancakes (page 179).

Serves 6 to 8

1½ cups water
½ cup plus 2 tablespoons sugar
½ teaspoon ground cinnamon, or 2 cinnamon sticks
3 pounds cooking apples (such as Granny Smith or Pippin), peeled, cored, and quartered
Zest of ½ lemon, cut into thin strips

Boiled Custard (page 169) for serving (optional)

1. In a large Dutch oven or saucepan, bring the water to a boil over medium-high heat. Add ½ cup of the sugar, and stir until dissolved. Add the cinnamon and lemon zest.
2. Add the apples, and stir to coat with the liquid. Bring to a boil, and then immediately reduce the heat to medium low. Cover and simmer for 15 to 20 minutes, until the apples are tender (but not mushy), occasionally basting them with the liquid.
3. Remove the apples to a serving dish, reserving the liquid in the pan. (If cinnamon sticks are used, remove and discard them.) Using a slotted spoon, remove and reserve the lemon zest and set aside to cool.
4. Add the remaining 2 tablespoons of sugar to the reserved cooking liquid, and bring to a boil over high heat. Boil uncovered until the liquid is reduced and syrupy. Set aside to cool briefly, and pour over the apples. Lay the reserved lemon zest over the apples.
5. Serve the compote warm or chilled as a side dish with Boiled Custard, if desired.

Stewed Pears, which are actually baked in red wine and sugar, are served on Martha Washington's States china, reproduced by Woodmere.

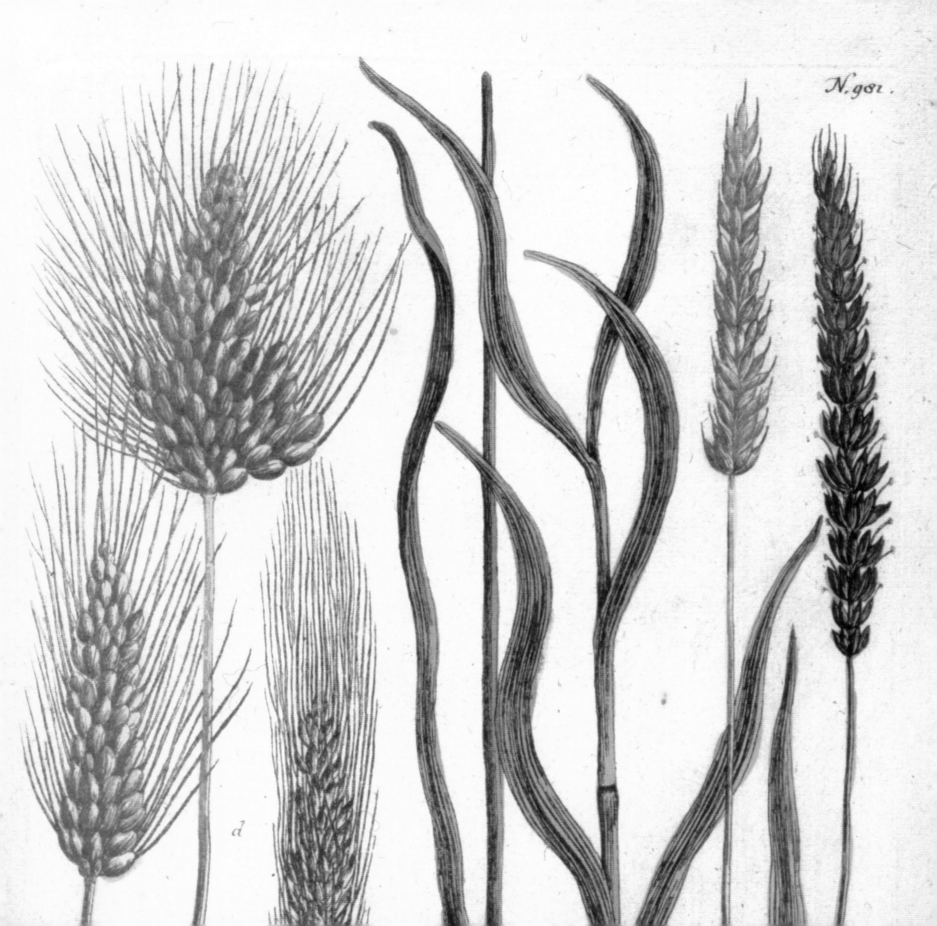

d

BREADS

Hot bread was an important food on Virginia tables, usually served at every meal. Housewives prided themselves on providing well-made breads to family members and guests alike, and numerous recipes for them appear both in published and manuscript form.

French Rolls

In genteel households, small rolls of French bread were individually tucked into linen napkins by each diner's plate for the beginning of the meal. This practice arose after King Charles II returned from exile in 1660 to reclaim the British throne, bringing various elements of French culture with him and consequently making them fashionable both in England and its colonies. Martha Washington's grandson, George Washington Parke Custis, noted the observance of this mealtime nicety at Mount Vernon in his memoirs.[1]

Recipes for French rolls are found in numerous cookbooks of the period. This one is derived from recipes by E. Smith and Mary Randolph.[2]

Makes about 20 rolls

1 teaspoon active dry yeast
¼ cup lukewarm water
¾ cup whole milk
2 tablespoons unsalted butter, softened
4 cups sifted all-purpose flour
2 teaspoons salt
2 large eggs
Melted butter for brushing

1. Sprinkle the yeast over the water, and set aside to proof for 5 to 10 minutes, or until the yeast bubbles.

2. Combine the milk and butter, and warm over low heat until the milk warms and the butter begins to melt. Remove from the heat, and set aside.

3. Sift the flour with the salt into a large bowl. Gradually blend in the warm milk, mixing together until combined. Add the eggs, one at a time, blending well after each addition. Stir the yeast and water together and add to the dough, mixing thoroughly. The dough will be sticky.

4. Turn the dough out onto a lightly floured surface and knead for about 10 minutes, until smooth and elastic. Shape the dough into a ball and place in a buttered bowl, turning to coat with butter. Cover with plastic wrap and set in a warm place to rise about 2 hours, or until doubled in bulk. Punch down the dough, cover with plastic wrap, and refrigerate for at least 8 hours, or overnight.

5. Grease two 9-inch French-roll or round cake pans with vegetable shortening.

6. To finish the rolls, break off pieces of dough, each about the size of a large egg. Shape into rounds, and arrange about ½ inch apart in the prepared pans. Cover with towels, and set aside to rise again in a warm place until doubled, about 1 hour.

7. Preheat the oven to 400°F. Position the rack in the upper third of the oven.

8. Bake the rolls for 15 to 20 minutes, or until golden brown. Turn out of the pans onto a wire rack to cool slightly.

9. Brush the rolls with melted butter and serve warm. They are best eaten directly out of the oven but will keep for about a day. Store leftover cooled rolls in plastic wrap or aluminum foil. To warm the rolls, set them on a baking sheet and heat in a 250°F oven for 10 to 15 minutes.

OPPOSITE:
Several varieties of wheat, as illustrated in the Taalryk register *(ca. 1748), published by German apothecary and botanist Johann Wilhelm Weimann.*

Hoecakes

———

Family members and visitors alike testified that hoecakes were among George Washington's favorite foods. He invariably ate them at breakfast, covered with butter and honey, along with hot tea—a "temperate repast" enjoyed each morning.[3]

Years after Washington's death, Nelly Custis Lewis described her method for preparing a yeast-risen version of hoecakes in a letter to her close friend Elizabeth Bordley Gibson. "Make it by candlelight," she wrote, "& let it remain [by a warm hearth] until the next morning." Describing the baking method, she wrote: "[D]rop [the batter] a spoonful at a time on a hoe or griddle (as we say in the South). When done on one side turn the other—the griddle must be rubbed . . . with a piece of beef suet."[4]

"A Box of China for Lady Washington" was among the goods that arrived in Philadelphia in 1796 with Dutch merchant Andreas Everardus van Braam Houckgeest. The porcelain service, in the States pattern, included this covered cup and saucer and features the monogram MW, and state names in a chain motif, to celebrate the unification of the American colonies. The inscription on these pieces, which translates "[Our Union is our] Glory, and [our] Defense against Him," suggests Van Braam's strong belief in the formation of the United States as well as his scorn for the colonies' former ruler, King George III.

Makes about fifteen 4- to 6-inch hoecakes

½ teaspoon active dry yeast
2½ cups white cornmeal, divided
3 to 4 cups lukewarm water
½ teaspoon salt
1 large egg, lightly beaten

Melted butter for drizzling and serving
Honey or maple syrup for serving

1. Mix the yeast and 1¼ cups of the cornmeal in a large bowl. Add 1 cup of the lukewarm water, stirring to combine thoroughly. Mix in ½ cup more of the water, if needed, to give the mixture the consistency of pancake batter. Cover with plastic wrap, and refrigerate for at least 8 hours, or overnight.
2. Preheat the oven to 200°F.
3. When ready to finish the hoecakes, begin by adding ½ to 1 cup of the remaining water to the batter. Stir in the salt and the egg, blending thoroughly.
4. Gradually add the remaining 1¼ cups of cornmeal, alternating with enough additional lukewarm water to make a mixture that is the consistency of waffle batter. Cover with a towel, and set aside at room temperature for 15 to 20 minutes.
5. Heat a griddle on medium-high heat, and lightly grease it with lard or vegetable shortening. Preparing 1 hoecake at a time, drop a scant ¼ cup of the batter onto the griddle and cook on one side for about 5 minutes, or until lightly browned. With a spatula, turn the hoecake over and continue cooking another 4 to 5 minutes, until browned.
6. Place the hoecake on a platter, and set it in the oven to keep warm while making the rest of the cakes. Drizzle each one with melted butter.
7. Serve the hoecakes warm, drizzled with melted butter and honey or maple syrup.

Hoecakes, swimming in honey and butter, were one of George Washington's favorite break-fasts. This simple treat, made with cornmeal, is served here on classic Blue Canton by Mottahedeh.

Rice Pancakes

Although Nelly Custis omitted sugar in her recipe for these lovely, delicate pancakes, published cookbooks of the period often suggested "strewing" sugar over them before sending them to the table.[5] E. Smith, for one, additionally recommended garnishing them with orange, a suggestion also included here.[6] This recipe can be readily doubled.

Makes about 15 pancakes

1½ cups cooked rice
2 cups heavy cream
2 tablespoons unsalted butter, melted, plus more for cooking
2 large eggs, well beaten
½ cup sifted all-purpose flour
1 teaspoon ground cinnamon
¼ teaspoon ground nutmeg
½ to 1 teaspoon salt

Sugar for sprinkling (optional)
Orange slices for garnish

1. Combine the rice, cream, and butter. Add the eggs, stirring together until well blended.
2. Sift the flour with the cinnamon, nutmeg, and salt, and blend thoroughly into the rice mixture. Cover the batter and refrigerate for at least 2 hours, or up to 8 hours.
3. Preheat the oven to 200°F.
4. When you are ready to cook the pancakes, remove the batter from the refrigerator and whisk together well. Melt about 1 tablespoon of butter in a skillet set over medium-high heat. When the butter is sizzling, add a small amount of batter to the pan to test the heat level. If necessary, reduce the heat to medium before cooking the pancakes.
5. For each rice pancake, pour about ¼ cup of the batter into the prepared pan. Cook for 2 to 3 minutes, or until bubbles appear on the surfaces and the edges of the pancakes are lightly browned. Using a spatula, carefully turn the pancakes over and cook about 2 minutes more, until done. Transfer the finished pancakes, separated by parchment paper, to an ovenproof platter, and set them in the oven to keep warm. Prepare the remaining pancakes, adding more butter to the pan as needed.
6. To serve, lightly sprinkle the rice pancakes with sugar, if desired, and garnish with orange slices.

Rice pancakes
Boil half a lb of Rice to a jelly in water, when cold mix it with a pint of cream, 8 eggs well beaten, a desert spoonful of beaten mace, cinnamon or nutmeg, stir in 8 ozs butter creamed, & as much flour as will make the batter thick enough, fry in butter, or as little lard as possible. —
Potatoe fritters
Beat the yolks of 6 eggs very light, add to them a quart of milk, boil as many Irish potatoes as will make a quart, skin & beat them very fine, put them into the milk 2 eggs, & thicken with flour, the thickness of common fritters batter, beat all till

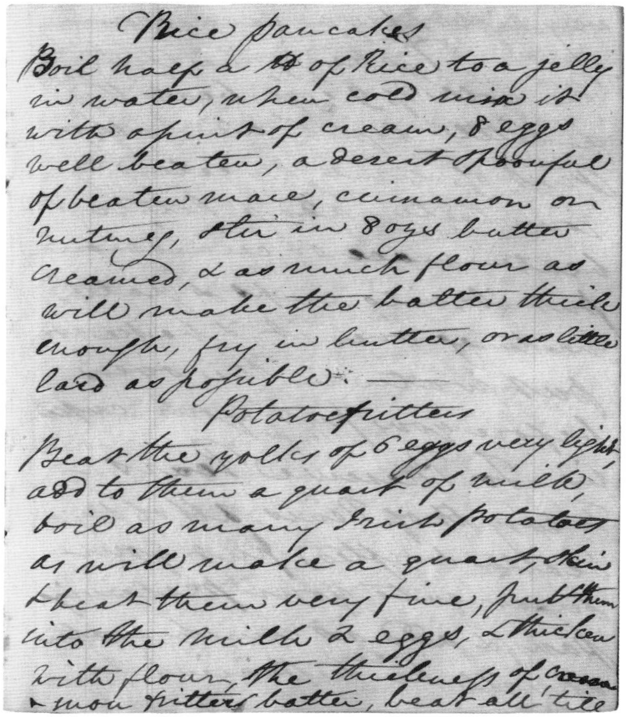

These original recipes for rice pancakes and potato fritters are in the handwriting of Nelly Custis Lewis, granddaughter of Martha Washington. Nelly lived with her grandparents after her father, Martha's son, John (Jacky) Parke Custis, died in 1781. As an adult, Nelly kept a housekeeping manual that included these and many other recipes.

Mrs. Fitzhugh's Buns

———◆———

This recipe for these slightly sweet and spicy buns is adapted from one in a small group of manuscripts in the Mary Custis Lee Papers at the Virginia Historical Society, Richmond.[7] Forgotten for more than a century, these papers were found in 2002 in two wooden trunks at the Burke and Herbert Bank and Trust Company in Alexandria, Virginia. Included are letters, legal papers, journals, and other significant documents, all collected by Mary Custis Lee, eldest daughter of Robert E. Lee. The recipe likely came from Ann Randolph Fitzhugh, the mother-in-law of George Washington Parke Custis.

Makes 12 buns

2 teaspoons active dry yeast
½ cup lukewarm water, divided
½ cup plus 1 tablespoon sugar, divided
2¾ cups sifted all-purpose flour
½ teaspoon ground mace
½ teaspoon ground nutmeg
1 teaspoon ground cinnamon
¼ teaspoon ground coriander
¼ teaspoon salt
2 tablespoons unsalted butter, softened
1 large egg
¼ cup lukewarm milk

1. Sprinkle the yeast over ¼ cup of the water, add 1 teaspoon of the sugar, and set aside to proof until bubbly, about 5 minutes.

2. Sift the flour, mace, nutmeg, cinnamon, coriander, and salt together into a large mixing bowl.

3. Stir together ¼ cup of the remaining sugar with the butter. Add to the spiced flour, mixing with your fingers until crumbly.

4. Whisk the egg together with the remaining ¼ cup plus 2 teaspoons of sugar. Make a well in the center of the flour mixture, and pour in the egg and sugar, proofed yeast, and milk. Stir until well mixed, adding enough of the remaining water to make a soft dough. Put the dough in a buttered bowl, turning to coat with butter. Cover with plastic wrap and a towel, and set aside in a warm place to rise for 1½ to 2 hours, until doubled.

5. Grease a 12-cup muffin pan with vegetable shortening. Push down the dough with a wooden spoon. Divide into 12 pieces, shape into balls, and place in the prepared pan. Cover with a towel, and set aside to rise for about 45 minutes, until doubled.

6. Preheat the oven to 375°F. Position the rack in the upper third of the oven.

7. Bake for 12 to 15 minutes, or until the buns are lightly browned. Watch carefully, as they can easily burn. Immediately remove the buns from the pan, and place on a wire rack to cool.

As the Revolutionary War drew to a close, Washington asked his nephew Bushrod Washington, then studying law in Philadelphia, to learn whether fused silver plate "is fashionable and much used in genteel houses in France and England." Once Bushrod wrote back in the affirmative, his uncle acquired an extensive set of silver-plated wares, including this basket for serving bread as well as cake and other sweetmeats during dessert.

George Washington presided at a table known for its convivial atmosphere, where conversation was "always free, and always agreeable" and where numerous toasts, both ceremonious and sentimental, were offered.[1] Wines that included port, claret, and especially Madeira could be found, along with brandy, beer, and punch.

This tall-stemmed glass vessel may have been one of the many "enameled" wine glasses George Washington acquired for his table in the 1760s and 1770s. The term enameled *refers to the opaque white glass rods embedded in the stem, which glassmakers fashioned into a dazzling variety of spirals and twists. Washington and his guests may have used this small one-ounce glass to partake of strong, sweet liquors after dinner or tea.*

To Make an Excellent Cherry Bounce

Among the few recipes known to have been used by the Washington family is this one for cherry bounce, a brandy-based drink popular in the eighteenth century. It seems to have been such a favorite of General Washington's that he packed a "Canteen" of it, along with Madeira and port, for a trip west across the Allegheny Mountains in September 1784.[2]

This fruity, spiced cordial requires a bit of work and time, but the result is well worth the effort. After pitting, halving, and mashing the cherries, be prepared to set away the sweetened brandied juice for twenty-four hours and then again for about two weeks after infusing it with spices. Enjoy small glasses of cherry bounce at room temperature, and keep the remainder on hand in the refrigerator.

Makes about 3 quarts

10 to 11 pounds fresh sour cherries, preferably Morello,
  or 3 jars (1 pound, 9 ounce) preserved Morello cherries
4 cups brandy
3 cups sugar, plus more as needed
2 cinnamon sticks, broken into pieces
2 to 3 cloves
1 (¼-inch) piece fresh whole nutmeg

1. Pit the cherries, cut them in half, and put them in a large bowl. Using a potato masher, carefully mash the fruit to extract as much juice as possible. Strain the juice through a large fine-mesh strainer, pressing the fruit with a sturdy spoon. (You should have about 8 cups.) Reserve

To Make Excellent Cherry Bounce.

Extract the juice of 20 pounds well ripen'd Morrella Cherrys
add to this 10 quarts of old French brandy and sweeten it with
White Sugar to your taste.— To 5 gallons of this mixture add
one ounce of Spice Such as Cinnamon, Cloves and Nutmegs of
each an Equal quantity Slightly bruis'd and A pint and
half of Cherry kirnels that have been gently broken in a
Mortar— After the liquor has fermented let it Stand close—
Stoped for a month or Six weeks then bottle it. remembering
to put a lump of Loaf Sugar into each bottle. —

*This original recipe was written in an unknown
hand and inserted in a pocket-size memo book
belonging to Martha Washington. Cherry Bounce
was a favorite libation of George Washington.*

the mashed cherries in the freezer or refrigerator for later use. If using jarred cherries, drain the fruit and set the juice aside before halving and mashing the cherries. Add any pressed juice to the reserved jarred juice.

2. In a lidded 1-gallon glass jar, combine the juice with the brandy and sugar, stirring to dissolve the sugar. Cover with the lid, and set aside in the refrigerator for 24 hours, occasionally stirring or carefully shaking the jar.

3. Bring 2 cups of the juice to a simmer over medium heat. Taste the sweetened juice and add more sugar, if desired. Stir in the cinnamon sticks, cloves, and nutmeg. Then cover, and simmer for about 5 minutes. Remove from the heat, and set aside to cool to room temperature. Strain, and discard the spices.

4. Stir the spiced juice back into the 1-gallon glass jar with the reserved sweetened juice. Cover loosely with the lid, and set aside for at least 2 weeks before serving, occasionally shaking the jar with care.

5. Serve at room temperature in small cordial or wine glasses. Store the remaining cherry bounce in the refrigerator.

This colorful punch bowl, made in Jingdezhen, China, around 1735–57, was likely brought to Mount Vernon by Martha Washington from her first marriage, to Daniel Parke Custis. With its delicate design, exquisitely executed in vibrant overglaze enamels of the famille rose *palette, it is the oldest and perhaps finest piece of Chinese export porcelain known to have been owned by the Washingtons. This vessel can hold up to five gallons of drink.*

Punch

Punch has been a popular drink for four centuries. East India merchants introduced it to Britain in the late 1600s. William Byrd II, who founded the city of Richmond, referred to punch as "a very good, pleasant and healthful drink," and Virginians enjoyed the beverage at various social gatherings.[3]

Punch is often mentioned in connection with the Washingtons, who served it at many of their receptions and as part of offering a hospitable welcome to guests at Mount Vernon. For example, Julian Niemcewicz, who visited from Poland in 1798, noted that when he arrived, Martha Washington "appeared after a few minutes, welcomed us most graciously and had punch served."[4]

This sweet and tart libation comes together quickly and easily. Be advised, however, that it needs to be put in the refrigerator for several hours so the ingredients can marry and the punch can chill completely.

Makes about 2 quarts

Juice of 5 limes
Water as needed
1½ cups dark brown sugar
4 cups dark rum
2 cups French brandy

1. Mix the lime juice with an equal amount of water in a lidded 1-gallon jar. Add the sugar, and stir until dissolved. Stir in the rum and brandy, mixing until combined. Cover with the lid, and refrigerate for at least 3 hours, or until well chilled.

2. To serve, place ice rings adorned with lime slices, if desired, in a large bowl, and pour in the punch.

Glasses of Cherry Bounce and syllabub, garnished with raspberries, were popular and refreshing treats at the Washingtons' table.

To Mull Wine

———— ◆ ————

Mulled wine has been popular for hundreds of years, imbibed not only on festive occasions but also because of its healthful ingredients. The inclusion of egg yolks in the hot, spiced drink seems to have disappeared by the nineteenth century, as that ingredient is rarely found in later recipes. When using this eighteenth-century recipe from Elizabeth Raffald, take care in combining the yolks with the hot wine and in pouring the mixture back and forth between two saucepans; this will quickly stop the egg yolks from cooking as well as aerate the thickened drink. Raffald recommended pouring the wine "several times till it looks fine and bright."[5] When correctly prepared, the mixture will indeed appear smooth and velvety.

Over the years, some cooks have suggested buying special pans for making mulled wine. Isabella Beeton, writing more than eighty years after Raffald, recommended the use of "small tin warmers" that could be "purchased for a trifle," noting they were "more suitable than saucepans."[6]

This hot, rich wine is delicious served on its own. It can also be served, as Raffald recommended, in the traditional manner—in chocolate cups (small mugs) with "dry toast cut in long narrow pieces."[7]

Makes about 1½ quarts

1 teaspoon ground nutmeg
4 cups dry red wine, divided
About 1 cup sugar, plus more as needed
6 large egg yolks

Dry toast strips for serving (optional)

1. Stir the nutmeg into 3 cups of the wine. Add the sugar and bring to a boil over medium-high heat, stirring frequently to dissolve the sugar. Remove from the heat as soon as the mixture boils. Taste the sweetened wine and add more sugar, if desired.

2. In the bowl of an electric mixer, beat the egg yolks until they are thick and lemon colored. Mix in the remaining 1 cup of wine. Slowly add the egg mixture to the hot, spiced wine, stirring constantly to prevent the egg yolks from curdling. When the mixture is well combined, pour it back and forth between two saucepans to cool it quickly and incorporate some air.

3. Heat the mulled wine over low heat, stirring constantly, until it is hot and begins to thicken. Make sure the wine remains just below a simmer to prevent the egg yolks from curdling. As soon as it thickens, pour it back and forth between two saucepans several times to cool it quickly and incorporate some air.

4. Serve the mulled wine immediately in mugs or heat-proof glasses, accompanied by toast strips, if desired.

To Make Very Fine Syllabub

Syllabub was another fashionable drink in Colonial America. Known in England since Tudor times, it was sipped or spooned from "special syllabub glasses, so that the effect" of highly whipped cream above, "contrasting with the clear liquid below could be fully appreciated."[8] Whether consumed as a spooned dessert or as a sipped beverage, syllabub has not lost its appeal in modern times. This version is based on popular eighteenth-century recipes by E. Smith and Elizabeth Raffald.[9]

Makes about 6 cups

2½ cups heavy cream
¾ cup sugar
Juice and zest of 1 large lemon
1 cup sweet white wine
½ cup cream sherry

1. Combine the cream, sugar, and lemon zest in the bowl of an electric mixer.
2. Combine the lemon juice, white wine, and sherry, blending together well. Mixing on low speed, slowly pour into the cream mixture, whipping for about 10 minutes until the syllabub is light and foamy.
3. Cover the bowl with plastic wrap, and set in the refrigerator to chill for about 8 hours, or overnight, to let the flavors blend together. Stir the syllabub at least once while chilling to make sure the ingredients are thoroughly combined.
4. Pour the chilled syllabub into small wine glasses, cover with plastic wrap, and refrigerate for at least 8 hours, or overnight.
5. To serve, place the chilled glasses of syllabub on dessert plates set with long-handled spoons.

To Make Lemonade

The Washingtons served simple refreshments at their Friday-night receptions during the presidential years, including nonalcoholic beverages such as orangeade and lemonade.[10] Recipes for lemonade came to England from France and, by the early eighteenth century, were widely used there.[11] English recipes often called for adding white wine to basic lemonade, as is the case in this refreshingly tart recipe from Elizabeth Raffald.

This lemonade is less sweet than those we drink today. Add the two cups of sugar called for, and then stir in more if you want it sweeter—or enough, in Raffald's words, "as will make it pleasant."[12] She also suggested adding white wine and orange juice to the basic recipe. The lemonade is delicious without them, but the wine and juice turn this simple citrus beverage into a refreshing libation.

Makes about 6½ cups

Juice and zest of 6 large lemons
4½ cups water, divided, plus more as needed
2 cups sugar, plus more as needed
2 cups medium-dry white wine (optional)
Juice of 1 orange (optional)

1. Put the zest in a medium saucepan, and pour in 2 cups of the water. Cover and bring to a boil. Immediately turn off the heat and let cool to room temperature.
2. Stir in the lemon juice, add the sugar, and stir to dissolve. Strain, and add enough of the remaining water and more sugar, if desired, to suit your taste.
3. Stir in the wine and orange juice, if desired, and chill for at least 1 hour before serving.

To Make Chocolate Cream

Fashionable chocolate pots and cups were used at Mount Vernon. In 1792, while living in Philadelphia with the president, Martha Washington wrote to her niece Fanny, who lived at the plantation, regarding an order of foodstuffs that were to be sent there: "I wish you would let me know," Mrs. Washington inquired, "which you will reather have chocolate in cakes or the shells. . . . I will send that you like best." In 1794 she noted that there were two barrels of chocolate shells in a storeroom at Mount Vernon.[13] Earlier that same year, Burgess Ball, son-in-law of Washington's brother Charles, wrote to the president requesting two or three bushels of the chocolate shells, "such as we've frequently drank Chocolate . . . at Mt. Vernon, as my Wife thinks it agreed with her better than any other Breakfast."[14]

Posset—a term dating to the fifteenth century—was a warm drink that combined heated milk with some type of spirits, such as wine or beer, and was occasionally enriched with beaten eggs. It was thought to be a remedy for minor ailments, such as a head cold. Its consistency is similar to that of syllabub and eggnog. Posset was served in special cups, as coffee and tea were. Posset cups are unique, however, in having two handles.

This chocolate cream, which is similar to posset, is lusciously thick and rich. Serve it in posset or demitasse cups with a bit of the froth spooned on top. "[L]ay the frothed cream upon them," Elizabeth Raffald advised in her recipe. "It makes a pretty picture."[15]

Makes 5 to 6 cups

1 cup water
5¼ ounces semisweet chocolate, grated
¾ cup sugar, or more as needed
4 cups heavy (whipping) cream

1. In the top of a double boiler, heat the water until very warm. Gradually add the chocolate, stirring constantly until melted. Blend in the sugar, and continue to stir until thoroughly dissolved. Add 1 cup of the cream, and continue to heat, stirring to blend. Stir in additional sugar, if desired.

2. Transfer the chocolate to a large saucepan, and stir in the remaining cream. Whisk over medium heat until scalding (just below the boiling point).

3. Use a chocolate mill, whisk, or immersion blender to froth the chocolate cream. Pour into posset or demitasse cups, and spoon the froth on top.

RIGHT:
This tall and elegant silver chocolate pot was made by London silversmith John Carter II for Martha Washington's son, John Parke (Jacky) Custis, and his bride, Eleanor Calvert, at the time of their wedding in 1774.

Chocolate cream, a popular eighteenth-century beverage, is served here in large Blue Canton teacups reproduced by Mottahedeh.

OVERLEAF:
A breakfast of asparagus and eggs (see recipe, page 126), fresh fruit, and muffins is served on the Mansion's east lawn as the sun rises over the Potomac.

About the Contributors

****

STEVEN T. BASHORE is Mount Vernon's Manager of Historic Trades, the department in charge of the gristmill, distillery, and blacksmith shop as well as the George Washington—Pioneer Farmer interpretive site. He holds a B.A. in history from the University of Texas at Arlington, and has traveled extensively abroad to research windmills and water mills. He has operated historic water mills for nearly two decades and, from 2001 to 2003, managed the restoration of the water-powered gristmill at Stratford Hall Plantation in Stratford, Virginia. He lectures often on eighteenth-century milling, farming, distilling, and industry. Besides making various products at Mount Vernon's gristmill, Bashore coordinates whiskey production, which began at the distillery in 2009.

CAROL BORCHERT CADOU is Mount Vernon's Robert H. Smith Senior Curator and Vice President for Collections. As the executive in charge of collections efforts, she developed the exhibition concepts and content for six galleries that debuted as part of the Donald W. Reynolds Museum and Education Center in 2006, collaborating with curators, designers, and other colleagues. Cadou earned an M.A. from the University of Delaware's Winterthur Program in Early American Culture and is the author of *The George Washington Collection: Fine and Decorative Arts at Mount Vernon* (2006).

NANCY CARTER CRUMP is the author of *Hearthside Cooking: Early American Southern Cuisine Updated for Today's Hearth and Cookstove* (2008) and *Hearthside Cooking: An Introduction to Virginia Plantation Cuisine* (1986). Her work has focused on many aspects of Southern culinary history, including historic authors of the domestic arts and the diet of Native Americans in North Carolina's Albemarle region. She has conducted culinary research for the Museum of the Cape Fear, Wilmington, North Carolina; Weston Manor, Hopewell, Virginia; and the Shirley and Tuckahoe plantations, both in Virginia. Crump founded the Culinary Historians of Virginia.

STEPHEN A. McLEOD is Assistant to the President and CEO at Mount Vernon. He holds a B.A. in communications from the University of Alabama, Tuscaloosa, and an M.A. in history, with additional certification in museum studies, from Florida State University, Tallahassee. He has worked with the Florida Department of State's Division of Historical Resources and England's National Trust. McLeod was general editor of *The Mount Vernon Ladies' Association: 150 Years of Restoring George Washington's Home* (2010).

J. DEAN NORTON, Director of Horticulture, began working at Mount Vernon at age sixteen. In 1977, having earned a B.S. in ornamental horticulture from Clemson University in South Carolina, he took up full-time duties at the estate. The main focus of his research is on eighteenth-century gardens. He has lectured both nationally and abroad and is the recipient of numerous conservation honors, including the American Horticultural Society's Professional Award in 2006. Norton serves on the boards of several historic sites and is president of the Southern Garden History Society.

DENNIS J. POGUE, Mount Vernon's Vice President for Restoration and Preservation, has managed reconstruction of the estate's distillery, sixteen-sided treading barn, and blacksmith shop as well as restoration of various rooms in the Mansion. He holds an M.A. in American studies from George Washington University and a Ph.D. in anthropology, with an emphasis in historical archaeology, from American University, Washington, D.C. His books include *Archaeology at George Washington's Mount Vernon, 1931–1987* (1988); *George Washington's Gristmill at Mount Vernon*, co-authored with Esther C. White (2005); and *Founding Spirits: George Washington and the Beginnings of the American Whiskey Industry* (2011).

WALTER SCHEIB graduated with honors from the Culinary Institute of America, Hyde Park, New York, and served as the White House's executive chef from 1994 until 2005. He was hired by First Lady Hillary Clinton, who was impressed by the distinctively American menu he had developed for the renowned Greenbrier resort in West Virginia. At the White House, his culinary creations were served to a host of dignitaries, including Tony Blair, Jacques Chirac, Nelson Mandela, Boris Yeltsin, and Diana, Princess of Wales. Scheib is co-author (with Andrew Friedman) of *White House Chef: Eleven Years, Two Presidents, One Kitchen* (2007).

MARY V. THOMPSON is Mount Vernon's Research Historian. She specializes in such topics as everyday life on the estate, food customs, religious practices, the Washington and Custis families, slavery, hired and indentured workers, and domestic animals. She organized the traveling exhibition *Treasures from Mount Vernon: George Washington Revealed* (1999–2000) and is the author of *In the Hands of a Good Providence: Religion in the Life of George Washington* (2008). Thompson holds a B.A. in history from Samford University, Birmingham, Alabama, and an M.A. in history from the University of Virginia, Charlottesville.

ESTHER C. WHITE directs Mount Vernon's archaeology program, which is designed to research, preserve, and interpret the buried resources at George Washington's home. Over the past two decades, she has excavated the estate's distillery, upper garden, and south grove midden while studying daily life at Mount Vernon, changes to its landscape, and the plantation economy. She holds a B.A. in history from the University of North Carolina, Chapel Hill; an M.A. in anthropology, with specialization in historical archaeology, from the College of William and Mary, Williamsburg, Virginia; and a Ph.D. in archaeology from the University of Leicester, England.

Chapter Notes

FREQUENTLY CITED SOURCES AND ABBREVIATIONS

Adams
New Letters of Abigail Adams, 1788–1801, ed. Stewart Mitchell (Boston: Houghton Mifflin, 1947).

AW
Anthony Whitting/Whiting, Mount Vernon farm manager (1790–93). He spelled his own surname Whitting, but Washington habitually wrote it as Whiting.

Baker
William Spohn Baker, *Washington after the Revolution, 1784–1799* (Philadelphia: J. B. Lippincott, 1898).

Beautiful Nelly
Patricia Brady, ed., *George Washington's Beautiful Nelly: The Letters of Eleanor Parke Custis Lewis to Elizabeth Bordley Gibson, 1794–1851* (Columbia: University of South Carolina Press, 1991).

Belden
Louise Conway Belden, *The Festive Tradition: Table Decoration and Desserts in America, 1650–1900* (New York: W. W. Norton, 1983).

Berard
Augusta Blanche Berard to Mrs. Mary Berard, Apr. 18, 1856, "Arlington and Mount Vernon, 1856, as Described in a Letter of Augusta Blanche Berard," ed. Clayton Torrence, *Virginia Magazine of History and Biography* 57, no. 2 (Apr. 1949): 140–75.

Brookes Journal
R. W. G. Vail, ed., "A Dinner at Mount Vernon: From the Unpublished Journal of Joshua Brookes (1773–1859)," *New-York Historical Society Quarterly* 31, no. 2 (Apr. 1947): 72–85.

Buhler
Kathryn C. Buhler, *Mount Vernon Silver* (Mount Vernon, Va.: MVLA, 1957).

Carson
Jane Carson, *Colonial Virginia Cookery* (Williamsburg, Va.: Colonial Williamsburg, 1968).

CB
Clement Biddle, Philadelphia merchant. GW's business agent in that city (1780s and 1790s).

Davidson
Alan Davidson, *The Oxford Companion to Food* (Oxford: Oxford University Press, 1999).

Decatur
Stephen Decatur, Jr., *Private Affairs of George Washington: From the Records and Accounts of Tobias Lear, Esquire, His Secretary* (Boston: Riverside Press, 1933).

Detweiler
Susan Gray Detweiler, *George Washington's Chinaware* (New York: Harry N. Abrams, 1982).

EB/EBG
Elizabeth Bordley/Elizabeth Bordley Gibson, lifelong friend of NCL.

EPCL
Elizabeth (a.k.a. Eliza) Parke Custis Law, MW's eldest granddaughter. Older sister of GWPC and NCL.

FBW/FBWL
Frances (a.k.a. Fanny) Bassett Washington/Fanny Basset Washington Lear, MW's niece.

Fithian
Philip Vickers Fithian, *Journal and Letters of Philip Vickers Fithian, 1773–1774: A Plantation Tutor of the Old Dominion*, ed. with an introduction by Hunter Dickinson Farish (Williamsburg, Va.: Colonial Williamsburg, 1957).

Glasse
A Lady [Hannah Glasse], *The Art of Cookery, Made Plain and Easy* (1747; facsimile, Totnes, England: Prospect Books, 1995). Editions published in 1765 and 1796 are also cited in the present book.

GM
Gouverneur Morris, American legislator and diplomat. U.S. minister to France (1792–94) and GW's purchasing agent there.

GW
George Washington

GWD
Donald Jackson and Dorothy Twohig, eds., *The Diaries of George Washington*, 6 vols. (Charlottesville: University Press of Virginia, 1976–79).

GWPC
George Washington Parke Custis, MW's grandson.

GWPC Recollections
George Washington Parke Custis, *Recollections and Private Memoirs of Washington, by His Adopted Son, George Washington Parke Custis, with a Memoir of the Author, by His Daughter; and Illustrative and Explanatory Notes, by Benson J. Lossing* (1860; repr., Bridgewater, Va.: American Foundation Publications, 1999).

Hess
Karen Hess, *Martha Washington's Booke of Cookery* (New York: Columbia University Press, 1981).

Kettilby
Mary Kettilby, *A Collection of above Three Hundred Receipts in Cookery, Physick, and Surgery*, 5th ed. (London: Printed for the Executrix of Mary Kettilby, 1734).

Lady's Companion
[Anonymous], *The Lady's Companion: Containing Upwards of Three Thousand Different Receipts in Every Kind of Cookery*, 6th ed., vol. 1 (London: Printed for J. Hodges and R. Baldwin, 1753).

Leslie, 1830
Eliza Leslie, *Seventy-five Receipts for Pastry, Cakes, and Sweet-meats*, 3rd ed. (Boston: Munroe and Franklin, 1830).

Leslie, 1973
Eliza Leslie, *Directions for Cookery in Its Various Branches* (1837; facsimile of 1848 edition, New York: Arno Press, 1973).

LGWMV
Library, George Washington's Mount Vernon Estate, Museum, and Gardens

LW
Lund Washington, GW's distant cousin and Mount Vernon farm manager (1765–ca. 1785).

LWT
John C. Fitzpatrick, ed., *The Last Will and Testament of George Washington and Schedule of His Property to Which Is Appended the Last Will and Testament of Martha Washington*, rev. ed. (Mount Vernon, Va.: MVLA, 1992).

Maclay
Kenneth R. Bowling and Helen E. Veit, eds., *The Diary of William Maclay and Other Notes on Senate Debates* (Baltimore: Johns Hopkins University Press, 1988).

MV
Mount Vernon

MVLA
Mount Vernon Ladies' Association of the Union

MVLA AR
Mount Vernon Ladies' Association of the Union Annual Report

MW
Martha Washington

NC/NCL
Eleanor (a.k.a. Nelly) Parke Custis Lewis, MW's youngest granddaughter.

Niemcewicz
Julian Ursyn Niemcewicz, *Under Their Vine and Fig Tree: Travels through America in 1797–1799, 1805, with Some Further Account of Life in New Jersey*, trans. and ed. Metchie J. E. Budka (Elizabeth, N.J.: Grassman Publishing, 1965).

Paston-Williams
Sara Paston-Williams, *The Art of Dining: A History of Cooking and Eating* (London: National Trust Enterprises Limited, 1993).

PGW Col.
W. W. Abbot, Dorothy Twohig, and Beverly H. Runge, eds., *The Papers of George Washington, Colonial Series*, 10 vols. (Charlottesville: University Press of Virginia, 1983–95).

PGW Rev.
W. W. Abbot, Dorothy Twohig, Philander D. Chase, and Beverly H. Runge, eds., *The Papers of George Washington, Revolutionary War Series*, 19 vols. (Charlottesville: University Press of Virginia, 1985–).

PGW Con.
W. W. Abbot, ed., *The Papers of George Washington, Confederation Series*, 6 vols. (Charlottesville: University Press of Virginia, 1992–97).

PGW Pres.
Dorothy Twohig, Mark Mastromarino, and Jack D. Warren, eds., *The Papers of George Washington, Presidential Series*, 16 vols. (Charlottesville: University Press of Virginia, 1987–).

PGW Ret.
Dorothy Twohig, Philander D. Chase, Beverly H. Runge, Frank E. Grizzard, Jr., et al, eds., *The Papers of George Washington, Retirement Series*, 4 vols. (Charlottesville: University Press of Virginia, 1998–99).

PGW Digital
The Papers of George Washington Digital Edition, ed. Theodore J. Crackel (Charlottesville: University of Virginia Press, 2007).

PMW
"Worthy Partner": The Papers of Martha Washington, comp. Joseph E. Fields (Westport, Conn.: Greenwood Press, 1994).

Prussing
Eugene E. Prussing, *The Estate of George Washington, Deceased* (Boston: Little, Brown, 1927).

Raffald
Elizabeth Raffald, *The Experienced English Housekeeper* (London: R. Baldwin, 1775).

Randolph
Mary Randolph, *The Virginia House-Wife*, ed. Karen Hess (1824; facsimile, Columbia: University of South Carolina Press, 1983).

RL
Robert Lewis, GW's nephew and his secretary during the presidency.

Rundell
By a Lady [Maria Rundell], *A New System of Domestic Cookery: Formed upon Principles of Economy, and Adapted to the Use of Private Families* (London: Printed for John Murray, Fleet-Street; J. Harding, St. James Street; and A. Constable and Company, Edinburgh, 1808).

RW
Richard Washington, London merchant. GW's business agent there (1755–65).

Schmit
Patricia Brady Schmit, ed., *Nelly Custis Lewis's Housekeeping Book* (New Orleans: Historic New Orleans Collection, 1982).

Smith
E. Smith, *The Compleat Housewife; or, Accomplish'd Gentlewoman's Companion*, 15th ed. (London: Printed for R. Ware and others, 1753).

Taylor
E. Taylor, *The Lady's, Housewife's, and Cookmaid's Assistant; or, the Art of Cookery* (Berwick-upon-Tweed, England: Printed by H. Taylor for R. Taylor, Bookseller, 1769).

TL
Tobias Lear, GW's private secretary (1785–92) and military secretary (1798). Married FBW and Frances (a.k.a. Fanny) Henley, both nieces of MW.

Trusler
[John Trusler], *The Honours of the Table; or, Rules for Behaviour during Meals* (London: Literary-Press, 1788).

WGW
The Writings of George Washington from the Original Manuscript Sources, 1745–1799, 39 vols., ed. John C. Fitzpatrick (Washington, D.C.: U.S. Government Printing Office, 1931–44).

WHAB
"Washington's Household Account Book, 1793–1797," *Pennsylvania Magazine of History and Biography*, 29, no. 4 (1905): 385–406; 30, nos. 1–4 (1906): 30–56, 159–86, 309–31, 459–78; 31, nos. 1–3 (1907): 53–82, 176–94, 320–50.

Wilson
C. Anne Wilson, *Food and Drink in Britain* (New York: Harper and Row, 1974).

WP
William Pearce, Mount Vernon farm manager (1793–96).

FOREWORD

1. GW to George William Fairfax, June 25, 1786, in PGW Con., 4:128.
2. GWPC Recollections, 168.
3. TL to George A. Washington, May 3, 1789, in PGW Pres., 2: 248.
4. GWPC Recollections, 421–22.
5. GW to the Marquis de Lafayette, Jan. 29, 1789, in PGW Pres., 1: 264.
6. Ashbel Green and Joseph Huntington Jones, *The Life of Ashbel Green, V.D.M.* (New York: Robert Carter and Brothers, 1849), 266–67. See also GWPC Recollections, 435n.
7. NCL to EBG, Feb. 23, 1823 (typescript, LGWMV).

"THAT HOSPITABLE MANSION"
Welcoming Guests at Mount Vernon

1. Entries for Dec. 13, 1773, and Apr. 3, 1774, in Fithian, 29, 90.
2. Charles Varlo, Oct. 1784, as quoted in Baker, 17n–18n.
3. Douglas Sinclair Robertson, ed., *An Englishman in America, 1785: Being the Diary of Joseph Hadfield* (Toronto: Hunter-Rose, 1933), 12, 13.
4. "An Account of a Visit Made to Washington at Mount Vernon, by an English Gentleman, in 1785," in *Pennsylvania Magazine of History and Biography* 17, no. 1 (1893): 77, 81.
5. GW to Mary Ball Washington, Feb. 15, 1787, in PGW Con., 5: 35.
6. GW to TL, July 31, 1797, in PGW Ret., 1: 281.
7. Entry for June 30, 1785, in GWD, 4: 157.
8. Drawn from Washington's diaries, the information offered here must be read with the understanding that there were not 677 separate individuals visiting the Washingtons in 1798. For example, Dr. James Craik frequently came for dinner and an overnight stay. Martha Washington's two eldest granddaughters and their families were often at Mount Vernon, too. With respect to the total figures, I have tried to determine the impact of houseguests on the food-preparation and housekeeping staffs, both of which Mrs. Washington supervised. I went through the diaries and, for each day, counted the number of extra people in the house, first for dinner and then for overnight. So, for example, if Thomas and Martha Parke Custis Peter came for five days, I counted them as two extra people on five days, for a total of ten. The largest number of single-day guests in 1798 was the twenty-seven who came for dinner on July 12 (GWD, 6: 307).
9. For these Christmas guests, see entries for Dec. 25–28, 1785, in GWD, 4: 255, 255n, 256, and 256n.
10. Entry for Feb. 1, 1773, in GWD, 3: 159.

11. Entry for Aug. 26, 1785, in GWD, 4: 186.
12. GW to James McHenry, Secretary of War, May 29, 1797, in WGW, 35: 455.
13. Entry for Mar. 21, 1786, in GWD, 4: 296.
14. GW to George William Fairfax, June 25, 1786, in PGW Col., 4: 128.
15. GW to WP, Dec. 7, 1794, in WGW, 34: 53.
16. GW to AW, Nov. 18, 1792, in WGW, 32: 233.
17. GW to WP, Oct. 6, 1793, in WGW, 33: 111.
18. GW to James Anderson, June 11, 1798; Anderson to GW, June 19, 1798, in PGW Ret., 4: 322, 346.
19. Entry for June 11, 1759, in Andrew Burnaby, *Travels through the Middle Settlements in North America in the Years 1759 and 1760* (1775; repr., New York: Augustus M. Kelley, 1970), 79, 80.
20. Entry for July 13, 1777, in *The Journal of Nicholas Cresswell, 1774–1777* (New York: Dial Press, 1924), 255.
21. Thomas Lee Shippen to his father, Sept. 16, 1790, as quoted in Robert A. Lancaster, Jr., *Historic Virginia Homes and Churches* (Philadelphia: J. B. Lippincott, 1915), 362.
22. George Grieve, as quoted in Marquis de Chastellux, *Travels in North America in the Years 1780, 1781, and 1782*, 2 vols., rev. trans., with an introduction and notes by Howard C. Rice, Jr. (Chapel Hill: University of North Carolina Press for the Institute of Early American History and Culture, Williamsburg, Va., 1963), 2: 595n.
23. Robertson, ed., *An Englishman in America*, 12, 13.
24. Entries for May 21 and June 5, 1798, in Niemcewicz, 86, 103.
25. Elkanah Watson, *Men and Times of the Revolution; or, Memoirs of Elkanah Watson, including Journals of Travels in Europe and America, from 1777 to 1842*, ed. Winslow C. Watson (New York: Dana and Company, 1856), 243–44.
26. MW to FBW, Aug. 29, 1791, in PMW, 233.
27. George Augustine Washington to GW, Apr. 15, 1792, in PGW Pres., 10: 269.

HERCULES THE COOK

1. Entry for Feb. 18, 1786, in GWD, 4: 277.
2. Berard: 162; Decatur, 169; Marie Kimball, *The Martha Washington Cookbook* (New York: Coward-McCann, 1940), 34.
3. MW to FBW, June 4 and Aug. 29, 1791, in PMW, 231, 233.
4. Entry for Sept. 9, 1787, in MV Store Book, Jan. 1–Dec. 31, 1787 (typescript, LGWMV).
5. GW to TL, Nov. 22, 1790, in PGW Pres., 6: 682.
6. GWPC Recollections, 422, 423.
7. Paston-Williams, 108, 221–22, 232. For more on this sanctioned money-earning by cooks, both enslaved and free, see Annette Gordon-Reed, *The Hemingses of Monticello: An American Family* (New York: W. W. Norton, 2008), 209–10.

8. GWPC Recollections 422–23.
9. TL to GW, June 5, 1791, in PGW Pres., 8: 232.
10. GW to WP, Nov. 14, 1796, in WGW, 35: 279.
11. See Weekly Reports for Jan. 7, 14, 20, and 28, 1797, and Feb. 11 and 25, 1797, in MV Farm Accounts, Jan. 7–Sept. 10, 1797 (bound Photostat, LGWMV); and Weekly Report for Feb. 18, 1797, in MV Weekly Reports, Jan. 10, 1795–Mar. 18, 1797 (bound Photostat, LGWMV). I thank Philadelphia journalist Craig LaBan for alerting me to several of these references in a Nov. 10, 2009, phone conversation.
12. GW to TL, Mar. 10, 1797, in PGW Ret., 1: 27.
13. Louis-Philippe, King of France, 1830–1848, *Diary of My Travels in America*, trans. Stephen Becker (New York: Delacorte Press, 1977), 32.

SERVING THE WASHINGTONS' TABLE

1. Louis-Philippe, King of France, 1830–1848, *Diary of My Travels in America*, trans. Stephen Becker (New York: Delacorte Press, 1977), 32, 35.
2. GW to WP, May 1, 1796, in WGW, 35: 34.
3. GW to WP, Dec. 13, 1795, in WGW, 34: 393–94.
4. GW to TL, Aug. 31, 1794, in Tobias Lear, *Letters and Recollections of George Washington* (New York: Doubleday, Page, and Company, 1906), 79.
5. Entry for Feb. 18, 1786, in GWD, 4: 277.
6. Detweiler, 112, 118.
7. Henry Wansey, *An Excursion to the United States of North America, in the Summer of 1794* (Salisbury, England: J. Easton, 1798), 112.
8. Brookes Journal: 76.
9. Trusler, 10–15.
10. Reminiscences of the Reverend Ashbel Green, as quoted in GWPC Recollections, 436n.

MARTHA WASHINGTON, HOUSEWIFE

1. Elizabeth Fox-Genovese, *Within the Plantation Household: Black and White Women of the Old South* (Chapel Hill: University of North Carolina Press, 1988), 118; Paston-Williams, 234.
2. For an example of a female family member cooking a special dish for guests, see NCL to EBG, June 25, 1823 (manuscript and typescript, LGWMV). The kettle is in the Mount Vernon collection (W-2870).
3. J. P. Brissot de Warville, Nov. 1788, as quoted in Baker, 113.
4. GWPC Recollections, 455.
5. Ibid., 509.
6. Berard: 162.
7. GWPC Recollections, 514.
8. Entry for Dec. 17, 1768, in GWD, 2: 115; Ledger A, 288a (Photostat, LGWMV).
9. LW to GW, Mar. 12, 1783 (typescript, LGWMV).
10. MW to Mrs. Elizabeth Powel, May 1, 1797, in PMW, 301; Meunier is identified on p. 302n4.

11. GW to Bushrod Washington, Oct. 23, 1797, in PGW Ret., 1: 422 and 1: 422n2. For Nelly's boast, see NC to EB, Mar. 18, 1797, in *Beautiful Nelly*, 32.

MARTHA WASHINGTON'S COOKBOOKS

1. The manuscript, edited by Karen Hess, was published by Columbia University Press in 1981 as *Martha Washington's Booke of Cookery*; see pp. 3–7 and 447–63 for the history of this family heirloom. An earlier version, which includes adaptations of the original recipes, was published as Marie Kimball, *The Martha Washington Cookbook* (New York: Coward-McCann, 1940). Selected recipes from the "Booke of Cookery" manuscript were published in *Leaves from the Table of George and Martha Washington* (Hammondsport, N.Y.: Taylor Winery, 1940); and *Martha Washington's Booke of Cookery: Being Recipes of the Washington Family, 1759–1799* (Kansas City, Mo.: Andrews and McMeel, 1992).

2. Hess, 7; Glasse, viii, xiv, xv. Martha Washington's original copy of *The Art of Cookery, Made Plain and Easy* is now in the LGMWV. A second copy is in the collection of Tudor Place, Washington, D.C., the home of Mrs. Washington's second granddaughter, Martha Parke Custis Peter. Both copies descended in Mrs. Peter's family.

3. NCL to Charles M. Conrad, Jan. 9, 1835 (typescript, LGWMV); NCL to EBG, Oct. 21, 1825 (typescript, LGWMV); "The finest lip salve in the World—Mrs[.] M[.] Washingtons recipe," [NCL] to Natalie, Mathilde, Clementine, Oscar, and Edward [Lafayette], Dec. 17, 1824 (Photostat, LGWMV).

4. "Memoirs of a Monticello Slave as Dictated to Charles Campbell by Isaac," in James A. Bear, Jr., ed., *Jefferson at Monticello* (Charlottesville: University Press of Virginia, 1967), 3.

5. The Jefferson cookbook was published as Ann Parks Marshall, ed., *Martha Washington's Rules for Cooking* (Washington, D.C.: Ransdell, 1931); for the recipes in it attributed to Mrs. Washington, see pp. 17, 37, 40–41, 47, 52–53, 58, 61, 68, 73, 75, 86, 93, 107, 111, 113, 119, 122, 127, 132, 134, 145, 147, and 156.

6. Both Nelly's and Mrs. Lee's manuscript cookbooks have been published, the first as Patricia Brady Schmit, ed., *Nelly Custis Lewis's Housekeeping Book* (New Orleans: Historic New Orleans Collection, 1982) and the second as Anne Carter Zimmer, ed., *The Robert E. Lee Family Cooking and Housekeeping Book* (Chapel Hill: University of North Carolina Press, 1997); the lip salve and remedy for worms are found on pp. 80 and 107, respectively, of the former volume.

ICE CREAM

1. Belden, 145.

2. Entry for May 16, 1784, in GW, Ledger B (bound Photostat, LGWMV), 198a.

3. Decatur, 253; entries for June 25, 1795, and Mar. 28, 1796, in WHAB 31: 56, 178.

4. Abigail Adams to her sister, Mary Smith Cranch (Mrs. Richard Cranch) Aug. 9, 1789, in Adams, 19.

5. Entry for Aug. 27, 1789, in Maclay, 136–37.

6. Prussing, 435.

7. Glasse, 168.

8. These two china services are detailed in Detweiler, 124, 126, 128, 145. An icery was a large, covered serving piece that kept ice cream or fruit cool during meals. Atop its lid was a well that could be filled with ice.

TEA ON THE PIAZZA

1. Thomas G. Cary, *Memoir of Thomas Handasyd Perkins* (Boston: Little, Brown, 1856), 199.

2. Prussing, 413.

3. George Washington Motier Lafayette (1779–1849) was sent to America during his father's five-year imprisonment by leaders of the French Revolution. For more about the young Lafayette's stay, see entry for March 9, 1797, in GWD, 6: 236–37n.

4. Elizabeth Wescott to her mother, Patience Wescott, June 27, 1796, as quoted in Rebekah Hockley Wheeler Baker, "Home Life at Mount Vernon" (paper read to Interstate Meeting of the Colony of New England Women, Delmonico's restaurant, New York, ca. 1908, n.p.; typescript, LGWMV).

5. GW to RL, June 26, 1796, in WGW, 35: 101.

"SERVED UP IN EXCELLENT ORDER"
Everyday Dining at Mount Vernon

1. For more on breakfast times at Mount Vernon, see Elizabeth Wescott to her mother, Patience Wescott, June 27, 1796, as quoted in Rebekah Hockley Wheeler Baker, "Home Life at Mount Vernon" (paper read to Interstate Meeting of the Colony of New England Women, Delmonico's restaurant, New York, ca. 1908, n.p.; typescript, LGWMV). Typical breakfast times in Virginia in the eighteenth century were one to two hours later than at Mount Vernon; see Carson, 12; Marie Kimball, *Thomas Jefferson's Cookbook* (Charlottesville: University Press of Virginia, 1976), 23; William Howard Adams, *Jefferson's Monticello* (New York: Abbeville Press, 1983), 226; and Fithian, entry for Dec. 15, 1773, 31.

2. NCL to EBG, Feb. 23, 1823 (typescript, LGWMV); Berard: 162; GWPC Recollections, 165–66, 384–85; Adams, *Jefferson's Monticello*, 226–27.

3. GWPC Recollections, 386.

4. Ibid., 509; Sally Foster Otis to Mrs. Charles W. Apthorp, Jan. 13, 1801 (manuscript, Massachusetts Historical Society, Boston; typescript, LGWMV).

5. NC to EB, n.d. (1794?), in *Beautiful Nelly*, 19.

6. For studying, see reminiscences of the Reverend Ashbel Green, as quoted in GWPC Recollections, 435n. For hunting, see GW to GWPC, Jan. 7, 1798, in PGW Ret., 2: 4–5.

7. Winthrop Sargent, entry for Oct. 13, 1793, in PGW Pres., 14: 209; Adams, *Jefferson's Monticello*, 226; Fithian, entry for Dec. 15, 1773, 31.

8. Entry for July [18,] 1796, in *The Virginia Journals of Benjamin Henry Latrobe, 1795–1798*, 2 vols., ed. Edward C. Carter II and Angeline Polites (New Haven, Conn.: Yale University Press for the Maryland Historical Society, 1977), 1: 171.

9. Entry for Jan. 2, 1802, in *Life Journals and Correspondence of Rev. Manasseh Cutler, LL.D.*, 2 vols., ed. William Parker Cutler and Julia Perkins Cutler (Cincinnati, Ohio: Robert Clarke and Company, 1888), 2: 56.

10. Burgess Ball to GW, Feb. 13, 1794, in PGW Pres., 15: 227.

11. Latrobe, July [18,] 1796.

12. Sargent, Oct. 13, 1793.

13. Stacy Gibbons Moore, "Established and Well Cultivated: Afro-American Foodways in Early Virginia," *Virginia Cavalcade* 39, no. 2 (Autumn 1989): 78–79.

14. Entry for June 5, 1798, in Niemcewicz, 103.

15. NCL to EBG, Feb. 23, 1823; GWPC Recollections, 166–67, 386.

16. Latrobe, July [18,] 1796.

17. Entry for Aug. 28, 1786, in GWD, 5: 31–32.

18. Friedrich Wilhelm Hoeninghaus to Johann Heinrich Hoeninghaus, Mar. 18, 1798 (typescript, LGWMV). After her husband's death, Martha Washington continued offering late-morning breakfasts to guests who had not yet eaten. See entry for Jan. 2, 1802, in *Life Journals and Correspondence of Rev. Manasseh Cutler*, ed. Cutler and Cutler, 2: 56; and James Hillhouse to Mrs. Rebecca Hillhouse, Jan. 4, 1802 (Photostat and typescript, LGWMV).

19. GWPC Recollections, 446; Berard: 162. For Thomas Jefferson's comparable practice of riding about his plantation between breakfast and dinner—a circuit of twelve to fifteen miles—see Adams, *Jefferson's Monticello*, 227.

20. Entry for May 21, 1798, in Niemcewicz, 85. For a definition of peach cheese, see Belden, 120.

21. Prussing, 417.

22. "Private sales, which took place up stairs among the Legatees, to be settled on the final adjustment without interest," July 22, 1802 (Photostat, LGWMV).

23. NCL to EBG, Feb. 23, 1823; Berard: 162.

24. NCL to EBG, Apr. 29, 1823, in *Beautiful Nelly*, 134. For dinner hours elsewhere in Virginia, see Carson, 6; Audrey Nöel Hume, *Colonial Williamsburg Archaeological Series, No. 9: Food* (Williamsburg, Va.: Colonial Williamsburg Foundation, 1978), 9; Kimball, *Thomas Jefferson's Cookbook*, 23; and entry for Dec. 15, 1773, in Fithian, 31.

25. GW to Bushrod Washington, July 24, 1797, in PGW Ret., 1: 272.

26. NCL to EBG, Feb. 23, 1823; NCL to EBG, Apr. 29, 1823, in *Beautiful Nelly*, 134; entry for June 2, 1798, in Niemcewicz, 96; GW to GWPC, Jan. 7, 1798, in PGW Ret., 2: 5.

27. Elizabeth Wescott to Patience Wescott, June 27, 1796, in Baker, "Home Life at Mount Vernon."

28. GW to George William Fairfax, July 17, 1763, in PGW Col., 7: 231.

29. GWPC Recollections, 446.

30. GW to TL, Sept. 10, 1797, in PGW Ret., 1: 345.

31. GW to GWPC, in PGW Ret., 2: 5.

32. GWPC Recollections, 169.

33. Pierre-Etienne Duponceau, "A Visit to Mount Vernon in 1780," in *George Washington as the French Knew Him: A Collection of Texts*, ed. and trans. Gilbert Chinard (1940; repr., New York: Greenwood Press, 1969), 19.

34. Olney Winsor to his wife, Hope Winsor, Mar. 31, 1788, in Jean B. Lee, ed., *Experiencing Mount Vernon: Eyewitness Accounts, 1784–1865* (Charlottesville: University of Virginia Press, 2006), 55.

35. Archibald Robertson [Dec. 1791 or Jan. 1792?], as quoted in Baker, 232n.

36. Entry for July 3, 1799, in John E. Latta journal (typescript, LGWMV). In this way, the table at Mount Vernon was probably similar to that at Monticello, which has been described as "not 'lavish' according to plantation standards of the day," although a former family slave recalled that Thomas Jefferson "never would have less than eight covers at dinner if nobody [was] at the table but himself" (see Adams, *Jefferson's Monticello*, 227).

37. Hamilton B. Staples, ed., "A Day at Mount Vernon, in 1797," paper read at American Antiquarian Society semiannual meeting, Boston, Apr. 1879 (Worcester, Mass.: Press of Charles Hamilton, 1879; typescript, LGWMV). 8–11.

38. Brookes Journal: 75, 76.

39. Entry for Dec. 27, 1773, in Fithian, 42. For similar prayers elsewhere in Virginia, see Lauren F. Winner, *A Cheerful and Comfortable Faith: Anglican Religious Practice in the Elite Households of Eighteenth-Century Virginia* (New Haven, Conn.: Yale University Press, 2010), 119. For the fact that it was considered bad manners to leave the table before the meal-ending prayer, see Trusler, 17.

40. Staples, "A Day at Mount Vernon," 8; entry for July 3, 1799, in Latta journal.

41. For prayers said during presidential dinners, see reminiscences of the Reverend Ashbel Green, as quoted in GWPC Recollections, 435n–436n, and Baker, 138. For the quotations about prayers at table during the war, see Claude Blanchard, July 1781, "An Intimate Portrait of Washington," in *Washington as the French Knew Him*, 66.

42. Trusler, 10; see also entry for Dec. 27, 1773, in Fithian, 42.

43. Entry for June 5, 1798, in Niemcewicz, 102.

44. Archibald Robertson, [Dec. 30 or 31, 1791], in Baker, 232n. The ladies do seem to have left the table before the gentlemen during more formal public dinners in the executive residence. (Maclay, entry for Aug. 27, 1789, 137; and reminiscences of Ashbel Green, as quoted in GWPC Recollections, 436n.)

45. NCL to EBG, Feb. 23, 1823.

46. Elizabeth Wescott to Patience Wescott, June 27, 1796, in Baker, "Home Life at Mount Vernon."

47. Thomas Handasyd Perkins, July 1796, in Thomas G. Cary, *Memoir of Thomas Handasyd Perkins; Containing Extracts from His Diaries and Letters* (Boston: Little, Brown, 1856), 199–200.

48. Entry for June 5, 1798, in Niemcewicz, 103.

49. Belden, 248–50; Carson, 12–13; GWPC Recollections, 388.

50. Sargent entry for Oct. 12, 1793, in PGW Pres., 14: 208n–209n.

51. GWPC Recollections, 453. Thomas Jefferson's day at Monticello tended to end much as Washington's did, with paperwork between dinner and teatime, reading or conversation with guests after tea, and bed at 10 p.m. See Adams, *Jefferson's Monticello*, 228.

52. [Robert Hunter, Jr.], Nov. 16, 1785, in "An Account of a Visit Made to Washington at Mount Vernon, by an English Gentleman, in 1785," *Pennsylvania Magazine of History and Biography* 17, no. 1 (1893), 78–79.

53. Elizabeth Wescott to Patience Wescott, June 27, 1796, in Baker, "Home Life at Mount Vernon."

54. Latrobe, July [18,] 1796.

55. Carson, 12; Hume, *Food*, 9; entry for Dec. 15, 1773, in Fithian, 32. In Britain at the end of the eighteenth century, less fashionable people were still eating dinner in mid-afternoon and often had an evening supper that included bread, cheese, cold meats, and pies. See Jennifer Stead, "Georgian Britain," in Peter C. D. Brears et al, *A Taste of History: 10,000 Years of Food in Britain* (London: English Heritage in association with the British Museum Press, 1997), 229.

DINING ROOMS AT MOUNT VERNON

1. Mark E. Wenger, "The Dining Room in Early Virginia," in Thomas Carter and Bernard L. Herman, eds., *Perspectives in Vernacular Architecture* (Columbia: University of Missouri Press, 1989), 3: 149–59.

2. Robert F. Dalzell and Lee Baldwin Dalzell, *George Washington's Mount Vernon: At Home in Revolutionary America* (New York: Oxford University Press, 1998), 104–6, 113–15.

3. *Mount Vernon Historic Structure Report*, 3 vols. (Albany, N.Y.: Mesick-Cohen-Waite Architects, 1993), 1: 79-81.

4. "An Inventory of the Estate of Lawrence Washington, 7–8 March 1753" (LGWMV).

5. Dalzell and Dalzell, *George Washington's Mount Vernon*, 246–47.

6. Allan Greenberg, *George Washington, Architect* (Singapore: Andreas Papadakis, 1999), 69.

7. Dalzell and Dalzell, *George Washington's Mount Vernon*, 104–6.

8. Ibid., 113–15.

9. GW to LW, Sept. 30, 1776, in PGW Rev., 6: 442.

10. GW to John Rawlins, Aug. 29, 1785, in PGW Con., 3: 207.

11. Greenberg, *George Washington, Architect*, 69–71.

12. Dalzell and Dalzell, *George Washington's Mount Vernon*, 88–89.

13. Tobias Lear's Narrative Accounts of the Death of George Washington, the Diary Account, Dec. 14, 1799, in PGW Ret., 4: 552.

THE KITCHEN AT MOUNT VERNON

1. Carl R. Lounsbury, *An Illustrated Glossary of Early Southern Architecture and Landscape* (New York: Oxford University Press, 1994), 201; Camille Wells, "The Eighteenth-Century Landscape of Virginia's Northern Neck," *Northern Neck of Virginia Historical Magazine* (Dec. 1987): 4231–32; Donald W. Linebaugh, "'All the Annoyances and Inconveniences of the Country': Environmental Factors in the Development of Outbuildings in the Colonial Chesapeake," *Winterthur Portfolio* 29, no. 1 (Spring 1994): 1–18.

2. Dennis J. Pogue, "Mount Vernon: Transformation of an Eighteenth-Century Plantation System," in Paul A. Shackel and Barbara J. Little, eds., *Historical Archaeology of the Chesapeake* (Washington, D.C.: Smithsonian Institution Press, 1994), 101–114.

3. Dennis J. Pogue, "Archaeology at George Washington's Mount Vernon, 1931–2006," *Archeological Society of Virginia Quarterly Bulletin* 61, no. 4 (Dec. 2006): 165–75.

4. Pogue, "Mount Vernon: Transformation."

5. W. K. Bixby, ed., *Inventory of the Contents of Mount Vernon* ([privately printed] 1810), 41–44.

THE COOKS' DAY, 1790S

1. Various sources were used in writing this section. Especially helpful were GWPC Recollections and Berard: 162. Also of particular value was Pat Gibbs, "Daily Schedule for an Eighteenth-Century Cook," *Colonial Williamsburg Interpreter* 7, no. 3 (May 1986): 1–2. Other sources included: letters of George and Martha Washington (WGW and PMW); descriptions of Mount Vernon by visitors Sally Otis Foster (1801) and Winthrop Sargent (1793) (typescripts, LGWMV); and a list dated July 22, 1802, of private sales held after Martha Washington's death (Photostat, LGWMV).

SMOKEHOUSE

1. Weekly Reports, Dec. 23 and 30, 1786, in MV Weekly Reports, Nov. 26, 1785–Dec. 30, 1786; Weekly Report, Dec. 11, 1790, in MV Weekly Reports, Apr. 19, 1789–Sept. 17, 1791 (bound Photostats, LGWMV).
2. WP to GW, May 31, 1795 (typescript, LGWMV).
3. LW to GW, Jan. 31, 1776, in PGW Rev., 3: 232.
4. "Cash Rcd. on act. of Genl. Washington," Aug. 3, 1778, in Lund Washington Account Book, 1774–1786 (typescript, LGWMV), 76b.
5. GW to the Marquis de Lafayette, June 8, 1786, in PGW Con., 4: 104–5.
6. GW to William Hambly, July 28, 1798, in PGW Ret., 2:459.
7. GWPC Recollections, 388–89.
8. GW to WP, July 13, 1794, in WGW, 33: 430.
9. Ham and other meats served are noted in a letter that Theophilus Bradbury, a guest at that meal, wrote to his daughter, Mrs. Thomas Hooper, on Dec. 26, 1795; it is quoted in Anne Hollingsworth Wharton, *Martha Washington* (New York: Charles Scribner's Sons, 1897), 233–34.

FOOD ON THE FRONTIER

1. Entry for Apr. 8, 1748, in GWD, 1: 19.
2. Entries for Mar. 23 and 25, 1748, and Dec. 27, 1753, in GWD, 1: 13, 15, 156.
3. Entries for Oct. 22 and 28, 1770, and Nov. 2, 1770, in GWD, 2: 295–96, 304, 307–8.
4. Entry for Sept. 22, 1784, in GWD, 4: 32.

DINING UNDER CANVAS

1. Joseph M. Thatcher and Maurice H. O'Brien, *George Washington Slept Here . . . But Where Did He Sleep?: A Furnishing Plan for Washington's Headquarters State Historic Site, Newburgh, New York* (Waterford, N.Y.: New York State Office of Parks, Recreation and Historic Preservation, Bureau of Historic Sites, 1985), 117–23, 125.
2. Ibid., 122–23.

3. *George Washington's Military Equipment* (Mount Vernon, Va: MVLA, 1963), 20.
4. Frank E. Grizzard, Jr., *George Washington: A Biographical Companion* (Santa Barbara, Calif.: ABC-CLIO, 2002), 305.
5. General Orders, Sept. 6, 1775, Mar. 4, 1778, Sept. 1, 6, and 7, 1782, in PGW Rev., 1: 419; 14: 53; and WGW, 25: 103, 133, 135.
6. GW to Dr. John Cochran, Aug. 16, 1779, in WGW, 16: 116–17.
7. François Marbois (later Marquis de Barbé-Marbois), as quoted in *George Washington as the French Knew Him: A Collection of Texts*, ed. and trans. Gilbert Chinard (Princeton, N.J.: Princeton University Press, 1940), 76–77.
8. Thatcher and O'Brien, *George Washington Slept Here*, 133. Bennet's words are from a letter to his mother dated Apr. 15, [1783].

"AN EXCELLENT TABLE"
The Art of Dining at Mount Vernon

1. Entry for July 13, 1777, in *The Journal of Nicholas Cresswell, 1774–1777* (New York: Dial Press, 1924), 255.
2. Prussing, 411; invoice to RW, Apr. 15, 1757, in PGW Col., 4:134; invoice from RW, Nov. 10, 1757, in PGW Col., 5: 50; invoice from Robert Cary and Co., Feb. 13, 1764, in PGW Col., 7: 293; Sales of Furniture at Belvoir, Aug. 15, 1774 (Photostat, LGWMV).
3. GW to Bushrod Washington, Sept. 22, 1783, in WGW, 27: 160.
4. Prussing, 411. Washington's order specified "1 Mahogony Case with 16 Square Bottles in it, each bottle holding a Gallon; and the case to stand upon a frame supported by 4 Legs from the foot of which to the Top of the case let be 2 feet 4 inches N.B. let the Bottles be very Strong." Invoice to Robert Cary and Co., Sept. 28, 1760, in PGW Col., 6: 462. In 1761 Washington received "A Neat Mahogony Square Case with 16 Gallon Bottles in ditto with ground Stoppers Brass lifting handles & brass Casters." Invoice from Robert Cary and Co., Mar. 31, 1761, in PGW Col., 7:27. The case and nine of the bottles, supplied by Philip Bell, survive in the Mount Vernon collection, without a stand (W-187/a–k).
5. Prussing, 411–12. Surviving original prints in the Mount Vernon collection include: *David Rittenhouse* (1796), by Edward Savage, after a painting by Charles Willson Peale; and *The Washington Family* (ca. 1790–98), by Edward Savage and David Edwin, after a painting by Savage (W-125 and W-2363, respectively).

6. Prussing, 410. Original paintings and prints in the Mount Vernon collection include: *Morning* and *Evening* (both ca. 1793), by William Winstanley (W-1179 and W-1180, respectively); *The Great Falls of the Potomac* (ca. 1797) and *The Passage of the Pato'k thro' the blew mountain at the confluence of that River with the Shan'h* (ca. 1797), by George Beck (W-2 and W-3, respectively); the engraving *Louis Seize Roi des Français, Restorateur de la Liberte* (1790), by Charles Clement Balvay Bervic (W-767); the engravings of *The Death of General Montgomery* (1798), by Johan Frederik Clemens and *The Battle of Bunker's Hill* (1798), by Johann Gotthard von Muller, both after John Trumbull (W-1407/a,b); and the eighteenth-century pastel *The Virgin Mary*, by an unknown artist (2003.024).
7. Prussing, 410. Washington began constructing the large dining room in 1775; it was completed about 1787. The interior work, papering, and painting were not finished until about 1789, however. For more on the room, see Mesick, Cohen, Waite Architects, "Mount Vernon Historic Structure Report," 3 vols. (1993), 2: 349–73 (LGWMV). For more on the chairs John Aitken supplied, see Carol B. Cadou, *The George Washington Collection: Fine and Decorative Arts at Mount Vernon* (Manchester, N.H.: Hudson Hills Press, 2006), 182. Additional original furnishings from the large dining room in the collection include one of the large looking glasses (W-28), two candlestands (W-1/a, b), a sideboard (W-94), two of the wall-mounted Argand lamps (W-13), and the marble mantelpiece (W-940) with its Worcester porcelain garniture (W-972/a, b; W-2260/a, b).
8. "A Dinner at Mount Vernon—1799," from the unpublished journal of Joshua Brookes, as excerpted in MVLA AR 1947, 24. The original manuscript is in the collection of the New-York Historical Society, New York.
9. Porcelain services in use at Mount Vernon in 1799 and noted in the inventory compiled after George Washington's death include the "Fine Image China," the tea-and-coffee service provided by the Comte de Custine-Sarreck, a Chinese export service decorated with the insignia of the Society of the Cincinnati, a Chinese export service provided by Andreas Everardus van Braam Houckgeest, the French ware purchased from the Comte de Moustier, and "the blew & white china in common use" that Martha Washington noted in her will. LWT, 58. For more on these services, see Cadou, *George Washington Collection*, 44–45, 89, 108–111, 148, 149, and Detweiler, 24–31, 67–77, 73–80, 82–97, 123–34, 151–58. For the silver urn, tongs, and cream pail, see Cadou, *George Washington Collection*,

46–47, 62–63, 114–15. For Washington's April 1784 order of silver tea ware, including an image of one sugar pail, see Buhler, 44–47.

10. For more on this silver coffeepot, see Cadou, *George Washington Collection*, 116–17. For more on the Comte de Moustier's French porcelains, see Detweiler, 123–34.

11. Manasseh Cutler, Jan. 2, 1802, in William E. Curtis, "Mount Vernon in 1802: Description of a Visit to "Lady" Washington; At the General's Tomb; How the Grounds Looked over a Century Ago" (typescript, LGWMV).

12. Henry Wansey, *An Excursion to the United States of North America in the Summer of 1794*, 2nd ed. (Salisbury, England: J. Easton, 1798), 112.

13. In March 1761, Washington received from Richard Farrer of London "1 Glass Pyramid with 8 arms" and "1 Salver." Invoice from Robert Cary and Co., Mar. 31, 1761, in PGW Col., 7: 29. For earlier orders as well as porcelain seasons and muses, see Cadou, *George Washington Collection*, 48–49, 50–51.

14. GM to GW, Jan. 24, 1790, in PGW Pres., 5: 48–49.

15. GW to GM, Oct. 13, 1789, in PGW Pres., 4: 177–78.

16. GM to GW, Jan. 24, 1790, in PGW Pres., 5: 48.

17. Theophilus Bradbury to his daughter Mrs. [Thomas] Hooper, Dec. 26, 1795, as quoted in *Christmas with George Washington, 1776–1799* (Philadelphia: Franklin Printing, 1954), [4–5].

18. Entry for Nov. 16, 1785, in *Quebec to Carolina in 1785–1786: Being the Travel Diary and Observations of Robert Hunter, Jr., a Young Merchant of London*, as excerpted in Research Notebook 15 (Early Descriptions ante 1800) (LGWMV).

19. For salvers, wine coasters, and wine coolers, see Cadou, *George Washington Collection*, 118–19, 114, and 144–45, respectively. In 2007 an additional four-bottle wine cooler (2007.012.001) and one of Washington's bottle rollers (2007.012.002) came to light and entered the collection.

20. Entry for Nov. 16, 1785, in *Quebec to Carolina in 1785–1786*.

PRESIDENTIAL DINING

1. Entries for Aug. 27, 1789, Jan. 14, Mar. 4, May 6, and July 8, 1790, and Jan. 20, 1791, in Maclay, 137, 182, 212, 261, 315, 364–65.

2. Entry for Aug. 27, 1789, in Maclay, 136–37.

3. Theophilus Bradbury to his daughter, Mrs. Thomas Hooper, Dec. 26, 1795, as quoted in Detweiler, 112, 118, and in Anne Hollingsworth Wharton, *Martha Washington* (New York: Charles Scribner's Sons, 1897), 233–34. The full letter was reproduced in the *Pennsylvania Magazine of History and Biography* 8, no. 2 (June 1884): 226–27.

4. Entry for June 11, 1789, in Maclay, 74.

LEVÉES

1. Decatur, 43–44; GWPC Recollections, 492n.

2. Rufus Wilmot Griswold, *The Republican Court; or, American Society in the Days of Washington* (New York: D. Appleton and Company, 1855), 215–16; Decatur, 43, 44; Abigail Adams to her sister, Mary Smith Cranch (Mrs. Richard Cranch), Aug. 9, 1789, in Adams, 19; GWPC Recollections; 432n.

3. Entry for June 5, 1789, in Maclay, 70.

4. GWPC Recollections, 395–96.

5. Entry for Aug. 7, 1789, in RL diary (July 4–Sept. 1, 1789, typescript, LGWMV).

SOUTH GROVE MIDDEN

1. GW to LW, Aug. 19, 1776, in PGW Rev., 6: 84–85.

2. Invoices from RW, Aug. 20, 1757, and Thomas Knox, Sept. 28, 1757, in PGW Col., 4: 378, 427.

3. Invoice from Thomas Knox, Aug. 18, 1758, in PGW Col., 5: 399–400.

4. Detweiler, 30.

SETTING THE TABLE

1. Belden, 19–21; Carson, 6–9.

2. For dish crosses, see Belden, 48–49. For Washington's French silver dish cross, see Buhler, 57.

3. Belden, 21; Carson, 9–10; Paston-Williams, 257, 258–59.

4. For Washington's purchases of knives and forks, see Buhler, 12, 14, 15, 16, 34, and 86. For the purchase of the porcelain-handled flatware, see Detweiler, 50. For the purchases of other silver utensils, see Buhler, 18, 21, 32, 33, 35, 60–62, and 65–68.

5. Belden, 19–21.

6. Trusler, 24.

7. Belden, 21.

8. Entry for Jan. 20, 1791, in Maclay, 365.

9. Helen Maggs Fede, *Washington Furniture at Mount Vernon* (Mount Vernon, Va.: MVLA, 1966), 25, 27; Buhler, 50–53, 55, 59–60, 71–72.

10. The general descriptions of typical eighteenth-century dining practices here are drawn from Belden, 21; Carson, 9–10; and Paston-Williams, 234, 252, 256, 257–58.

11. Belden, 21; Carson, 7.

12. Paston-Williams, 261–63.

13. Belden, 30.

14. GW, invoice to Robert Cary and Co., Sept. 27, 1763, and invoice from Robert Cary and Co., Feb. 23, 1764, in PGW Col., 7: 256, 289. See also Detweiler, 51–53.

FRANK LEE THE BUTLER

1. "Cash Accounts," May 3, 1768, in PGW Col., 8: 82, 83n. For the fact that Frank was mulatto, see GW to WP, Oct. 27, 1793, in PGW Pres., 14: 293.

2. GW to Albin Rawlins, Jan. 31, 1798, in PGW Ret., 2: 62.

3. Frank had earlier been a waiter; see entry for Feb. 18, 1786, in GWD, 4: 277.

4. Linda Baumgarten, *What Clothes Reveal: The Language of Clothing in Colonial and Federal America* (Williamsburg, Va.: Colonial Williamsburg Foundation in association with Yale University Press, 2002), 128–32; GW to RW, Dec. 6, 1755, enclosure, invoice [Dec. 6, 1755], in PGW Col., 2: 208, 209.

5. MW to FBW, July 1, 1792, and Aug. 4, 1793, as quoted in PMW, 238, 250.

6. GW to AW, Feb. 3 and 10, 1793, in WGW, 32: 330, 341; MW to FBW, Aug. 4, 1793, in PMW, 250; GW to WP, Dec. 28, 1794, in WGW, 34: 74; GW to AW, Dec. 9, 1792, in PGW Pres., 11: 487; GW to AW, Nov. 4, 1792, in PGW Pres., 11: 333; GW to WP, Dec. 4, 1796, in WGW, 35: 307.

7. Entry for Feb. 18, 1786, in GWD, 4: 281, 282; GW, Negros Belonging to George Washington in his own right and by Marriage, in PGW Ret., 4: 529, 530. For Frank and Lucy's quarters, see GW to WP, Oct. 27, 1793, in PGW Pres., 14: 293.

8. Ledger B (bound Photostat, LGWMV), 330a, 344a, 367a. Slaves were allowed to sell chickens, eggs, and produce from their gardens. They could also sell fish and game they caught while "off duty" as well as items they made during hours when not at work.

9. LWT, 2–4.

10. For the breakdown of the ownership of the slaves, see Negros Belonging to George Washington in his own right and by Marriage, and A List of Negros Hired from Mrs[.] French [June 1799], in PGW Ret., 4: 528–40. For information about the dower slaves, see PGW Col., 6: 215n3, 217–20, 219n8; and PGW Ret., 4: 494n2.

11. *Alexandria Gazette*, July 30, 1821.

12. GWPC Recollections, 389.

"AN ABUNDANCE OF EVERY THING"
Mount Vernon's Fruit and Vegetable Gardens

1. GW to AW, Feb. 3, 1793, in PGW Pres., 32: 327.

2. GW to AW, May 12, 1793, in PGW Pres., 32: 459.

3. GW to WP, Sept. 21, 1794, in PGW Pres., 33: 503.

4. MW to FBW, July 1, 1792, in PMW, 238.

5. Thomas Mawe and John Abercrombie, *The Universal Gardener and Botanist; or, a General Dictionary of Gardening and Botany* (London: Printed for G. Robinson and T. Cadell, 1778), n.p.

6. Entry for Mar. 24, 1762, in GWD, 1: 295.

7. Entry for Mar. 30, 1763, in GWD, 1: 317.

8. Baron Ludwig von Closen, "A Visit to Mount Vernon," *William and Mary Quarterly*, 3rd ser., 10, no. 2 (Apr. 1953): 229.

9. Mawe and Abercrombie, *Universal Gardener and Botanist*, n.p.

10. GW to Robert Adam, Nov. 22, 1771, in PGW Col., 3: 77.

11. Entry for Nov. 14, 1788, in GWD, 5: 422.

12. George A. Washington to GW, Mar. 26, 1790, in PGW Pres., 35: 47.

13. GW to WP, May 15, 1796, in PGW Pres., 35: 47.

14. GW to RL, June 26, 1796, in PGW Pres., 35: 101.

15. Reports for Mar. 17, Apr. 21, and June 2, 1798, in Weekly Reports of General Washington's Gardener, Jan. 7, 1797–Jan. 26, 1799 (bound transcript, LGWMV), 16, 18, 20.

16. Invoice from Robert Cary and Co., Nov. 17, 1766, in PGW Col., 7: 470.

17. Reports for Jan. 26 and May 26, 1798, in Weekly Reports of General Washington's Gardener, Jan. 7, 1797–Jan. 26, 1799 (bound transcript, LGWMV), 13, 19.

18. Peter Stephen Duponceau, "The Autobiography of Peter Stephen Duponceau," *Pennsylvania Magazine of History and Biography* 63 (July 1939): 311–15.

19. Reports for Feb. 18, 1798, Dec. 30, 1797, and Jan. 6, 1798, in Weekly Reports of General Washington's Gardener, Jan. 7, 1797–Jan. 26, 1799 (bound transcript, LGWMV), 15, 12, 13.

20. Amariah Frost diary, as quoted in Moncure D. Conway, "Footprints in Washingtonland," *Harper's New Monthly Magazine* 78, no. 467 (Apr. 1889): 743.

THE UPPER GARDEN

1. Entry for July 3, 1799, in John E. Latta journal (typescript, LGWMV).

2. Entry for Mar. 22, 1762, in GWD, 1: 295

3. Entry for Feb. 9, 1785, in GWD, 4: 86–88; entry for Feb. 12, 1785, in GWD, 4: 89–90; entry for Mar. 4, 1785, in GWD, 4: 98; entry for Mar. 14, 1785, in GWD, 4: 102; entry for Apr. 1, 1785, in GWD, 4: 111–12; entry for Apr. 4, 1785, in GWD, 4: 112–13; entry for Oct. 26, 1785, in GWD, 4: 213–14; entry for Nov. 18, 1785, in GWD, 4: 232–34; entry for Feb. 11, 1786, in GWD, 4: 273–74.

4. Entry for June 2, 1798, in Niemcewicz, 97–98; MV Gardener's Weekly Reports, Apr. 7, May 5, and June 9, 1798 (typescript, LGWMV).

GEORGE WASHINGTON'S BOOKS ON GARDENING

1. Philip Miller, *The Abridgement of the Gardeners Dictionary* (London: n.p., 1768); GW to Governor George Clinton, Apr. 20, 1785, in PGW Con., 28: 135.

2. Mac Griswold, *Washington's Gardens at Mount Vernon* (Boston: Houghton Mifflin, 1999), 63–64; Steven Parissien, *Palladian Style* (London: Phaidon

Press, 1994), 226; John Rhodehamel, "Langley's Book of Gardening," MVLA AR (1984), 26–29.

3. Batty Langley, *New Principles of Gardening: The Laying out and Planting of Parterres, Groves, Wildernesses, Labyrinths, Avenues, Parks, etc.* (London: Printed for A. Bettesworth and J. Batley, 1728); Niemcewicz account, as cited in Jean B. Lee, ed., *Experiencing Mount Vernon: Eyewitness Accounts, 1784–1865* (Charlottesville: University of Virginia Press, 2006), 75.

FOOD PRESERVATION

1. Schmit, 25.

2. Sarah F. McMahon, "Laying Foods By: Gender, Dietary Decisions, and the Technology of Food Preservation in New England Households, 1750–1850," in Judith A. McGaw, ed., *Early American Technology: Making and Doing Things from the Colonial Era to 1850* (Chapel Hill: University of North Carolina Press, 1994), 171–75, 172n.

3. MW to FBW, July 1, 1792, in PMW, 238.

4. Weekly Report, Oct. 27, 1792, in MV Weekly Reports, Jan. 8, 1792–Nov. 8, 1794 (bound Photostat, LGMWV), 63.

5. Dennis J. Pogue, "New Light on the Mansion Basement," MVLA AR 1994, 22–23; GW to AW, Dec. 9, 1792, in PGW Pres., 11: 487.

6. Weekly Reports, Nov. 4, 11, and 18, 1786, in MV Weekly Reports, Nov. 26, 1785–Dec. 30, 1786 (bound Photostat, MVLA), 51, 52, 53, 55; "Dogue Run Farm . . . Contra," 1797, and "Union Farm . . . Contra," 1797, in MV Farm Ledger, 1797–1798 (bound Photostat, LGWMV), 6, 8; Weekly Reports, Oct. 27, 1792, and Nov. 8, 1794, in MV Weekly Reports, Jan. 8, 1792–Nov. 8, 1794, 63, n.p.

7. Schmit, 25.

8. "To keep green pease till Christmas" and "Another way to preserve green pease," in [Hannah Glasse,] *The Art of Cookery, Made Plain and Easy* (London: Printed for A. Millar, J. and R. Tonson, W. Strahan, T. Caslon, T. Durham, and W. Nicoll, 1765), 310.

9. Weekly Report, Nov. 4, 1786, in MV Weekly Reports, Nov. 26, 1785–Dec. 30, 1786, 50–51.

10. GW to David Stuart, Dec. 24, 1785, in PGW Con., 3: 479–80; GW, Mar. 15–17 and 30, 1786, in GWD, 4: 294–95, 301.

11. Schmit, 25, 26.

12. For pickle recipes, see Glasse, 260–71. For the number of pickle pots in the Mansion, see "In the Cellar," in *Estate of George Washington*, 434. For the Martha Washington quote, see MW to FBW, July 1, 1792, in PMW, 239.

13. Schmit, 27–28; Hess, 228–31, 237–40, 253–55, 276.

14. Pierre-Etienne Duponceau, "A Visit to Mount Vernon in 1780," in *George Washington as the French*

Knew Him: A Collection of Texts, ed. and trans. Gilbert Chinard (1940; repr., New York: Greenwood Press, 1969), 19.

15. GW to WP, May 4, 1794, in WGW, 33: 352; MW to FBWL, May 24, 1795, in PMW, 288.

16. LW, "Cash pd. on Acct. of Genrl. Washington," [June] 1783, Lund Washington Account Book, 1774–1786 (typescript, LGWMV), 122a.

17. GW to WP, Feb. 9, 1794, in WGW, 33: 266–67.

MILLING FLOUR AT MOUNT VERNON

1. Charles B. Kuhlmann, *The Development of the Flour-Milling Industry in the United States* (Boston and New York: Houghton Mifflin, 1929), 16.

2. Entry for June 6, 1771, in GWD, 3: 36.

3. GWPC Recollections, 166–67, 386.

4. GW to Robert Cary and Co., Aug. 12, 1771, in PGW Col., 8: 516–17.

5. GW to Robert Lewis and Sons, Apr. 12, 1785, in PGW Con., 2: 493–94.

6. Ibid.

7. GW to William Roberts, June 17, 1799, in PGW Ret., 4: 132–33.

8. GW to CB, Jan. 23, 1799, in GW Papers, Series 2: Letterbook 21 (Library of Congress, Washington, D.C.)

DRINK AND BE MERRY
Liquor and Wine at Mount Vernon

1. GW to Thomas Green, Mar. 31, 1789, in PGW Pres., 1: 468.

2. William J. Rorabaugh, *The Alcoholic Republic: An American Tradition* (Oxford: Oxford University Press, 1979), 25, 95–122.

3. Ibid., 110–12; invoice from RW, Aug. 20, 1757, in PGW Col., 4: 380; invoice from Thomas Knox, Aug. 18, 1758, in PGW Col., 5: 400.

4. Invoice from RW, Aug. 20, 1757, in PGW Col., 4: 380; invoice from Thomas Knox, Aug. 18, 1758, in PGW Col., 5: 400; invoice to Robert Cary and Co., Sept. 28, 1760, in PGW Col., 6: 463; invoice from Robert Cary and Co., Mar. 31, 1761, in PGW Col., 7: 24; enclosure, invoice to Robert Cary and Co., Oct. 12, 1761, in PGW Col., 7: 77; enclosure, invoices to Robert Cary and Co., Nov. 15, 1762, in PGW Col., 7: 165. During this period, the liquid capacities for barrels and casks were generally standardized: pipe (126 gallons), hogshead (63 gallons), tierce (42 gallons), and barrel (31.5 to 34 gallons). See James I. Walsh, "Capacity and Gauge Standards for Barrels and Casks of Early America," *Chronicle of the Early American Industries Association* 52, no. 4 (Dec. 1999): 151–54. On several occasions, however, Washington specified that the "hogsheads" of rum he purchased

or sold held between 111 and 125 gallons; see MV Accounts Kept by John Kirkpatrick and Lund Washington, 1772–1787 (LGWMV), 51–52, 152, 155.

5. GW to the Marquis de Lafayette, Jan. 29, 1789, in PGW Digital, 264; GW to CB, July 20, 1788, in PGW Con., 6: 387; TL to GW, Oct. 31, 1790, in PGW Pres., 6: 606; GW to TL, in PGW Pres., Nov. 7, 1790, 6: 635.

6. Cash Accounts, June 16, 1774, in PGW Col., 10: 76; GW to the Marquis de Lafayette, June 8, 1786, in PGW Con., 4: 105; GW to the Comte de Moustier, Dec. 15, 1788, in PGW Pres., 1: 181; MV Farm Accounts, 1797–1801 (LGWMV), 45.

7. Entry for June 5, 1798, in Niemcewicz, 103; enclosure, invoice to Robert Cary and Co., May 1, 1759, in PGW Col., 6: 318; G. Deneale to Colonel Joseph May, July 21, 1802 (Photostat, LGWMV).

8. David Hancock, Oceans of Wine: Madeira and the Emergence of American Trade and Taste (New Haven, Conn.: Yale University Press, 2009), 112, 115–24; GW to Wakelin Welch and Son, Aug. 16, 1789, in PGW Pres., 3: 479; GW Household Account Book, 1793–1797 (LGWMV), 33.

9. GW to Philip Mazzei, July 1, 1799, in WGW 15: 347; entry for Mar. 21, 1763, in GWD 1: 315; John Marsden Pintard to GW, Jan. 24, 1786, in PGW Con., 3: 522–23; entry for Nov. 20, 1771, in GWD 3: 73; GW to AW, Jan. 13, 1793, in PGW Pres., 11: 630–31.

10. Rorabaugh, Alcoholic Republic, 64–69; Frederick H. Smith, Caribbean Rum: A Social and Economic History (Gainesville: University Press of Florida, 2005), 80–81; entry for July 3, 1799, in John E. Latta journal (typescript, LGWMV); entry for June 2, 1798, in Niemcewicz, 96.

11. MV Store Account, 1787 (LGWMV), 25–33; MV Farm Accounts, 1797–1799 (LGWMV), 147; MV Farm Accounts, 1797–1801 (LGWMV), 33.

12. William Thornton to GW, Oct. 6, 1797, in PGW Ret., 1: 386; GW to Thornton, Oct. 10, 1797, in PGW Ret., 1: 401.

13. Agreement between GW and Philip Bater, Apr. 23, 1787, MV Farm Accounts, 1797–1801 (LGWMV), 46.

14. GW to Robert Lewis and Sons, Apr. 12, 1785, in PGW Con., 2: 493–94; GW to Robert Lewis and Sons, Feb. 1, 1785, in PGW Digital, 317.

15. Reminiscences of the Reverend Ashbel Green, as quoted in GWPC Recollections, 169; Robert Hunter, Jr., Quebec to Carolina in 1785–1786: Being the Travel Diary and Observations of Robert Hunter, Jr., a Young Merchant of London (1943), repr. in Jean B. Lee, ed., Experiencing Mount Vernon: Eyewitness Accounts, 1784–1865 (Charlottesville: University of Virginia Press, 2006), 28–30.

16. GW to WP, Dec. 7, 1794, in WGW 34: 53; GW to WP, Nov. 23, 1794, in WGW 34: 41–42.

17. GW to James Anderson, Jan. 8, 1797, in WGW

35: 352–53; GW to John Fitzgerald, June 12, 1797, in PGW Ret., 1: 180; Fitzgerald to GW, June 12, 1797, in PGW Ret, 1: 181; GW to Anderson, June 18, 1797, in PGW Ret., 1: 193; MV Farm Accounts, 1797–1799 (LGWMV); MV Farm Accounts, 1797–1801 (LGWMV); Henry Lee, "Funeral Oration on the Death of General Washington" (1800), as quoted in William M. S. Rasmussen and Robert Tilton, George Washington: The Man behind the Myths (Charlottesville: University Press of Virginia, 1999), 262.

BARBECUES

1. Jane Carson, Colonial Virginians at Play (Williamsburg, Va.: Colonial Williamsburg Foundation, 1989), 14. See also Randolph, xxvii–xxviii. For hints that, a few years earlier, Virginia barbecues had had more of a potluck-supper quality, see Landon Carter, Sept. 5, 1772, The Diary of Colonel Landon Carter of Sabine Hall, 1752–1778, ed. with an introduction by Jack P. Greene, 2 vols. (Charlottesville: University Press of Virginia for the Virginia Historical Society, 1965), 2: 722.

2. Allan B. Magruder, John Marshall (Boston and New York: Houghton Mifflin and the Riverside Press, 1898), 267.

3. Randolph, 63.

4. For Jefferson's cultivation of cayenne pepper and its use in Virginia, see Randolph, 282–83. For Washington's purchases of this pepper, see invoice from Robert Cary and Co., Mar. 15, 1760, and GW to Daniel Jenifer Adams, July 20, 1772, in PGW Col., 6: 399 and 9: 70. For Washington planting cayenne at Mount Vernon, see the entries for June 13 and 29, 1785, in GWD, 4: 152, 153n, 157.

5. For Washington's attendance at prewar barbecues, see entries for May 27, 1769, Aug. 4, 1770, Sept. 4 and 18, 1773, and May 7 and Aug. 27, 1774, in GWD, 2: 154, 261; 3: 203, 204, 248, 271.

6. Britannia Wellington Peter Kennon, Dec. 19, 1899, in "Reminiscences of Britannia Peter Kennon (1815–1911), recorded by her grandson Armistead Peter, Jr. (1870–1960)," Tudor Place Archives (Photostat, LGWMV).

7. Entry for Aug. 4, 1770, in GWD, 2: 261.

8. For Washington bringing guests home after a barbecue, see entries for Sept. 4–5 and 18, 1773, and May 7, 1774, in GWD, 3: 203, 204, 248. For Washington as a guest after a barbecue, see entries for May 27, 1769, and Aug. 4, 1770, in GWD, 2: 154, 261.

9. Entry for May 7, 1774, in GWD, 3: 248, 248n.

10. Charles Willson Peale, as quoted in entry for Dec. 28, 1773, in GWD, 3: 221n; see also Carson, Colonial Virginians at Play, 79–81.

FISHERIES

1. Donald B. Leach, "George Washington: Waterman-Fisherman, 1760–1799," Historical Society of Fairfax County, Virginia, Yearbook 28 (2002): 18–19. By comparison, in 1797, a year when fishery profits were £165, net profits for the entire plantation were £898. See MV Farm Accounts, 1797–1799 (LGWMV), 87–88.

2. Leach, "Waterman-Fisherman": 13–14.

3. Ibid.: 19; MV Ledger B (bound Photostat, LGWMV), 42; MV Farm Accounts, 1797–1799 (LGWMV), 87–88; MV Accounts Kept by John Kirkpatrick and Lund Washington, 1772–1787 (LGWMV), 15b, 52.

EXOTIC FOODS AND BEVERAGES

1. LW to GW, Mar. 18 and Aug. 19, 1778, in PGW Rev., 14: 221, 16: 334.

2. LW to GW, Apr. 1, 1778, in PGW, Rev., 14: 382.

3. GW to the Marquis de Lafayette, Jan. 29, 1789, in PGW Pres., 1: 264.

DAIRYING

1. GW to WP, Nov. 2, 1794, in WGW, 34: 12.

2. Audrey Nöel Hume, Food: Colonial Williamsburg Archaeological Series, No. 9 (Williamsburg, Va.: Colonial Williamsburg Foundation, 1978), 49–50.

3. Kenneth F. Kiple and Virginia Himmelsteib King, Another Dimension to the Black Diaspora: Diet, Disease, and Racism (Cambridge, England: Cambridge University Press, 1981), 83

4. For Washington's purchases of milk before and after 1759, see entries for July 4 and Oct. 25, 1755, Apr. 28, 1756, Sept. 20, 1758, and Aug. 1769, in Ledger A (bound Photostat, LGWMV), 22a, 24a, 28a, 52a, 295a; and Jan. 2, 1794, in WHAB, 30: 159.

5. For Washington's purchases of milk pans and other dairy implements in the 1760s and 1790s, see GW, Enclosure: Invoice to Robert Cary and Co., Sept. 28, 1760; invoice from Robert Cary and Co., Mar. 31, 1761; GW, Enclosure: Invoices to Robert Cary and Co., Nov. 15, 1762; invoice from Robert Cary and Co., Apr. [23,] 1763; GW, Enclosure: Invoice to Robert Cary and Co., Sept. 20, 1765; invoice from Robert Cary and Co., Dec. 20, 1765, in PGW Col., 6: 462; 7: 29, 165, 198, 404; entry for Jan. 5, 1761, in Washington Invoices and Letters, 1755–1766 (bound Photostat, LGWMV); entries for Aug. 11, 1794, and Mar. 16, 1795, in WHAB 30: 314, 470; entries for Apr. 3, 1797, June 22, 1798, and Aug. 17, 1798, in MV Farm Ledger, 1797–1798 (bound Photostat, LGWMV), 86, 165, 182; and Detweiler, 49–50.

6. Dennis J. Pogue and Esther C. White, "Summary Report on the 'House for Families' Slave Quarter Site (44 Fx 762/40–47), Mount Vernon

Plantation, Mount Vernon, Virginia" (unpublished paper prepared for the MVLA, Dec. 1991), 19, 23.

7. See reports of Mansion House slaves for Aug. 22, 1789, Dec. 12, 1789, Mar. 13 and 20, July 10, Sept. 11 and 18, 1790, in MV Weekly Reports, Apr. 19, 1789–Sept. 17, 1791 (bound Photostat, LGWMV); July 27 and Aug. 3 and 10, 1793, in MV Weekly Reports, Jan. 8, 1792–Nov. 8, 1794 (bound Photostat, LGWMV); and June 23 and 30, 1798, in MV Farm Accounts 2, Mar. 31, 1798–Jan. 7, 1799 (bound Photostat, LGWMV).

8. GW to WP, Feb. 9, 1794, in PGW Pres., 15: 204.

9. For these purchases, see entries for June 22 and Aug. 17, 1798, in MV Farm Ledger, 1797–1798, 165, 182.

10. Dorothy Hartley, *Lost Country Life* (New York: Pantheon, 1979), 103.

11. GW to AW, Dec. 9, 1792, in PGW Pres., 11: 487; entries for Mansion House Farm, June 23 and 30, 1798, in MV Farm Accounts 2, Mar. 31, 1798–Jan. 7, 1799; "Negros Belonging to George Washington in his own right and by Marriage" [June 1799], in PGW Ret., 4: 529, 530.

12. GW to James Anderson (of Scotland), Apr. 7, 1797, in PGW Ret., 1: 80.

13. "Agreement with Edward Violet" [Aug. 5, 1762], in PGW Col., 7: 145.

14. See account with Andrew Jameson's Bakery, June 17 and July 24, 1797, in MV Farm Ledger, 1797–1798, 63.

15. MW to FBW, Aug. 4, 1793 (typescript, LGWMV).

16. See account of the Dairy at J. A's [farm manager James Anderson], 1797, in MV Farm Ledger, 1797–1798, 15, 16.

17. GW to James Anderson, Dec. 10, 1799, in PGW Ret., 4: 457.

THE SLAVE DIET

1. Entry for June 4, 1798, in Niemcewicz, 100–101. Slaves were allowed to sell chickens, eggs, and produce from their gardens. They were also permitted to sell fish and game they caught while "off duty" as well as items made during hours when they were not at work.

2. GW to Arthur Young, June 18[–21], 1792, and GW to WP, Dec. [23], 1793, in PGW Pres., 10: 461 and 14: 611.

3. U.S. Bureau of the Census, *Historical Statistics of the United States: Colonial Times to 1957* (Washington, D.C.: U.S. Government Printing Office, 1960), 755, 774.

4. Kenneth F. Kiple and Virginia Himmelsteib King, *Another Dimension to the Black Diaspora: Diet, Disease, and Racism* (Cambridge, England: Cambridge University Press, 1981), 88–93.

5. Ledger A, Jan. 1758 (Photostat; LGWMV), xxii; LW Account Book, July 1775 (typescript, LGWMV), 49; Ledger B, Sept. 7 and 29, 1788; July 19, 1789; Mar. 28, 1791; Sept. 29, 1791; July 23, 1792; Aug. 2, 1792; Sept. 13 and 15, 1792; Oct. 3, 1792 (Photostat, LGWMV), 270a, 275a, 306a, 325a, 333a, 342a, 344a, 346a. As with food, slaves were issued very basic attire each year—equivalent to one set of winter clothes and one set of summer clothes. They had to obtain other such items they needed or wanted through purchase (see note 1 above) or trade.

6. MVLA Archaeological Artifact Catalogue: House for Families, 1984–1985; Stephen C. Atkins, "Mount Vernon: Identified Taxa" (unpublished paper, LGWMV, 1993), 1. For documentary evidence of hunting, see entries for Sept. 11, 1790, and Oct. 3, 1792, in Ledger B, 320a, 346a; entry for Jan. 19, 1787, in MV Storehouse Account Book, 1787 (typescript, LGWMV); GWPC Recollections, 457–58; and "Mount Vernon Reminiscences," *Alexandria (Va.) Gazette*, Nov. 10 or 16, 1835; Jan. 18, 22, and 25, 1876.

7. Atkins, "Mount Vernon: Identified Taxa," 1–3; Dennis J. Pogue, "The Archaeology of Plantation Life: Another Perspective on George Washington's Mount Vernon," *Virginia Cavalcade* 41, no. 2 (Autumn 1991): 76.

8. Pogue, "The Archaeology of Plantation Life," 76–78; Dennis J. Pogue and Esther White, "Summary Report on the 'House for Families' Slave Quarter Site (44 Fx 762/40–47), Mount Vernon Plantation, Mount Vernon, Virginia" (unpublished paper prepared for MVLA, Dec. 1991), 19.

9. MVLA Archaeological Artifact Catalogue, House for Families, 1984–1985; Pogue and White, "Summary Report," 13–36.

FAVORITE FOODS

1. GWPC Recollections, 421.

2. Ibid., 421–22.

3. TL to George Augustine Washington, May 3, 1789, in PGW Pres., 2: 248.

THE RECIPES

SOUPS

1. Wilson, 223–24.

2. Entry for Aug. 27, 1789, in Maclay, 136–37.

3. Glasse, 1796 ed., 177.

4. James McHenry to GW, Jan. 25, 1791, in PGW, Pres., 7: 283.

5. Randolph, 37–38.

6. Glasse, 1796 ed., 185.

7. Leslie, 1830, 96.

8. Kettilby, 9–10.

9. Glasse 1796 ed., 207.

VEGETABLES

1. Glasse, 1747 ed., 12.

2. Smith, 15.

3. Raffald, 78; Rundell, 163.

4. Rundell, 174.

5. Leslie, 1973, 183.

6. Glasse, 1796 ed., 140.

7. Glasse, 1747 ed., 98.

8. Carson, 7.

9. Glasse, 1747 ed., 98.

10. Ibid., ii.

11. Glasse, 1796 ed., 228.

12. Entry for Mar. 31, 1787, in GWD, 5: 125–26.

13. Mary Custis Lee Papers, 1694–1917, section 63, Virginia Historical Society, Richmond.

14. Rundell, 174.

15. Hess, 189.

16. Glasse, 1796 ed., 140.

17. GW to George A. Washington, June 3, 1787, in PGW, Con., 5: 218; GW to George A. Washington, June 10, 1787, in PGW, Con., 5: 224.

18. Glasse, 1796 ed., 233.

19. Entry for May 2, 1787, in GWD, 4: 149.

20. Glasse, 1796 ed., 30.

21. Entry for May 25, 1785, in GWD, 4: 145.

22. Entry for Apr. 25, 1788, in Robert Carter III Journal, Aug. 1784–Mar. 1789 (Robert Carter III Papers, Manuscript Division, Library of Congress, Washington, D.C.).

23. Glasse, 1747 ed., 104.

24. MW copy of *The Good Old Virginia Almanack for the Year of Our Lord, 1802* (LGWMV), n.p.

25. Glasse, 1747 ed., 57.

26. Taylor, 69.

27. Wilson, 360.

28. Glasse, 1747 ed., 59.

MEAT, POULTRY, AND FISH

1. Theophilus Bradbury to his daughter, Mrs. Thomas Hooper, Dec. 26, 1795, as quoted in Anne Hollingsworth Wharton, *Martha Washington* (New York: Charles Scribner's Sons, 1897), 234.

2. GW to AW, Aug. 29, 1791, in PGW Pres., 8: 468.

3. *Lady's Companion*, 171–72; Glasse, 1747 ed., 19.

4. *Lady's Companion*, 181.

5. Wilson, 220.

6. Glasse, 1747 ed., 13.

7. Glasse, 1796 ed., 204. For additional historic recipes, see Raffald, 158–59 and Randolph, 101.

8. Glasse, 1796 ed., 204.

9. Wilson, 85.

10. Glasse, 1747 ed., 20.

11. Smith, 90.

12. Samuel Johnson, *A Dictionary of the English Language* (1755; facsimile, London: Times Books, 1979), n.p.

13. Davidson, 181.

14. Johnson, *Dictionary*, n.p.

15. Smith, 18.

16. Wilson, 104.

17. Leslie, 1830, 94–95.

18. Johnson, *Dictionary*, n.p.

19. GWPC, as quoted in Berard: 162.

20. GW to William Hambly, July 28, 1798, in WGW, 36: 369.

21. Johnson, *Dictionary*, n.p.

22. Glasse, 1747 ed., 31.

23. Brookes Journal: 76.

24. Glasse, 1796 ed., 76–77.

25. Misson, *Misson's Memoirs and Observations in His Travels over England* (London: Printed for D. Browne, A. Bell, and others, 1719), 3–35.

26. David Humphreys to GW, Nov. 16, 1786, in PGW Con., 4: 374.

27. GW to David Humphreys, Dec. 26, 1786, in PGW Con., 4: 480.

28. *Newcastle Chronicle*, Jan. 6, 1770.

29. Glasse, 1747 ed., 73.

30. Raffald, 125–26.

31. GWPC Recollections, 451–52.

32. Entry for Feb. 24, 1768, in GWD, 2: 39.

33. Raffald, 59–60.

34. GWPC Recollections, 457.

35. Glasse, 1747 ed., 123.

36. R. Howe to Col. Webb, June 6, 1782, as quoted in "Notes," *Magazine of American History* 5, no. 3 (Sept. 1880): 221.

37. Randolph, 75.

38. Glasse, 1796 ed., 140.

39. Ibid., 95.

SAUCES

1. Randolph, 112–13.

2. Raffald, 59.

3. Randolph, 80.

4. *Lady's Companion*, 167.

5. Randolph, 112.

6. John Evelyn, *Aceteria: A Discourse of Sallets* (1699; facsimile, London: Prospect Books, 1982), 97–107.

7. Taylor, 69.

8. Randolph, 27–28.

9. Terms on which the farms at Mount Vernon may be obtained, Feb. 1, 1796, in WGW, 34: 444.

10. Glasse, 1796 ed., 34.

11. Hannah Mary Bouvier Peterson, *The National Cook Book: By a Lady of Philadelphia; a Practical Housewife* (Philadelphia: T. B. Peterson and Brothers, ca. 1866), 159–60.

12. Raffald, 258.

13. Rundell, 199.

PIES, PUDDINGS, FRITTERS, AND PANCAKES

1. Glasse, 1747 ed., 75–76.

2. Leslie, 1830, 23–24.

3. Leslie, 1973, 12.

4. GW to Dr. John Cochran, Aug. 16, 1779, in WGW, 16: 116–17.

5. Glasse, 1796 ed., 260.

6. Ibid., 261.

7. Wilson, 143; Davidson, 320–21.

8. Hess, 121–23.

9. Glasse 1796 ed., 249–50; Taylor, 197.

10. Glasse 1747 ed., 83; Randolph, 149.

CAKES AND SMALL CONFECTIONS

1. Raffald, 264.

2. Glasse, 1747 ed., 138.

3. Randolph, 191.

4. Glasse, 1747 ed., 139.

5. Davidson, 644.

6. Wilson, 148.

7. Kettilby, 78; Raffald, 177.

8. Glasse, 1747 ed., 141; Davidson, 722.

9. Invoice, Robert Cary and Co., to Estate of Daniel Parke Custis and consigned to Mrs. Martha Custis, Mar. 1759, in Washington Invoices and Letters, 1755–1766 (bound Photostat, LGWMV), [13]. Documentation of several subsequent Washington-household purchases of gingerbread: Robert Cary and Co. to GW, Oct. 12, 1761, in WGW, 2: 370; entries for Jan. 25 and Mar. 21, 1796, in WHAB 31: 77, 178.

10. Hess, 342–48; gingerbread recipe from Mary Anna Randolph Custis Lee Cookbook, ca. 1860–61, Virginia Historical Society, Richmond, Mss1 L5114d.

11. Leslie, 1830, 67.

12. Randolph, 173.

13. Martha [Parke] Custis, "To make a great Cake," n.d. [probably 1784–95] (manuscript, LGWMV).

CUSTARDS, ICE CREAMS, AND FRUIT

1. Wilson, 168.

2. NCL to EBG, June 25, 1823 (typescript, LGWMV).

3. Kettilby, iv.

4. Davidson, 80.

5. Glasse, 1796 ed., 335.

6. Raffald, 254.

7. Entries for Aug. and Sept. 1767, in GWD, 2: 27.

8. Randolph, 176.

9. Blair, Bannister, Braxton, Horner, and Whiting Papers, Special Collections Research Center, Earl Gregg Swem Library, College of William and Mary, Williamsburg, Va., Mss 39.1B58.

10. Randolph, 174.

11. Wilson, 169; Davidson, 313.

12. Glasse, 1747 ed., 79.

13. Ibid., 83–84.

14. Randolph, 154–55.

BREADS

1. GWPC Recollections, 435n, 436n.

2. Smith, 176; Randolph, 170.

3. GWPC Recollections, 166–67, 386; Winthrop Sargent, entry for Oct. 13, 1793, in PGW Pres., 14: 210; entry for June 5, 1798, in Niemcewicz, 103; NCL to EBG, Feb. 23, 1823 (typescript, LGWMV).

4. NCL and daughter Frances Parke Lewis to EBG, Jan. 1821 (manuscript, LGWMV).

5. NCL Housekeeping Book (bound manuscript, Butler Family Papers, Historic New Orleans Collection, folder 1632), 9.

6. Smith, 136, 138.

7. Mary Custis Lee Papers, 1694–1917, section 63, Virginia Historical Society, Richmond.

BEVERAGES

1. Marquis de Chastellux *Travels in North America in the Years 1780, 1781, and 1782*, 2 vols. (London: G. G. J. and J. Robinson, 1807), 1: 128.

2. Entry for Sept. 22, 1784, in GWD, 4: 32.

3. Wilson, 401; Richard Croom Beatty and William J. Mulloy, eds., *William Byrd's Natural History of Virginia: Or, the Newly Discovered Eden* (Richmond, Va.: Dietz Press, 1940), 92.

4. Entry for July 3, 1798, in Niemcewicz, 71.

5. Raffald, 311.

6. Isabella Beeton *The Book of Household Management* (London: S. O. Beeton, 1861), 891.

7. Raffald, 311.

8. Wilson, 171.

9. Smith, 198; Raffald, 207.

10. Decatur, 44; Abigail Adams to her sister, Mary Smith Cranch (Mrs. Richard Cranch), Aug. 9, 1789, in Adams, 19.

11. Wilson, 357.

12. Raffald, 333–34.

13. MW to FBW, Apr. 22, 1792, in PMW, 237; MW to FBW, July 14, 1794, in PMW, 272.

14. Burgess Ball to GW, Feb. 13, 1794, in PGW Pres., 15: 227.

15. Raffald, 248–49.

Illustration Credits

Index to People, Locations, and Objects

Index to Recipes, Beverages, and Foodstuffs

****

This index includes recipes by name and by category, and it lists ingredients, beverages, and foodstuffs mentioned throughout the book.

Page numbers in *italics* indicate illustrations.

Recipes by Name

Recipes by Category

Ingredients, Beverages, and Foodstuffs mentioned throughout the book

First edition, 2011

Published in the United States by
the Mount Vernon Ladies' Association
Post Office Box 110
Mount Vernon, Virginia 22121

Distributed by
The University of North Carolina Press
Chapel Hill, North Carolina 27515
1-800-848-6224
www.uncpress@unc.edu

Library of Congress Cataloging-in-Publication Data
Dining with the Washingtons : historic recipes,
entertainment, and hospitality from Mount
Vernon / essays by Carol Borchert Cadou . . .
[et al.] ; contributions by Steven T. Bashore and
Esther White ; recipes by Nancy Carter Crump ;
foreword by Walter Scheib ; Stephen A. McLeod,
editor.—1st ed.
    p. cm.
    Includes index.
    ISBN 978-0-8078-3526-5 (alk. paper)
1. Cooking, American—History—18th century.
2. Entertaining—United States—History—18th
century. 3. Washington, George, 1732–1799—
Homes and haunts. 4. United States—Social life
and customs—18th century. 5. United States—
History—Revolution, 1775–1783. 6. Cookbooks.
I. Cadou, Carol Borchert. II. Crump, Nancy
Carter. III. McLeod, Stephen A. (Stephen Archie),
1965– IV. Mount Vernon Ladies' Association of the
Union.
    TX715.D58664 2011
    641.5973—dc23   2011019451

The efforts of the following staff members at
George Washington's Mount Vernon Estate,
Museum, and Gardens were vital in creating
this book:

James C. Rees, *President and CEO*
Dawn M. Bonner, *Administrative Specialist for
    Collections*
Elizabeth Sumner Chambers, *Collections Manager*
Jill M. DeWitt, *Assistant Curator*
Amanda E. Isaac, *Curatorial Research Associate*
Anne M. Johnson, *Desktop Publishing Specialist*
Anne Kingery, *Project Conservator*
Michele Lee, *Librarian, Special Collections*
F. Anderson Morse, *Director for Development*
Julia Mosley, *Director of Retail*
Katherine Ridgway, *Conservator*
Susan P. Schoelwer, *Curator*
Laura B. Simo, *Associate Curator*
Joan Stahl, *Librarian*
Jennifer Van Horn, *Assistant Curator*

Book and jacket design: Julia Sedykh Design
Manuscript editor: Phil Freshman
Recipes editor: Jennifer Lindner McGlinn
Assistant manuscript editor: Susan C. Jones
Proofreaders: Phil Freshman, Stephen A. McLeod,
    and Caroline Rosier
Indexer: Monica S. Rumsey
Food photography: Renée Comet
Food photography stylist: Lisa Cherkasky
Printing and binding: C&C Offset Printing Co.,
    Ltd., China
This book was typeset in Adobe Caslon and
Monotype Bell.

ENDPAPER ILLUSTRATIONS
Front left: In 1789 Congress authorized the
purchase of carefully selected tableware for the
executive residence that included elegant ivory-
and silver-handled cutlery and flatware.
Front right: This saucer from the States pattern
porcelain service, presented to Martha Washington
by the Dutch East India Company in 1796, features
her monogram at its center.
Back left: In 1759 George Washington purchased
eight dozen "best hard mettle Plates [of assorted
sizes] with my Crest engraved."
Back right: Washington acquired this bone-handled
knife and fork for his own use, probably during the
Revolutionary War.

FRONTISPIECE
Plates produced by Crown Ducal in 1932 to com-
memorate the bicentennial of Washington's birth
include a scene based on the painting *Washington
and Lafayette at Mount Vernon, 1784* (see pages
16–17).

VERSO OF CONTENTS
This porcelain coffee cup and saucer, manufactured
at France's Sèvres factory, are from a 309-piece service that President Washington purchased in 1790
from the Comte de Moustier, the outgoing French
minister to the United States.

PAGE 235
The numerous cuts and notches on the surface of
this large (thirteen-inch diameter) wooden vessel
indicate that it was used as a chopping bowl. The
enslaved cooks at Mount Vernon prepared meals
for the Washingtons and their many visitors using
this rare surviving handmade container.

The President of the United States
and Mrs Washington, request the Pleasure of
Mr & Mrs Dalton & Miss Dalton's
Company to Dine, on Thursday next, at 4 o'Clock.

March 1st   1793

An answer is requested.